Gastric Sleeve Bariatric Cookbook: 300+ Tasty Recipes to Overcome Food Addiction and Avoid Regaining Weight after Surgery. Includes an 8-Week Meal Plan That Will Help You Take Care of Your New Stomach

ISBN 9798509600210

10 9 8 7 6 5 4 3 2 1

Gastric Sleeve

Bariatric

Cookbook

300+ Tasty Recipes to Overcome Food Addiction and Avoid Regaining Weight after Surgery. Includes an 8-Week Meal Plan That Will Help You Take Care of Your New Stomach

Sharon Rush

Table of Contents

Introduction

Introduction

When choosing to live a healthier lifestyle, bariatric surgery is a significant step and should not be taken lightly. These operations are always the final option for a specialist, but they effectively help people lose weight after other approaches have failed.

Gastric Sleeve bariatric surgery, also known as Sleeve Gastrectomy, is a restrictive operation that reduces the stomach's average size. This technique entails removing certain portions of the stomach to limit the number of calories consumed at one time. About 60-70 percent of the stomach is removed, resulting in a smaller and more banana-shaped stomach. Its average capacity of up to 48 oz. of food is reduced to around 10-15 ounces. This lowers total food intake, makes you feel full quickly, and can help you lose weight.

Many people believe that having bariatric surgery is all that is necessary to reduce weight. This is real, but most patients would find themselves back at square one with unhealthy dietary patterns. It is essential to develop new eating patterns to live a healthier lifestyle. Tracking your calories in a food journal, changing current recipes for healthier ingredients, or following the recipes in this cookbook are effective ways to develop and sustain healthy eating habits. Just follow the recipes and meal schedule in this book strictly, and you'll be on the way to a safe, happier lifestyle in no time. Although the choice to have this type of surgery is solely between you and your doctor, it is beneficial to be prepared before the procedure. Knowing what you can and can't cook, can help to alleviate some of the stress. To further shrink the size of your stomach, you'll be placed on a low-carb, high-protein diet in the weeks leading up to your operation. You'll be on a liquid diet for the two days leading up to the surgery. You have to go through four different step-down feeding stages after treatment, from liquid to solid foods. But that doesn't mean you can't be happy about what you eat. This book is designed to relieve some of the anxiety associated with these phases. There are 300 different recipes to choose from depending on where you are in the recovery journey. Various beverages and snacks will be available to you during the first week after surgery, as well as recipes that you will use for the remainder of your life.

The best part is that you can consume these before surgery, or at least before you start the liquid diet. Just because you have a small number of foods to choose from doesn't mean that you have to forego taste. All of these meals are rich in protein, allowing you to eat less and feel better for longer. You'll also find the serving amount, so you'll understand how many people you should feed with and how much you can consume. Just a note that nothing in this book can be taken as medical advice. This book is solely for informational purposes. For bariatric operations, only a specialist may assist you. Follow the surgeon's and doctor's instructions and guidelines before and after your operation.

Chapter 1: Basics of Sleeve Gastrectomy

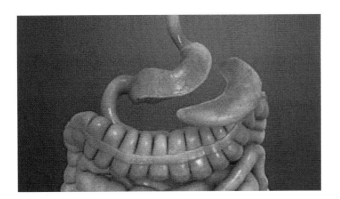

Perhaps you've done all to lose weight, even for the majority of your adult life, and nothing has succeeded. Maybe you've established an emotional attachment to food, which you switch to when you're sad or anxious. Alternatively, you might have suffered from your weight your whole life, and simply now, you need the care, knowledge, and advice that bariatric surgery provides, but weight loss surgery is not a quick fix. Many people think this way, but they don't know that maintaining weight loss requires a lifetime of commitment and healthy choices and that surgery isn't the solution. There's still the question of undergoing major surgery in and of itself. This necessitates a patient's lifestyle and nutrition to be entirely changed both before and after the procedure. Weight loss surgery will give you the confidence and mindset you have to lose more weight to hold it off in the long run. This is due to the fact that, based on the type of surgery you had, you would be unable to eat or ingest as many calories as you did prior to surgery. Furthermore, when implemented with dedication, the knowledge, social counseling, and assistance that you can get will help you transform your relationship with food and extra weight permanently. This will not only aid in safe weight reduction but will also help to prevent a number of other health complications linked to obesity.

The most famous weight reduction surgical bariatric procedure done in the United States and worldwide is Gastric Sleeve Surgery, commonly known as Vertical Sleeve Gastrectomy. This is a type of weight-loss surgery in which part of the stomach is removed, and the rest is fused to form a sleeve or banana shape. This operation reduces your stomach's scale to around a tenth of its original size, allowing you to consume less and feel full faster. Usually, 60-70 percent of the stomach is removed. Its normal volume of up to 48 oz. of food is reduced to about 10-15 ounces. This lowers total food intake, makes you feel full quickly, and can help you lose weight. Many people believe that having bariatric surgery is all that is necessary to reduce weight. This is real, but most patients would find themselves back at square one with unhealthy dietary patterns. It is important to develop new eating patterns to live a healthier lifestyle. Tracking your calories in a nutrition plan, changing current recipes for healthier ingredients, or simply following the recipes in this cookbook are both helpful ways to develop and sustain healthy eating habits. So, follow the tips and meal schedule in this book religiously, and you'll be on the way to a safe, healthier lifestyle in no time.

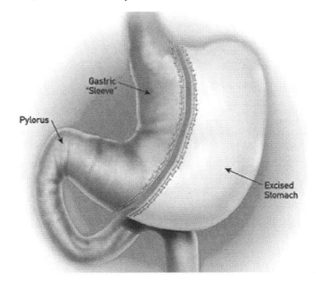

1.1 Difference between Gastric Sleeve and Gastric Bypass

By forming a narrow gastric pouch from the upper portion of the stomach, the gastric bypass laparoscopic technique limits food consumption and shortens the digestive tract. The intestine is surgically bound to this pocket, allowing food to flow into a small opening. The remainder of the stomach, as well as a part of the intestines, are bypassed. Gastric bypass surgery decreases the number of calories and nutrients absorbed from food by limiting the amount of food consumed.

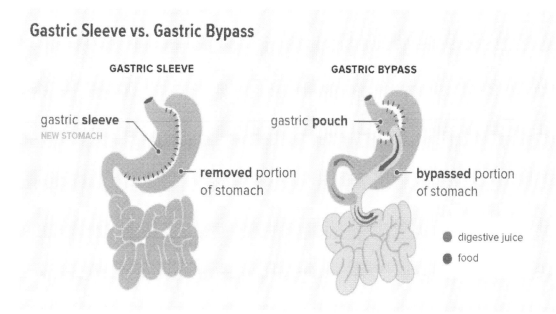

A sleeve gastrectomy involves developing a sleeve-shaped tube from a small part of the stomach and removing the rest of the stomach. Food enters the intestines directly through the new stomach tube. Nutrients and calories are absorbed naturally from food, but patients feel full faster and for longer. Sleeve gastrectomy is a laparoscopic procedure that may be used to permanently manage weight.

1.2 Benefits of Gastric Sleeve Bariatric Surgery

One of the most important reasons for bariatric surgery is severe obesity, although it is not the only one; other prominent reasons include:

- Improved Health-Weight loss surgery typically improves an individual's health and wellbeing. It lowers the risk of type 2 diabetes, coronary heart disease, stroke, and the risks of high cholesterol levels, particularly in obese people.

- Weight loss procedure has been shown to significantly improve fertility conditions. Following substantial weight loss regulates hormones, which improves fertility rates.

- Fewer Hunger Pangs: As 60-75 percent of your stomach is removed, the Ghrelin hunger hormone's amount is reduced. Ghrelin is a hunger hormone released in the gut that signals to the brain that it's time to eat. The lower your levels are, the more satisfied you will be and the simpler it will be to consume less calories.

- Hauling around excess weight places a lot of strain on the knees, creating pain and damage daily. Individuals may have greater mobility and a healthy body as a result of their weight loss.

13

No matter whether you've opted to have a sleeve gastrectomy, pay attention to your diet both before and after the procedure. The first year after the surgery is the most important. You must concentrate on weight management while not reverting to your old eating patterns. You must adhere to a lifestyle that is beneficial to your overall health. And ensure to make the following adjustments:

- Eat right. Eat three regular meals and two snacks every day.

1.3 Sleeve Gastrectomy Risks

Some bariatric surgery risks are:

- Anesthesia-related risks
- Chronic nausea
- Infection
- vomiting
- Acid reflux
- Dilation of esophagus
- Inability to consume certain foods.
- Failure to lose weight or weight gain.
- Blockage in stomach

Bariatric Surgery Long-Term Risks

Patients who undergo bariatric surgery face certain long-term complications, including:

- Low blood sugar
- Vomiting
- Malnutrition
- Ulcers
- Nausea and dizziness
- Hernias
- Bowel obstruction

- Drink plenty of water to keep hydrated, and avoid caffeine, alcohol, soda, and juices.
- Get enough rest. It is important that you sleep for at least 7 hours per night.
- At least once a week, keep track of your weight.
- Set aside at least 40 minutes a week to exercise.
- Take the multivitamins regularly.

How to reduce the risks associated with bariatric surgery?

Although all surgical procedures involve some risk, there are steps you should take to reduce the risk of adverse side effects from bariatric surgery. You will, for example, lower your body mass index (BMI), boost your workout, and stop smoking. To determine what is best for you, speak with your doctor regarding your options.

When weight-loss surgery doesn't work?

Long-term weight loss is possible with a sleeve gastrectomy. Your dietary changes determine the sum of weight you lose. Within two years, you can be able to lose up to 60% of your body weight, or perhaps more. If you don't make the necessary lifestyle improvements, you can gain weight even after surgery as if you are regularly binging on a high-calorie snack. You must make lasting positive dietary modifications and engage in daily physical activity and workouts to prevent regaining weight.

Following weight-loss surgery, it's important to have all of your regular follow-up appointments so that your doctor can monitor your improvement. If you don't lose weight or have problems following the operation, contact the doctor right away.

Chapter 2: Steps and Strategies for Success

The whole procedure for a Gastric Sleeve begins well before the patient enters the operating room. It's important to know what this type of surgery involves. You must not only be concerned with surgery, but you must also be cautious and follow all instructions given to you after and even before you enter the operating room. Some people believe that gastric sleeve is a miraculous cure and retains their current eating patterns. However, your new eating habits will begin before you have the surgery. Living on a strict diet ensures that the physician will be able to perform a laparoscopic surgery, which is both simpler and faster. This tends to keep the suffering to a minimum and allows the specialist to complete the job. To make it work, you must stick to your diet schedule to the full. Throughout the process of achieving the desired weight goal, caution must be taken.

2.1 Before the Surgery

This is a life-altering procedure. It can assist you with losing weight by altering you're eating habits before and after the treatment. You must pay close attention to your weight in the weeks leading up to the surgery. It's important not to gain weight because it would render the procedure's technical aspects even more complicated. It is required that you follow a strict liquid protein diet for two weeks before surgery. This lowers the odds of developing a fatty liver, which may render the treatment riskier. A fatty liver is caused by fat accumulation throughout the spleen and liver. Two weeks before the operation, you must adhere to a preoperative liquid diet. The diet includes the following items:

- Meal replacement shakes, and protein shakes.

- Juice made from vegetables.

- Sugar-free beverages (You can use sugar substitutes).

- Soups and broths of no solid particles.

- Extremely thin cream of rice or cream of wheat can be consumed.

- Drinks should be sipped steadily. Never take them with meals; instead, consume them 30 minutes after you've eaten a meal.

If you want to consume solids, you can have up to two portions of vegetables and lean meat, but your doctor must first know about it to give his or her approval. During this period, you can consume a variety of food substitutes and protein shakes. It is safer to inquire about the products that your doctor suggests. To make a protein shake, combine 1 scoop of protein powder with 1 cup of skim milk or water in a blender. It's ready to drink after 60 seconds of processing. However, if you gain a considerable amount of weight over this period, the doctor will have to reconsider your candidacy for the operation. There is a decent possibility that the operation will be canceled and rescheduled. You can only have protein shakes the day before the treatment. After 5 p.m., stick to plain drinks like water, Jell-O, soup, ginger ale, and tea. Do not eat or drink food after midnight so that the stomach is empty for the operation. You must drop 10 to 15 pounds before the surgery. You must lose 10% of your body weight if your BMI is greater than 55. Before beginning the operation, make the following preparations:

- Be prepared for a significant improvement in nutrition after the treatment. Slowly eat. Limit yourself to three meals and one to two snacks a day. Make a habit of chewing the food thoroughly.

- Ask others to assist you with food preparation and vitamins supplementation during the first few weeks following surgery.

- Learn the types of workouts you may do during the operation. Select the forms that you would be able to adhere to and enjoy.

- Remain in constant contact with a licensed dietitian. Check with him to see if you can consume the food you like or crave.

- Purchase the equipment you'll need to cook food and concoctions quickly following surgery.

- Do a thorough cleaning of your kitchen, removing the foods that you won't be able to consume after the surgery and substituting them with the diet's prescribed foods. Purchase the following items prior to surgery:

- Meal replacement and protein shake that your doctor has approved.

- Vitamins and minerals recommended by the health team that is handling the

- Procedure

- Sugar-free flavors and sugar substitute

- Canned broth

- Jell-O, yogurt, popsicles, and pudding with no sugar added.

- Soups with a smooth texture

- Freezer bags, small food containers, kitchen utensils

- Food processor or blender

PRE-BARIATRIC DIET MEAL PLAN

	Time	Item
☐	8:00 AM	Approved Protein Supplement
☐	9:00 AM	8 oz Water or Herbal Tea
☐	10:00 AM	8 oz Water
☐	11:00 AM	Approved Protein Supplement
☐	12:00 PM	8 oz Broth or Miso
☐	1:00 PM	8 oz Water
☐	2:00 PM	8 oz Water
☐	3:00 PM	Approved Protein Supplement
☐	4:00 PM	8 oz Water
☐	5:00 PM	8 oz Water
☐	6:00 PM	Approved Protein Supplement
☐	7:00 PM	8 oz Broth or Miso
☐	8:00 PM	Sugar-Free Popsicle
☐	9:00 PM	8 oz Water or Herbal Tea

Medical Disclaimer: This is for educational purposes only and not intended to be medical advice. Please refer all questions to your surgeon.

2.2 After the Surgery

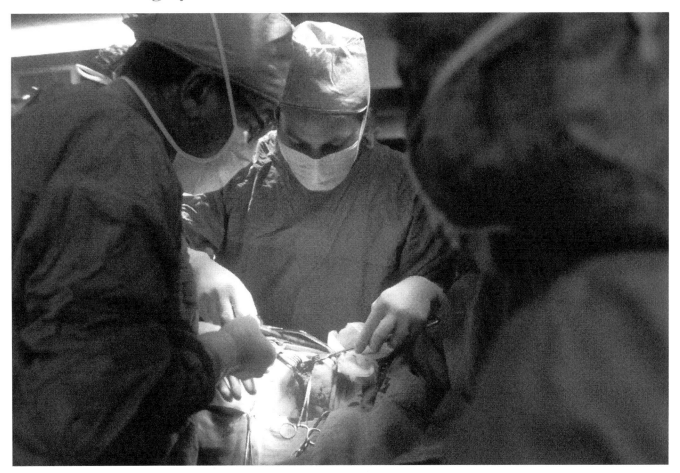

The treatment will reduce the size of your stomach by up to 70%. This is a good way to lose weight because it suppresses your appetite and makes you feel satisfied even after limited meals. Since the surgery, you may not lose weight immediately. You can improve your eating habits and what you consume on a long-term basis. When it comes to your diet, you'll go through stages to make yourself recover. You will limit what you consume and how much you eat first, thus ensuring that you get enough vitamins and nutrients. Once your body has recovered, you may need to eat a more limited yet nutritionally healthy diet. To avoid complications after surgery, adhere to the following guidelines:

- Take your time chewing your food. To be safe, chew your food until it has the same consistency as a liquid. If you do not do this, you will feel nauseated or vomit due to the blockages caused by food that was not thoroughly chewed.

- Eat and drink in a very slow manner. The ideal time that you must allot for each meal is 30 minutes. You might vomit or get nauseated when you eat or drink too quickly.

- Drink 30 to 60 minutes before and after meals. You cannot drink with your meals. Your stomach will become overloaded, which may lead to expansion and split.

- Do not eat or drink more than what your doctor recommends. While you are still in the healing process, you have to avoid gaining weight. This can cause a rupture in the stomach, which will jeopardize your surgery.

- Avoid food that has high sugar content and the kinds with too many calories but minimal nutrients. They can affect the number of nutrients you are getting, making it harder for you to lose weight.

- Drink lots of fluids in a slow manner. Avoid dehydration at all costs. You need to consume 3 to 4 oz. of water in between meals. You can also take low-calorie beverages suitable for the diet. Once you become dehydrated due to the insufficient fluids that your body is getting, you will likely suffer from diarrhea and vomiting.

- Take the recommended minerals, vitamins, and liquid supplements. Follow the kind of diet that is suitable for your recovery stage. The kinds of diet plans depend on your recovery stage.

- Eat what your doctor tells you to eat after your surgery, which will consist of a lot of liquid. If you eat regular food too early or eat sugary or fat food, you may damage your stomach or harm yourself.

- Depending on which kind of surgery you have and what type of work you do, you could be back to work as soon as two weeks after surgery if you do not lift anything heavy.

- Wait about four weeks before you exercise or lift weights to decrease the chance that you will get a hernia in the wound.

- Let your doctor check on your progress at the scheduled times. He'll see whether or not you are on schedule in your weight loss goals.

- You should try out new recipes so that you can stay on your diet plan. It will not bore you with your food to turn you back to your old eating habits.

2.3 The Five Stages of Eating After Bariatric Surgery

You should follow the surgical team's advice to the core as they know you, the treatment you've had, and the medical history. They do, however, suggest that you should consume in five stages:

- **Stage 1:** Clear Liquids

- **Stage 2:** Full Liquids

- **Stage 3:** Pureed Foods

- **Stage 4:** Soft Foods

- **Stage 5:** Eating Well for Life

Food Cravings

During the first few days after surgery, you might notice that you've lost your cravings, meals don't excite you, and that the thought of trying new foods makes you feel nauseous. This is entirely normal; the body undergoes rapid hormonal and physical changes after surgery, and it can take some time before you revert to your former self and become interested in the foods you used to eat. However, this may be a positive thing since it allows you to wean yourself off unhealthy food options and train the body to crave nutritious meals, which can help you lose weight.

Maintain a strict diet regimen; food can be seen as nothing more than nourishment for the body. You will drop weight quicker than you think if you put a little effort and thought into what you put in your stomach, avoid high-calorie snacks, and adjust pre-existing meals to include nutritious ingredients. Consider your long-term progress.

2.4 Nutritional Concern

You have no desire to consume large portions of food after the surgery, and the body struggles to fulfill the normal dietary requirements. Bariatric patients can select from a wide variety of products. To further improve your immune function, your doctor can prescribe a few vitamins and nutrients.

Some recommendations include:

- **Liquids**

One of the most critical aspects of this surgery is the restriction on the amount of food that can be consumed at one time. This aids weight loss because patients cannot eat as much as they used to, particularly in the days and weeks after surgery. The first week is all about drinking plenty of water and taking protein supplements. Vitamins will be provided to patients two weeks after their bariatric surgery.

However, just as the stomach can no longer support large quantities of food, it can no longer handle large amounts of liquids. To avoid dehydration, patients are only allowed small sips of water during the day. The most critical part is staying hydrated after weight-loss surgery during the first weeks.

If patients' fluid consumption is restricted in one sitting, it's essential that they have access to fluids during the day. One way to ensure the patients are getting enough water is to have a water bottle with them. Often water bottles have measurements on the side such that patients will still see how much water they have left.

During the first few weeks on the new diet, water can also make the stomach feel whole. Water, on the other hand, cannot be used to quell hunger pangs. Drinking too much at once will induce nausea, belching, and discomfort. Keep in mind that the body is constantly adjusting to the smaller stomach. The recommended amount of liquid a day is 64 to 100 oz., with the amount increasing as you go through your post-op diet phase.

Being well hydrated often entails being cautious of the beverages that patients consume. Although coffee is mainly made up of water, caffeinated drinks are also diuretics, which enhance the need for water. Carbonated drinks irritate the stomach, induce reflux, and cause the pouch to spread out with time.

Sugary drinks don't help you lose weight either, but water and other sugar-free drinks do. Not only is staying hydrated during the recovery process essential; it is also one of the keys to leading a healthy lifestyle.

Hydration aids fat absorption, aids in removing contaminants from the body, leaves joints and muscles primed, and improves the skin's health.

- **Protein Supplements**

Protein is the essential macronutrient to consume post-operatively. The building block of muscle and tissue is protein. It's essential to consume enough protein even on a low-calorie diet. You will feel energized, lose more weight while retaining muscle, and have longer post-meal satisfaction if you consume enough protein. Protein takes longer to absorb than carbs and has fewer calories than fat. As you still have to consume water and protein-rich foods after surgery. As time goes by, you have to gradually incorporate more blended meals into your diet. Protein can be consumed at any meal for the rest of one's life to reduce weight and heal initially and sustain weight loss over time. For protein intake, consume eggs, poultry (chicken, turkey without skin, lean nitrate-free chicken or turkey sausages, ground chicken, turkey breast), both fish and seafood, low fat or nonfat dairy products (low-fat Greek yogurt, 1% or nonfat cottage cheese, 1% or nonfat milk and cheese), lean beef (if tolerated) beginning for three months post-op (sirloin, loin, round roast), low fat or nonfat dairy products (low-fat Greek yogurt, 1% or nonfat cottage Protein intake should be between 60 and 100 gram a day. Specific guidelines are made depending on the optimal body weight and the stage of the post-op diet. High-fat dairy ingredients (cream or whole milk), high-fat beef and pork cuts (pork sausage, bacon, bologna, salami, pork ribs, and ground beef) skin-on poultry should be avoided.

- **Carbohydrates**

Carbohydrates (also known as "carbs") get a poor reputation after weight reduction surgery. Even the most experienced bariatric physicians will also impose restrictions on their patients, such as "No more than twenty carbs a day" or "Never consume white foods like rice, bread, or pasta ever."

Also, after bariatric surgery, carbs remain the preferred energy source in the diet. Here is why:

- Inadequate carbohydrate consumption can be one reason for low energy in bariatric patients in the first few months following surgery.

- Consume enough carbohydrates and spare protein, so protein isn't converted to fuel the brain.

- Nutrient-dense carbohydrates include vegetables, fruits, and whole grains.

- Fiber-rich carbs help you avoid constipation, helps you feel fuller, and remain fuller for longer.

- Fiber-rich carbohydrates also help to maintain a steadier blood sugar level, reducing sugar cravings.

- According to scientific analysis, six months after weight reduction surgery, the optimum amount of carbohydrates for long-term performance is about 90 grams per day.

An indication of a day's food consumption that provides 90 grams of carbohydrate is as follows:

- 3 fruit servings (1 orange, pear, peach, ½ grapefruit, medium banana, 15 grapes = 1 serving)

- 3 vegetable servings (1 serving = 1 cup raw or ½ cup cooked)

- 2 servings grains or starchy vegetables (1 slice of bread, ½ cup hot cereal, a small potato, ½ cup peas or corn)

That may seem like a lot of food after bariatric surgery, particularly if you're not hungry or if you're too concentrated on having enough fluid and nutrition that you don't have much space for carbohydrate-rich foods.

- **Fat**

Fat, like carbohydrates and protein, is a macronutrient. Fat is essential not just in our bodies but also in our diet. Dietary fat is essential for the absorption of fat-soluble vitamins A, D, E, and K. Furthermore, certain essential fatty acids (omega 3s and omega 6s) are not generated by our bodies and must be consumed instead. At nine calories per gram, fats are the most calorie-dense among all macronutrients and in the balanced variety, so portion sizes must be carefully monitored. Processed foods marketed as fat-free or reduced-fat can be avoided since they sometimes substitute fat with more sugar or sodium to increase the taste. For fat satisfaction, eat avocado, chia seeds, fatty fish, other seafood and shellfish, flaxseed extra virgin olive oil, almonds, walnuts, peanuts, and all-natural nut butter. The amount of fat consumed every day should be kept to a minimum at first. Fat consumption should not exceed 25-30% of daily calories for anybody, regardless of whether or not they have had weight reduction surgery.

- **Multivitamins**

Your body requires multiple vitamins to make up for the lost nutrients. Multivitamins should contain folic acid, copper, and iron. Brands like Bariatric Fusion and Bari melts are recommended.

  - **Vitamins B12** Bariatric procedures make it difficult for the body to release adequate levels of B12 to aid digestion. A B12 deficiency can have no symptoms and, if left untreated, can lead to feelings of weakness, lightheadedness, and more; your doctor might recommend B12 vitamins in the form of pills, injections, and nasal sprays.

  - **Calcium citrate** Calcium is essential for bones, muscles, and nerve function. You might be prescribed calcium citrate to be taken in 500mg doses three times a day.

  - **Iron:** If your body fails to produce enough iron, you might be prescribed iron supplements. Early signs of an iron deficiency include heart palpitations, lightheadedness, dizziness, and fatigue. Note that it cannot be taken with calcium citrate and should only be taken on an empty stomach.

  - **Pain Medications:** Your doctor might recommend opioids or medication to help with the dull ache you might feel from time to time.

BEST LOW CARB SHAKES

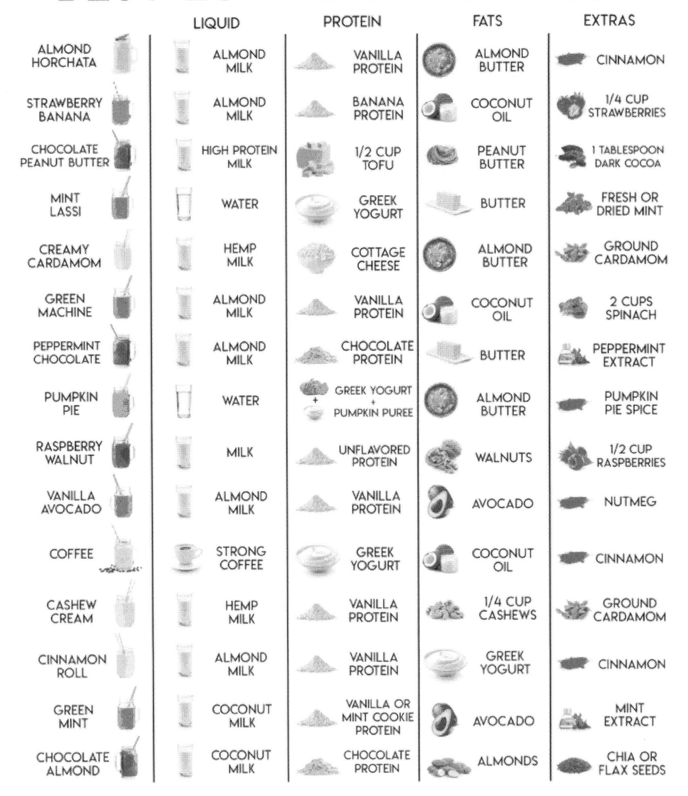

	LIQUID	PROTEIN	FATS	EXTRAS
ALMOND HORCHATA	ALMOND MILK	VANILLA PROTEIN	ALMOND BUTTER	CINNAMON
STRAWBERRY BANANA	ALMOND MILK	BANANA PROTEIN	COCONUT OIL	1/4 CUP STRAWBERRIES
CHOCOLATE PEANUT BUTTER	HIGH PROTEIN MILK	1/2 CUP TOFU	PEANUT BUTTER	1 TABLESPOON DARK COCOA
MINT LASSI	WATER	GREEK YOGURT	BUTTER	FRESH OR DRIED MINT
CREAMY CARDAMOM	HEMP MILK	COTTAGE CHEESE	ALMOND BUTTER	GROUND CARDAMOM
GREEN MACHINE	ALMOND MILK	VANILLA PROTEIN	COCONUT OIL	2 CUPS SPINACH
PEPPERMINT CHOCOLATE	ALMOND MILK	CHOCOLATE PROTEIN	BUTTER	PEPPERMINT EXTRACT
PUMPKIN PIE	WATER	GREEK YOGURT + PUMPKIN PUREE	ALMOND BUTTER	PUMPKIN PIE SPICE
RASPBERRY WALNUT	MILK	UNFLAVORED PROTEIN	WALNUTS	1/2 CUP RASPBERRIES
VANILLA AVOCADO	ALMOND MILK	VANILLA PROTEIN	AVOCADO	NUTMEG
COFFEE	STRONG COFFEE	GREEK YOGURT	COCONUT OIL	CINNAMON
CASHEW CREAM	HEMP MILK	VANILLA PROTEIN	1/4 CUP CASHEWS	GROUND CARDAMOM
CINNAMON ROLL	ALMOND MILK	VANILLA PROTEIN	GREEK YOGURT	CINNAMON
GREEN MINT	COCONUT MILK	VANILLA OR MINT COOKIE PROTEIN	AVOCADO	MINT EXTRACT
CHOCOLATE ALMOND	COCONUT MILK	CHOCOLATE PROTEIN	ALMONDS	CHIA OR FLAX SEEDS

2.5 Exercise Guidelines for Each Stage of Weight-loss Surgery

Increasing one's degree of health is the safest thing a weight-loss surgery candidate can do to prepare for success before and after surgery. The healthier their cardiovascular health is before the operation, the fewer problems they'll have before and afterward. The following pointers can be useful:

Preoperative Stage

- Make weight loss a top priority in your workout routine. Excess fat will make the procedure for weight reduction surgery more difficult. Many surgeons, in particular, demand that their patients drop a certain amount of weight before they operate.

- Start slowly and gradually increase your exercise for 30 to 60 minutes a day, six days a week.

- Exercises that place so much stress on the joints, such as leaping and jogging, should be avoided.

- Concentrate on low- to moderate-intensity aerobic activity.

- Place a greater emphasis on duration than intensity.

- For strength training, use light to reasonable weights and two to three pairs of 12 to 15 reps.

- Avoid joint discomfort; if an exercise causes you pain, strive to adjust it to not have to deal with it.

Post-operative Stage

After bariatric surgery, it's important to establish practical exercise goals. Eventually, 30 to 60 minutes of exercise a day, six days a week, would be the goal. However, getting there takes time, so begin with smaller objectives. Following gastric sleeve and gastric balloon surgeries, the immediate aim is to recover. Light physical exercise, on the other hand, is a vital aspect of the healing process.

Patients can begin walking as soon as they get home and continue to walk every day after surgery. After three to six weeks, patients may plan to begin a weekly workout schedule. Patients should begin low-impact exercises such as shoulder rolls, leg raises, and arm rotations two to four weeks after surgery. Aerobics are normally started one to three months after treatment, and strength training is introduced four months after that. When it comes to when and how to begin exercise after bariatric surgery, follow the doctor's instructions. Begin with sessions of 20 to 30 minutes every day. Start slowly and steadily raise your speed as your stamina improves. Consistency is the key to exercise after surgery. You don't need intense exercise to get results, although you need to adhere to a schedule. Here are a few suggestions about getting back into shape after surgery:

- Begin slowly and steadily raise the amount of time you spend exercising.

- Move around and drink fluids to relieve body pain.

- Buy a good pair of running shoes and gym attire.

- Before you begin exercising, warm up to gradually raise your heart rate and loosen your muscles.

- When you've finished working out, take some time to relax.

- If you have joint discomfort, stop immediately.

2.6 Gastric Sleeve Pouch Reset

It's important to remain committed to the prescribed diet and weight loss plan after gastric sleeve operation and stay consistent with your doctor's appointments. If you've had a relapse and are starting to gain weight after gastric sleeve surgery, a gastric sleeve pouch reset, also known as a VSG pouch reset, will help you get back on track. A gastric sleeve pouch reset is a meal plan designed to help a person's post-operative diet progress more quickly.

Following sleeve operation, a daily bariatric diet can have up to five phases and last anywhere from eight to ten weeks, based on the surgeon's recommendations. The reset, on the other hand, follows identical rules but lasts between 5 and 10 days. Simple liquids are introduced first, followed by full liquids, soft drinks, and then solids.

It's necessary to keep in mind that the pouch reset VSG isn't meant to be done every week or even every month. Instead, it's intended to assist you with returning to your post-eating habits. Keep in mind that the VSG pouch reset would not shrink your stomach, reduce hunger, or improve your feeling of fullness. It will assist you in regaining control of your eating habits and portion sizes. The gastric sleeve pouch reset, like the surgery, is a tool. And of this, it just works if you use it!

The pouch reset VSG comes in a variety of styles. Resets can be as short as 48 hours, as long as 5, and 10 days. After a gastric sleeve, here's an illustration of a 5-day pouch reset:

DAY 1: Clear Liquids
- o Water
- o Tea
- o Broth (chicken, vegetable, beef)
- o Sugar-free drinks
- o Unsweetened tea

DAY 2: Thick Liquids
- o Must drink 3 protein shakes. You can make as many servings of the vegetable soup as you want; just space them out every 2-3 hours.
- o 64 oz. of water or a sugar-free beverage
- o Low-calorie Soup

DAY 3: Soft Solid Foods
- o Soup (low fat)
- o 3 protein shakes

Choose 2 servings out of these soft solid protein options:
- o 6 oz. Greek yogurt: plain or flavored
- o ½ cup cottage cheese
- o 2 scrambled or poached eggs
- o ½ cup beans (whole or refried)
- o 4 oz. tofu

DAY 4: Firm Solid Foods
- o 3 protein shakes or soup (low fat)

Choose 2 Servings of protein/day:
- o 4 oz. tofu
- o 4 oz. chicken
- o 2 eggs
- o 4 oz. fish

Choose 2 Servings of fat/day:
- o 15 almonds
- o ½ avocado
- o 1 tablespoon peanut butter, butter, or oil

DAY 5: Whole Solids
On day 5, meal intake is the same as for day 4, except for the protein, especially lean protein (including pork, beef, and venison). Add 2 of your favorite servings:

- o ¼ cup berries
- o ¼ cup beans
- o ¼ cup quinoa
- o ¼ cup vegetables
- o ¼ cup sweet potato

2.7 Top Ten Tips from a Dietician

- Follow the five-stage post-surgery diet plan: Clear Liquids, Full Liquids, Pureed Foods, Soft Foods, and Eating Well for Life. Just go on to the next level if you're delighted with the current one and your surgeon has permitted you.

- Chew, chew, and chew again! From the start, it's important to chew your food thoroughly. Break food into little bits and chew at least twenty times per mouthful. You'll be able to handle bigger pieces of food as time goes by, but the chewing should remain thorough.

- Enjoy mealtimes with friends and relatives.

- Grazing contributes to overconsumption, so mealtimes should not last longer than half an hour. If you get into the habit of eating until you're full, waiting a few minutes, and then come back for more, you'll find yourself on a slippery slope.

- Eat three meals and two short, nutritious snacks every day. And use a kitchen scale, keep track of portion sizes.

- Eat a well-balanced and diverse diet. The most important thing to remember is to consume adequate nutrition, but carbohydrates and vegetables are also important.

- Patients should strive for 60 to 70 grams per day after a bypass or gastric sleeve and 80 to 120 grams per day after a duodenal switch. Hair loss and malnutrition may result if these requirements are not met.

- Don't forget to drink enough water. To avoid dehydration, drink plenty of water in between meals. Daily, drink six to eight 8-fluid-ounce bottles. These should be caffeine-free and low in calories.

2.8 Bariatric Kitchen

After surgery, the kitchen becomes your workshop. Fortunately, eating healthy would not require a complete kitchen makeover. To prepare fast, tasty meals and achieve long-term weight loss success, you just need a few essential staples and equipment pieces. Here's a list of which foods to exclude and which foods to substitute them with.

Toss it	Stock up
Vegetable oil	Extra virgin olive oil
All-purpose flour	Whole-what pastry flour
Sour Cream	low-fat plain Greek yogurt, hummus
Processed cheese and cheese spreads	Natural cheeses (mozzarella, cheddar, feta, etc.), cottage cheese
Canned Premade soups	Canned or dried beans for making homemade soups, low sodium broth
Juice	herbal tea
Hot dogs, bacon	Nitrate free natural chicken or turkey sausages
Potato chips and pretzels	Dehydrated vegetables/snap peas, kale chips
Flavored regular yogurt	Plain yogurt, lower sugar Greek yogurt
Fruit Snacks	Fresh Fruits, natural unsweetened applesauce, frozen fruit
Instant oatmeal packets	100% old fashioned rolled oats or steel-cut oats, unsweetened

2.9 Measuring Conversions

There are two widely employed measuring schemes in nutrition: Metric and US Customary.

Weight (mass)	
Metric (grams)	**US contemporary (oz.)**
14 grams	½ ounce
28 grams	1 ounce
85 grams	3 oz.
100 grams	3.53 oz.
113 grams	4 oz.
227 grams	8 oz.
340 grams	12 oz.
454 grams	16 oz. or 1 pound

Volume (liquid)	
Metric	**US Customary**
0.6 ml	1/8 tsp
1.2 ml	¼ tsp
2.5 ml	½ tsp
3.7 ml	3/4 tsp
5 ml	1 tsp
15 ml	1 tbsp
30 ml	2 tbsp
59 ml	2 fluid oz. or ¼ cup
118 ml	½ cup
177 ml	3/4 cup
237 ml	1 cup or 8 fluid oz.
1.9 liters	8 cups or ½ gallon

Oven Temperatures	
Metric	**US contemporary**
121° C	250° F
149° C	300° F
177° C	350° F
204° C	400° F
232° C	450° F

2.10 Foods to avoid after surgery

The long-term aim after surgery is to return to normalcy, consume most foods in moderation. Abdominal pain or vomiting during surgery is a common concern for patients. Some foods should be stopped entirely within the first three months after surgery to eliminate this situation; however certain foods may be gradually introduced as the body responds to the new stomach.

- **Liquids:** Carbonated beverages, alcohol caffeinated beverages, fruit juices, any sugary beverages.

- **Carbohydrates:** Rice, pasta doughy bread products (untoasted bread), dried fruits, skin-on fruits, fresh pineapples, popcorn, dry fibrous cereals such as granola and bran cereal

- **Fats:** Raw nuts/seeds, fried foods, greasy foods (skin-on poultry, fat-on meat), peanut and other kinds of nut butter (sticky)

- **Proteins:** Dry, tough meat and poultry, any breaded or deep-fried proteins

- **Other Foods:** Asparagus stalks, raw celery, coconut, Sugar-sweetened sauces/ condiments, cookies, and candies.

Chapter 3: Meal Plan

Planning your meals in advance is a smart way to get your post-operative diet to a good start. After surgery, you will feel exhausted with the sudden adjustments your body is undergoing, and meal preparation will be only one more thing on your mind. However, knowing what you're going to consume ahead of time renders food shopping comfortable and eliminates the burden of being home late from work with nothing to eat.

Some patients don't prepare meals before surgery because they don't have time or aren't a priority. Some people skip meal prep after surgery because they aren't interested in eating and might not be hungry.

It's essential to have a regular schedule in place to ensure that you have enough fluids, nutrient vitamins, and protein so that you don't skip meals and have to play catch-up later. Plan for a four- to six-hour break between meals, with a glass of High Protein Milk or a protein shake as a snack in between. Cook once and consume the food at least twice, according to an essential preparation guide. The majority of the recipes in this book make enough for your whole family to eat and still have leftovers for lunch the next day. Some recipes can be preserved in limited portions for later use.

The eight-week meal plans below can be seen as a guide to make food preparation simpler after surgery. Feel free to substitute your meal options based on your personal preferences and available time. Always follow the surgery center's post-operative instructions. These meal plans are supposed to be used as a roadmap, and since the exact servings you eat will differ, you should make sure you get enough protein.

3.1 Week 1 and Week 2: Liquid Diet

Weeks one and two are primarily for liquids. The most important thing to do in the first two weeks following surgery is to stay hydrated. Dehydration is one of the most frequent early postoperative problems, and it can easily make you feel down and out. Getting enough fluids in the early weeks lays the foundation for long-term water consumption, which can help you lose weight faster. Here are a few primary considerations to keep in mind.

As it comes to hydration, water comes first, followed by protein-rich drinks. Water, other clear liquids, and protein-rich shakes account for at least 64 oz. of fluid a day. Make sure there are no seeds or pulp in some shakes or smoothies.

If you're consuming the protein shake in its entirety at mealtimes, consider adding high-protein milk. Between meals, try to increase the day's protein consumption by making two protein shake servings and storing the second serving in the refrigerator for the next day.

Week 1 Meal Plan

Day 1:

- **Breakfast:** Commercial Protein Shake, with at least 20 g protein
- **Lunch:** Guava Smoothie
- **Dinner:** Double Fudge Chocolate shake

Day 2:

- **Breakfast:** Protein-Packed Peanut butter shake
- **Lunch:** Commercial Protein Shake, with at least 20 g protein
- **Dinner:** Double Fudge Chocolate shake

Day 3:

- **Breakfast:** High Protein Fruit Smoothie
- **Lunch:** Vanilla Bean Probiotic Shake
- **Dinner:** Commercial Protein Shake, with at least 20 g protein

Day 4:

- **Breakfast:** Commercial Protein Shake with at least 20 g protein
- **Lunch:** Double Fudge Chocolate shake

- **Dinner:** Vanilla Bean Probiotic Shake

Day 5:

- **Breakfast:** Vanilla Bean Probiotic Shake
- **Lunch:** Commercial Protein Shake, with at least 20 g protein
- **Dinner:** Protein-Packed Peanut butter shake

Day 6:

- **Breakfast:** High Protein Fruit Smoothie
- **Lunch:** Double Fudge Chocolate shake
- **Dinner:** Commercial Protein Shake, with at least 20 g protein

Day 7:

- **Breakfast:** Commercial Protein Shake, with at least 20 g protein
- **Lunch:** Vanilla Bean Probiotic Shake
- **Dinner:** Double Fudge Chocolate shake

Suggested Snack

Water / Calorie-free beverages

Day 1:
- **Breakfast:** Double Fudge Chocolate shake
- **Lunch:** High Protein Fruit Smoothie
- **Dinner:** Commercial Protein Shake, with at least 20 g protein

Day 2:
- **Breakfast:** Strawberry-Banana Protein Smoothie
- **Lunch:** Chunky Monkey Smoothie
- **Dinner:** Vanilla Apple Pie Protein Shake

Day 3:
- **Breakfast:** Vanilla Apple Pie Protein Shake
- **Lunch:** Commercial Protein Shake with at least 20 g protein
- **Dinner:** Guava Smoothie

Day 4:
- **Breakfast:** Commercial Protein Shake with at least 20 g protein
- **Lunch:** Berry Protein Shake
- **Dinner:** Double Fudge Chocolate shake

Day 5:
- **Breakfast:** Double Fudge Chocolate shake
- **Lunch:** Berry Protein Shake
- **Dinner:** Commercial Protein Shake, with at least 20 g protein

Day 6:
- **Breakfast:** Pumpkin Pie Bliss Protein Shake
- **Lunch:** Fresh Mango Smoothie
- **Dinner:** Vanilla Bean Probiotic Shake

Day 7:
- **Breakfast:** Pumpkin Pie Bliss Protein Shake
- **Lunch:** Vanilla Bean Probiotic Shake
- **Dinner:** Fresh Mango Smoothie

Suggested Snack
Water / Calorie-free beverages
High Protein Milk

3.2 Week 3: Pureed Diet

Pureed foods have a much thicker consistency than the liquids you've been consuming, giving you more choice in your diet. If you have a good food processor or blender, you can puree almost everything. Continue to prioritize consuming water first, providing enough nutrition second, and supplementing fruits and vegetables third during the pureed diet; at each meal, target for ¼ to ½ cup of meal. Since your sleeve will become filled more rapidly when you turn to more solid foods, the overall amount of food you consume will decrease. To meet the protein target, drink high-protein milk or a protein shake in between meals. To make pureed foods more interesting, use herbs and seasonings to flavor them. Try curry powder, taco seasoning, chili powder, or other seasoning blends (ideally low sodium). To puree the foods to the desired consistency, thin them with milk, Greek yogurt, water, or broth. Check to label closely before pureeing foods in catsup, BBQ sauce, or premade sauce since they contain calories and sugar.

Day 1:
- **Breakfast:** Scrambled Eggs
- **Lunch:** Tuna salad
- **Dinner:** Noodle less lasagna with Ricotta cheese

Day 2:
- **Breakfast:** Cinnamon Oatmeal
- **Lunch:** Black Beans Salad
- **Dinner:** Slow cooker Barbecue Shredded Chicken and mashed Cauliflower

Day 3:
- **Breakfast:** Greek Yogurt
- **Lunch:** Tuna Salad
- **Dinner:** Chicken Salad

Day 4:
- **Breakfast:** Scrambled Eggs
- **Lunch:** Shrimp Cocktail Salad

- **Dinner:** Slow cooker Barbecue Shredded Chicken and mashed Cauliflower

Day 5:
- **Breakfast:** Cinnamon Oatmeal
- **Lunch:** Tuna Salad
- **Dinner:** Noodle less lasagna with Ricotta cheese

Day 6:
- **Breakfast:** Greek Yogurt
- **Lunch:** Chicken Salad
- **Dinner:** Shrimp Cocktail Salad

Day 7:
- **Breakfast:** Scrambled Eggs
- **Lunch:** Black Beans Salad
- **Dinner:** Slow cooker Barbecue Shredded Chicken and mashed Cauliflower

Suggested Snack
High Protein Milk
Protein Shake

3.3 Week 4: Soft Diet

As you move from liquids to solid foods, keep in mind that you will become satiated more quickly and will not be able to consume the whole portion of food you intended to consume to fulfill your protein requirements. To help you achieve your protein target, drink high-protein milk, milk, or protein drinks in between meals. To develop healthy eating habits, focus on eating food at mealtimes. A protein shake may be used as a food replacement on occasion. Many people find it impossible to consume solid foods first thing every morning and prefer to drink a protein shake instead.

During this time, the portion size can differ. In one sitting, you should be able to consume around ½ cup (4 oz.) of food. To make sure you're consuming enough protein, adjust the nutrition facts information to the portion of food you're consuming.

Week 4 Meal Plan

Day 1:
- **Breakfast:** Wisconsin Scrambler with Aged Cheddar Cheese
- **Lunch:** Tuna salad
- **Dinner:** Herb Crusted Salmon

Day 2:
- **Breakfast:** Greek Yogurt
- **Lunch:** Herb Crusted Salmon
- **Dinner:** Whole Herbed Roasted Chicken in the slow cooker

Day 3:
- **Breakfast:** Wisconsin Scrambler with Aged Cheddar Cheese
- **Lunch:** Chicken and Lotus Root Soup
- **Dinner:** Creamy Chicken Soup with Cauliflower

Day 4:
- **Breakfast:** Cinnamon Oatmeal
- **Lunch:** Creamy Chicken Soup with Cauliflower
- **Dinner:** Leftovers

Day 5:
- **Breakfast:** Greek Yogurt
- **Lunch:** Cottage Cheese with peaches (without skin)

- **Dinner:** Tuna Noodle Casserole

Day 6:
- **Breakfast:** Wisconsin Scrambler with Aged Cheddar Cheese
- **Lunch:** Tuna Noodle Casserole
- **Dinner:** Chicken and Lotus Root Soup

Day 7:
- **Breakfast:** Cinnamon Oatmeal
- **Lunch:** Slow cooker Turkey Chili
- **Dinner:** Lemon-Parsley Crab Cakes

Suggested Snack
High Protein Milk
Protein Shake

3.4 Week 5: Soft Diet

This week, stick to the soft diet. If you're having trouble fulfilling your protein requirements, you may need to go back to a pureed or complete liquid diet for a meal or two, so you can consume a greater amount of food when it's liquid rather than soft. The food quality for the soft diet should be similar to what you'd expect, so you can quickly mash it with a fork. Continue to choose protein-rich foods first, followed by fruits and vegetables, and then all other foods.

Week 5 Meal Plan

Day 1:
- **Breakfast:** High Protein Pancakes
- **Lunch:** Lemon-Parsley Crab Cakes
- **Dinner:** Curried Zucchini Soup

Day 2:
- **Breakfast:** Soufflé Omelet with Mushrooms
- **Lunch:** Eggplant Rollatini
- **Dinner:** Baked fried Chicken Thighs and Roasted Root vegetables

Day 3:
- **Breakfast:** High- Protein Pancake
- **Lunch:** Chicken and Lotus Root Soup
- **Dinner:** Roasted Vegetables Quinoa Salad with Chickpeas

Day 4:
- **Breakfast:** Soufflé Omelet with Mushrooms
- **Lunch:** Roasted Vegetables Quinoa Salad with Chickpeas
- **Dinner:** Chicken, vegetable, and barley soup

Day 5:
- **Breakfast:** High- Protein Pancake
- **Lunch:** Curried Zucchini Soup
- **Dinner:** Mexican Taco Skillet with red peppers and Zucchini

Day 6:
- **Breakfast:** Greek Yogurt
- **Lunch:** Mexican Taco Skillet with red peppers and Zucchini

- **Dinner:** Leftovers

Day 7:

- **Breakfast:** Soufflé Omelet with Mushrooms
- **Lunch:** Cottage Cheese with fruit

- **Dinner:** Zoodles with Turkey Meatballs

Suggested Snack

High Protein Milk

Protein Shake

3.5 Week 6: Soft Diet

Consider how much protein you've been consuming until you start this week. Have a note of your protein goal. Are you meeting your regular targets with your meals and two cups of milk? As you get more solid protein from food, gradually reduce the usage of protein shakes and high-protein milk. Use snacks in between meals to complement total protein consumption if required but avoid consuming too many calories. During this time, the potions will change. In one sitting, you should be able to consume around ½ cup (4 oz.) of food. To ensure that you are consuming enough protein, change the nutrition facts details according to the portion of food you consume.

Week 6 Meal Plan

Day 1:

- **Breakfast:** Scrambled eggs
- **Lunch:** Zoodles with Turkey Meatballs
- **Dinner:** Seafood Cioppino

Day 2:

- **Breakfast:** Cherry Vanilla baked Oatmeal
- **Lunch:** Seafood Cioppino
- **Dinner:** Italian Eggplant Pizzas

Day 3:

- **Breakfast:** Greek Yogurt
- **Lunch:** Italian Eggplant Pizzas
- **Dinner:** Baked fish with pea puree

Day 4:

- **Breakfast:** Cherry Vanilla baked Oatmeal
- **Lunch:** Red Snapper Veracruz
- **Dinner:** Leftovers

Day 5:

- **Breakfast:** Scrambled eggs
- **Lunch:** Cottage cheese with fruits
- **Dinner:** Slow Cooker White Chicken chili

Day 6:

- **Breakfast:** Greek Yogurt
- **Lunch:** Slow Cooker White Chicken chili
- **Dinner:** Fried-less Fish fry with Cod and baked Zucchini Fries

Day 7:

- **Breakfast:** Cherry Vanilla baked Oatmeal
- **Lunch:** Fried-less Fish fry with Cod and baked Zucchini Fries
- **Dinner:** Mediterranean turkey Meatballs

Suggested Snack

1 cup Milk

High Protein Milk

Protein Shake

3.6 Week 7: General Diet

This week promises to be more interesting because the food you will now consume is becoming more varied in taste. Although if you're about to put the blender and food processor back and consume regular food again, pay attention to your sleeve. Depending on the body's tolerance, you might need to substitute a protein drink with a meal here and there. Stress, sleep deprivation, and sickness are all variables that will affect how much you can tolerate on any given day.

<u>Week 7 Meal Plan</u>

Day 1:
- **Breakfast:** Berry Wrap
- **Lunch:** Mediterranean turkey Meatballs
- **Dinner:** Baked Halibut with tomatoes

Day 2:
- **Breakfast:** Greek Yogurt
- **Lunch:** Baked Halibut with tomatoes
- **Dinner:** Coconut Curry Tofu Bowl

Day 3:
- **Breakfast:** Scrambled eggs
- **Lunch:** Coconut Curry Tofu Bowl
- **Dinner:** Baked fish with pea puree

Day 4:
- **Breakfast:** Andre's Hangry Eggs with Cauliflower
- **Lunch:** Mexican Stuffed Summer Squash
- **Dinner:** Leftovers

Day 5:
- **Breakfast:** Smoothie Bowl with Greek Yogurt and fresh berries
- **Lunch:** Cottage cheese with fruits
- **Dinner:** Chicken Cordon Bleu

Day 6:
- **Breakfast:** Andre's Hangry Eggs with Cauliflower
- **Lunch:** Chicken Cordon Bleu
- **Dinner:** Chicken nachos with sweet bell peppers

Day 7:
- **Breakfast:** Smoothie Bowl with Greek Yogurt and fresh berries
- **Lunch:** Chicken nachos with sweet bell peppers
- **Dinner:** Tuna Salad

Suggested Snack
1 cup Milk (High Protein Milk)

3.7 Week 8: General Diet

Congratulations on making it through week eight. Diet restrictions are most severe during the first two months of sleeve gastrectomy. Around week 8, you should be able to switch to a more varied diet that more closely resembles the meals you had before surgery. During this time, the portions will change. You should be able to consume up to 1 cup of food in a single sitting. To ensure you get enough protein, adjust the nutrition facts in detail to the portion of food you consume. If you find that the foods in the continued general diet are still not tolerable for you, go back and repeat an earlier week's diet, then consider adding certain foods again in a week or two. Continue to consume 1 cup of milk as a snack in between meals. Depending on the day, you may need to go to a protein shake and High Protein milk to fulfill your protein requirements. As time goes by, continue to drink pure 1% or nonfat milk to make it easier, save money, and avoid the extra calories that protein supplements provide because you can now satisfy your protein needs from whole foods.

Week 8 Meal Plan

Day 1:
- **Breakfast:** Boiled eggs and Avocado on Toast
- **Lunch:** Tuna Salad
- **Dinner:** Slow roasted Pesto Salmon

Day 2:
- **Breakfast:** Cinnamon Oatmeal
- **Lunch:** Slow roasted Pesto Salmon
- **Dinner:** Leftovers

Day 3:
- **Breakfast:** Boiled eggs and Avocado on Toast
- **Lunch:** Cottage Cheese with fruits
- **Dinner:** Baked fish with pea puree

Day 4:
- **Breakfast:** Cinnamon Oatmeal
- **Lunch:** Ranch Seasoned Crispy Chicken and Cheesy Cauliflower Casserole
- **Dinner:** Butternut Squash and black bean Enchiladas

Day 5:
- **Breakfast:** High protein Pancakes
- **Lunch:** Butternut Squash and black bean Enchiladas
- **Dinner:** Buffalo Chicken Wrap

Day 6:
- **Breakfast:** Greek Yogurt
- **Lunch:** Buffalo Chicken Wrap
- **Dinner:** Cauliflower Pizza and caramelized onions and chicken sausage

Day 7:
- **Breakfast** High protein Pancakes
- **Lunch:** Cauliflower Pizza and caramelized onions and chicken sausage
- **Dinner:** Tuna Salad

Suggested Snack

1 cup Milk (High Protein Milk)

Chapter 4: Liquid Recipes

1. High Protein Chicken Soup

Serves: 1

Total time: 15 minutes

Ingredients:

- 1/3 cup dry nonfat milk powder
- Unflavored protein powder: 2 scoops equal about 20 grams of protein.
- Warm water (to equal 4-6 oz.)
- 1 teaspoon low sodium chicken bouillon

Preparation:

Mix low sodium chicken bouillon, nonfat milk powder, and protein powder in a bowl. Add an ounce of warm water at a time and keep adding while mixing until you have a total of 4-6 oz. Serve at room temperature.

Nutrition information per serving: Calories: 160 kcal, Protein: 28 g, Total Carbs: 12 g, Dietary Fibers: 2 g, Total Fat: 1 g

2. High Protein Fruit Smoothie

Serves: 1

Total time: 3 minutes

Ingredients:

- ½ cup almond milk: unsweetened
- 1 scoop protein powder: unflavored
- ½ cup frozen unsweetened berries

Preparation:

In a blender, mix all ingredients until smooth. Pour in a serving cup and enjoy.

Nutrition information per serving: Calories: 145 kcal, Protein: 20 g, Total Carbs: 15 g, Dietary Fibers: 2 g, Total Fat: 1 g

3. High Protein Milk

Serves: 1

Total time: 3 minutes

Ingredients:

- ¼ teaspoon vanilla extract
- ½ cup (4 oz.) low-fat milk
- 2 scoops unflavored protein powder
- Cinnamon to garnish (added)

Preparation:

Combine all ingredients in a blender and process until smooth. Enjoy with a sprinkling of cinnamon on top.

Nutrition information per serving: Calories: 140 kcal, Protein: 24 g, Total Carbs: 6 g, Dietary Fibers: 0 g, Total Fat: 1 g

4. Mixed Vegetable Soup

Serves: 4

Total time: 25 minutes

Ingredients:

- 2 garlic cloves, crushed.
- Oil spray
- 5 cups low salt vegetable or chicken stock
- 1 onion, diced.
- Black pepper to taste (freshly ground)
- 1 teaspoon dried oregano

- 1 carrot, peeled, diced.
- ½ Zucchini, diced.
- 1 cup chopped green beans,
- ¼ cabbage, chopped.
- 1 teaspoon dried basil
- ¼ cauliflower, finely diced.
- 2 tablespoons tomato paste (no added salt)
- 1 cup chopped tomatoes.

Preparation:

Use an oil-sprayed saucepan, heat it. Cook the onion, carrots, and garlic for 5 minutes. Add remaining ingredients and get it to a boil, except the Zucchini. Cover, reduce to medium heat, and cook for 15 minutes or until the beans are soft. Cook, sometimes stirring until the Zucchini is soft. To taste, season with pepper.

Nutrition information per serving: Calories: 97 kcal, Protein: 4.5 g, Total Carbs: 11 g, Dietary Fibers: 6.5 g, Total Fat: 3 g

5. Double Fudge Chocolate Shake

Serves: 2

Total time: 5 minutes

Ingredients:

- 1 cup low-fat milk or unsweetened soy milk
- ½ cup low fat plain Greek yogurt
- 1 scoop (¼ cup) chocolate protein powder
- 2 tablespoons unsweetened cocoa powder
- ½ small banana
- ½ teaspoon vanilla extract

Preparation:

In a blender, combine yogurt, protein powder, cocoa powder, banana, vanilla, and milk. Blend until thick, creamy, and smooth for at least 2-3 minutes. Serve immediately or refrigerate for later usage.

Nutrition information per serving: Calories: 157 kcal, Protein: 20 g, Total Carbs: 18 g, Dietary Fibers: 3 g, Total Fat: 1 g

6. Vanilla Bean Probiotic Shake

Serves: 2

Total time: 5 minutes

Ingredients:

- 1 cup low-fat milk or unsweetened vanilla soy milk
- ¼ cup low fat plain Greek yogurt
- 1 scoop (¼ cup) vanilla protein powder
- ½ cup low-fat plain kefir
- 5 ice cubes
- 1 teaspoon vanilla extract

Preparation:

In a blender, combine yogurt, protein powder, kefir, ice cubes, vanilla, and milk. Blend until powder is well dissolved for at least 3-4 minutes. Serve immediately or refrigerate for later usage.

Nutrition information per serving: Calories: 153 kcal, Protein: 22 g, Total Carbs: 8 g, Dietary Fibers: 2 g, Total Fat: 3 g

7. Protein-Packed Peanut Butter Shake

Serves: 2

Total time: 5 minutes

Ingredients:

- 1 cup low-fat milk
- ½ cup low fat plain Greek yogurt
- ¼ cup nonfat ricotta cheese
- 1 scoop (¼ cup) chocolate protein powder
- 2 tablespoon powdered peanut butter
- 2 tablespoons cocoa powder

Preparation:

In a blender, combine yogurt, protein powder, ricotta, powdered peanut butter, cocoa powder, and milk. Blend until powder is well dissolved for at least 3-4 minutes. Serve immediately or refrigerate for later usage.

Nutrition information per serving: Calories: 215 kcal, Protein: 27 g, Total Carbs: 18 g, Dietary Fibers: 3 g, Total Fat: 3 g

8. Chunky Monkey Smoothie

Serves: 2

Total time: 5 minutes

Ingredients:

- 1 small banana frozen
- 1 cup unsweetened almond milk
- ½ cup low-fat plain Greek yogurt
- 1 scoop (¼ cup) chocolate protein powder
- 2 tablespoons powdered peanut butter.
- 1 cup ice cubes

Preparation:

In a blender, combine chocolate protein powder, banana, yogurt, powdered peanut butter, ice cubes, and milk. Blend until powder is well dissolved and no longer visible for at least 3-4 minutes. Serve immediately or refrigerate for later usage.

Nutrition information per serving: Calories: 194 kcal, Protein: 20 g, Total Carbs: 23 g, Dietary Fibers: 4 g, Total Fat: 4 g

9. Strawberry Banana Protein Smoothie

Serves: 2

Total time: 5 minutes

Ingredients:

- ½ cup frozen or fresh strawberries
- 1 small ripe banana
- 1 scoop (¼ cup) vanilla or unflavored protein powder
- 5 ice cubes
- 1 cup low-fat milk

Preparation:

Put all the ingredients together in a blender, blend until smooth for 3 to 4 minutes. If the mixture is too thick, add more milk. If the mixture is too thin, add less milk.

Nutrition information per serving: Calories: 131 kcal, Protein: 15 g, Total Carbs: 14 g, Dietary Fibers: 2 g, Total Fat: 1 g

10. Vanilla Apple pie protein Shake

Serves: 2

Total time: 5 minutes

Ingredients:

- 1 cup low-fat milk
- 1 scoop (¼ cup) vanilla protein powder
- 1 small apple, peeled, cored, and chopped.
- 1 teaspoon vanilla extract
- 2 teaspoons ground cinnamon
- ½ teaspoon ground nutmeg
- 5 ice cubes

Preparation:

In a blender, combine protein powder, apple, vanilla protein powder, cinnamon, nutmeg, ice cubes, and milk. Blend until powder is well dissolved and no longer visible for at least 3-4 minutes. Serve immediately or refrigerate for later usage.

Nutrition information per serving: Calories: 123 kcal, Protein: 14 g, Total Carbs: 14 g, Dietary Fibers: 1 g, Total Fat: 1 g

11. Berry Protein Shake

Serves: 2

Total time: 5 minutes

Ingredients:

- 1 cup low-fat milk or unsweetened soy milk
- 1 scoop (¼ cup) vanilla or plain protein powder
- 5 ice cubes
- 3/4 cup mixed frozen berries.

Preparation:

In a blender, combine protein powder, berries, ice cubes, and milk. Blend until powder is well dissolved and no longer visible for at least 3-4 minutes. Serve immediately or refrigerate for later usage.

Nutrition information per serving: Calories: 126 kcal, Protein: 15 g, Total Carbs: 14 g, Dietary Fibers: 3 g, Total Fat: 1 g

12. Fresh Mango Smoothie

Serves: 3

Total time: 10 minutes

Ingredients:

- 1 medium mango roughly chopped.
- 1 cup coconut milk
- 1 tablespoon walnuts, chopped.
- 1 teaspoon vanilla extract, sugar-free
- A handful of ice cubes

Preparation:

Peel the mango and cut it into small chunks. Set aside. Now, combine mango, coconut milk, walnuts, and vanilla extract in a blender and process until well combined and creamy. Transfer to a serving glass and stir in the vanilla extract. Add a few ice cubes and serve immediately.

Nutrition information per serving: Calories: 271 kcal, Protein: 3.4 g, Total Carbs: 21.7 g, Dietary Fibers: 3.7 g, Total Fat: 21 g

13. Milky Chai Latte

Serves: 2

Total time: 10 minutes

Ingredients:

- ½ teaspoons honey
- 1 teaspoon black tea leaves, powdered.
- ½ teaspoons cinnamon
- ½ teaspoons nutmeg
- 2 cloves
- 8 oz. almond/skim/soy milk

Preparation:

Combine the tea, honey, and spices and mix well. Add the milk to a small pot over low heat. Bring to a light simmer and add the tea mixture, mixing well continuously until the lumps have dissolved. Add cloves, reduce the heat, cover, and allow it to boil for 10 minutes. Pour through a sieve to get rid of the cloves and serve in your favorite mugs.

Nutrition information per serving: Calories: 62 kcal, Protein: 1 g, Total Carbs: 12 g, Dietary Fibers: 1 g, Total Fat: 1 g

14. Vegetable Consommé

Serves: 3

Total time: 1 hr.

Ingredients:

- 2 egg whites
- 14 oz. vegetable stock

Preparation:

Whisk the egg whites until they begin to foam slightly. Blend the egg whites with the vegetable stock until it is almost smooth. In a deep pan over low heat, add the stock. Bring to a simmer, constantly stirring, until the egg whites shape a crust on the surface. Scoop the egg white crust into a sieve lined with muslin or a clean tea towel (not washed with soap or detergent). Slowly pour the stock into the egg whites and sieve until enough of the liquid has passed through (don't force it). Return the liquid to the pan and heat it until it is warm (do not boil).

Nutrition information per serving: Calories: 20 kcal, Protein: 4 g, Total Carbs: 1 g, Dietary Fibers: 0 g, Total Fat: 0 g

15. Chicken Consommé

Serves: 4

Total time: 1 hr.

Ingredients:

- 2 egg whites
- 16 oz. homemade chicken stock

Preparation:

The procedure is the same for chicken consommé. Whisk the egg whites until they begin to foam slightly. In a separate bowl, whisk together the egg whites and chicken stock until smooth. In a deep pan over low heat, add the chicken stock. Bring to a simmer, constantly stirring, until the egg whites shape a crust on top. Scoop the egg white crust into a sieve lined with muslin or a clean tea towel (not washed with soap or detergent). Slowly pour the stock into the egg whites and sieve until enough of the liquid has passed through (don't force it). Return the liquid to the pan and heat it until it is warm (do not boil).

Nutrition information per serving: Calories: 51 kcal, Protein: 5 g, Total Carbs: 4 g, Dietary Fibers: 0 g, Total Fat: 1 g

16. Peppermint Tea

Serves: 4

Total time: 30 minutes

Ingredients:

- ½ cup pepper leaf, dried
- 4 cups hot water

Preparation:

Set Water on to boil. Once boiling, add peppermint leaves and remove them from heat. Cover and let rest for at least 5 minutes. Strain, serve and enjoy.

Nutrition information per serving: Calories: 34.2 kcal, Protein: 0.1 g, Total Carbs: 0 g, Dietary Fibers: 0 g, Total Fat: 0.0 g

17. Pecan Tea

Serves: 2

Total time: 20 minutes

Ingredients:

- 5 tablespoons pecan, grounded
- 1 cup water
- 1 teaspoon cinnamon

Preparation:

Heat a cup of water in a saucepan and then stir in the remaining ingredients. Serve hot.

Nutrition information per serving: Calories: 40 kcal, Protein: 1.51 g, Total Carbs: 1.4 g, Dietary Fibers: 0 g, Total Fat: 3.58 g

18. Ginger Tea

Serves: 2

Total time: 15 minutes

Ingredients:

- 3 tablespoons ginger root, grated
- 3 cups boiling water

Preparation:

Combine all ingredients and allow to rest. Covered for at least 10 minutes. Serve hot.

Nutrition information per serving: Calories: 26.8 kcal, Protein: 0.1 g, Total Carbs: 6.8 g, Dietary Fibers: 0 g, Total Fat: 0 g

19. Orange Vanilla Tea

Serves: 2

Total time: 10 minutes

Ingredients:

- ¼ teaspoons vanilla extract
- 2 medium peeled and sliced oranges
- ¼ cup water

Preparation:

Combine all ingredients in a saucepan and boil it. Remove from heat and let it rest for at least 5 minutes. Strain and serve hot.

Nutrition information per serving: Calories: 60 kcal, Protein: 1 g, Total Carbs: 14 g, Dietary Fibers: 3 g, Total Fat: 0 g

20. Peanut Tea

Serves: 2

Total time: 20 minutes

Ingredients:

- 5 teaspoons peanuts, grounded
- 1 teaspoon cinnamon
- 1 cup water

Preparation:

Heat a cup of water in a saucepan and then stir in the remaining ingredients. Serve hot.

Nutrition information per serving: Calories: 40 kcal, Protein: 1.51 g, Total Carbs: 1.4 g, Dietary Fibers: 2 g, Total Fat: 3.58 g

21. Chamomile Tea

Serves: 2

Total time: 5 minutes

Ingredients:

- 2 cups water
- 3 teaspoons dried chamomile

Preparation:

Take a saucepan and start heating water on high heat. Once the water starts boiling, switch off the heat and add the dried Chamomile. Keep it covered for a minute. Strain the chamomile tea into the teacups, swirl, and serve it.

Nutrition information per serving: Calories: 1 kcal, Protein: 0.0 g, Total Carbs: 0.4 g, Dietary Fibers: 0.7 g, Total Fat: 0 g

Chapter 5: Breakfast Recipes

1. Ginger Peach Smoothie

Serves: 4

Total time: 5 minutes

Ingredients:

- 1 tablespoon coconut oil
- 1 cup coconut milk
- 1 teaspoon fresh ginger, peeled.
- 1 tablespoon chia seeds
- 1 large peach, chopped.

Preparation:

Peaches must be washed and sliced in half. Remove the pit and cut the fruit into small chunks. Cut a small ginger knob. Peel and chop it into small pieces and put it aside. In a mixer, combine the peach, coconut milk, ginger, and coconut oil. Process until everything is well blended. Stir in the chia seeds and transfer them to a serving glass. Add ice if desired, and garnish with mint leaves if desired.

Nutrition information per serving: Calories: 201 kcal, Protein: 2.5 g, Total Carbs: 8.9 g, Dietary Fibers: 3.5 g, Total Fat: 19 g

2. Cherry Avocado Smoothie

Serves: 3

Total time: 5 minutes

Ingredients:

- 1 whole lime
- ½ ripe avocado, chopped.
- 1 cup sugar-free coconut water,
- 1 cup fresh cherries

Preparation:

Cut the avocado in half after peeling it. Remove the pit and cut the fruit into small bits. Refrigerate the remaining one and, for current usage, set a part of them aside. Using a large colander, rinse the cherries under cool running water. Remove the pits and cut each in half. Put it aside. Split the lime in half after peeling it. Place it aside. In a mixer, blend the avocado, cherries, coconut water, and lime. Transfer to a serving glass after pulsing to blend. Refrigerate for 10 minutes before serving with a few ice cubes.

Nutrition information per serving: Calories: 128 kcal, Protein: 1.7 g, Total Carbs: 17 g, Dietary Fibers: 3.8 g, Total Fat: 6.8 g

3. Green Tea Smoothie

Serves: 2

Total time: 10 minutes

Ingredients:

- 3 tablespoons green tea powder
- 1 cup grapes, white
- ½ cup kale, finely chopped.
- 1 tablespoon honey
- ½ teaspoon fresh mint, ground
- 1 cup water

Preparation:

Under cool running water, rinse the grapes. The pits should be drained and removed and set them aside. Wash the kale well in a big colander under cool running water. Drain well and cut into small pieces with a good knife. Mix 2 tablespoons of hot water with green tea powder. Soak in the water for 2 minutes and set it aside. In a blender, combine the mint, grapes, honey, kale, and water and mix until smooth. Add water and tea mixture. Allow 30 minutes to chill before serving.

Nutrition information per serving: Calories: 76 kcal, Protein: 2.3 g, Total Carbs: 18.3 g, Dietary Fibers: 2.2 g, Total Fat: 0.2 g

4. Guava Smoothie

Serves: 2

Total time: 5-7 minutes

Ingredients:

- 1 banana peeled and sliced.
- 1 cup baby spinach finely chopped.
- 1 cup guava, seeds removed, chopped.
- 1 teaspoon fresh ginger, grated.
- 2 cups water
- ½ medium-sized mango, peeled and chopped.

Preparation:

Peel the guava and cut it in half. Scoop out the seeds and wash them. Cut into small pieces and set aside. Rinse the baby spinach thoroughly under cold running water. Drain well and torn into small pieces. Set aside. Peel the banana and chop it into small chunks. Set aside. Peel the mango and cut it into small pieces. Set aside. Now, combine guava, baby spinach, banana, ginger, and mango in a juicer and process until well combined. Gradually add water and blend until all combine and creamy. Transfer to a serving glass and refrigerate for 20 minutes before serving. Enjoy!

Nutrition information per serving: Calories: 166 kcal, Protein: 3.9 g, Total Carbs: 39.1 g, Dietary Fibers: 7.8 g, Total Fat: 1.4 g

5. Egg, spinach, Tomato, and Mushroom Breakfast

Serves: 1

Total time: 10 minutes

Ingredients:

- 1 large field mushroom,
- 1 large egg
- 3 cherry tomatoes
- ½ cup baby spinach
- 2 teaspoons parsley/chives (finely chopped)

Preparation:

In a shallow bowl, combine the mushroom, 2 tablespoons of water, and balsamic vinegar splash. Microwave for 90 seconds, covered with glad wrap. In a small dish, crack the egg. Microwave for 35-40 seconds after adding 2 teaspoons of water and covering. Place the mushroom on a plate to serve. Poached egg, sliced tomatoes, and finely minced parsley/chives go on top. Add a pinch of salt and pepper to taste.

Nutrition information per serving: Calories: 365 kcal, Protein: 9.0 g, Total Carbs: 9.2 g, Dietary Fibers: 3.0 g, Total Fat: 6.7 g

6. Smoothie Bowl with Greek yogurt and Fresh Berries

Serves: 1

Total time: 10 minutes.

Ingredients:

- 1/3 cup fresh spinach
- 3/4 cup unsweetened vanilla almond milk or any low-fat milk
- ¼ cup low-fat plain Greek yogurt
- ½ scoop (1/8 cup) plain or vanilla protein powder
- ¼ cup fresh blueberries
- ¼ cup fresh raspberries
- ¼ cup frozen mixed berries
- 1 tablespoon sliced, slivered almonds.
- 1 teaspoon chia seeds

Preparation:

To a blender, add all smoothie ingredients and pulse until smooth. Blend for 4 to 5 minutes until the powder is well dissolved. Pour smoothie into a bowl, and top with desired ingredients.

Nutrition information per serving: Calories: 255 kcal, Protein: 20 g, Total Carbs: 21 g, Dietary Fibers: 8 g, Total Fat: 10 g

7. High Protein Pancake

Serves: 4

Total time: 10 minutes

Ingredients:

- 3 eggs
- 1 cup low-fat cottage cheese
- 1/3 cup whole-wheat pastry flour
- 1 ½ tablespoons coconut oil, melted.
- Non-stick cooking spray

Preparation:

Whisk the eggs gently in a wide mixing bowl. Just when mixed, whisk in the cottage cheese, flour, and coconut oil. Coat a large skillet or griddle with cooking spray and heat over low heat. Pour 1/3 cup batter into the skillet for each pancake using a measuring cup. Cook for 2-3 minutes, or until bubbles emerge on top of each pancake. Flip the pancakes and cook for another 1 to 2 minutes, or until golden brown on the other hand. Serve right away.

Nutrition information per serving: Calories: 182 kcal, Protein: 12 g, Total Carbs: 10 g, Dietary Fibers: 3 g, Total Fat: 10 g

8. Boiled Eggs and Avocado on Toast

Serves: 4

Total time: 15 minutes

Ingredients:

- 4 eggs
- 4 slices sprouted whole-wheat bread.
- 1 medium Avocado
- 1 teaspoon hot sauce
- Freshly ground Black pepper

Preparation:

Over high heat, get a large pot of water to a rapid boil. Set the timer for 10 minutes after carefully placing the eggs into boiling water with a spoon. To end the cooking process, immediately move the eggs from the boiling water to a strainer and run cold water over them. When the eggs are cool enough to touch, peel them and slice them into fourths lengthwise. The bread should be toasted. In a shallow bowl, mash the avocado with a fork and stir in the hot sauce. Top toasted bread with avocado mash and four egg slices. Season with black pepper.

Nutrition information per serving: Calories: 191 kcal, Protein: 10 g, Total Carbs: 15 g, Dietary Fibers: 5 g, Total Fat: 10 g

9. Yogurt Breakfast Popsicles

Serves: 6

Total time: 6 minutes

Ingredients:

- ½ cup regular or instant oats
- 1 cup mixed berries or chopped fruits.
- ½ cup milk 1% or skim
- 1 cup Greek yogurt, plain, non-fat

Preparation:

Combine the milk and yogurt in a mixing bowl. Divide the mixture between your popsicle molds. Fill each mold with a few berries. Divide the ½ cup oatmeal among each mold. Insert a wooden ice cream stick in each mold, then freeze the popsicles for at least 4 hours before serving. To remove the popsicles, run the mound under a little hot water until they come loose.

Nutrition information per serving: Calories: 75 kcal, Protein: 5 g, Total Carbs: 11 g, Dietary Fibers: 1.5 g, Total Fat: 0.6 g

10. Healthy Porridge Bowl

Serves: 2

Total time: 15 minutes

Ingredients:

- 100 g frozen or fresh blueberries
- 1 orange juice
- 150 g porridge oats
- 100 ml milk
- ½ banana, sliced.
- 2 tablespoons smooth almond butter
- 1 tablespoon goji berries or sliced almonds
- 1 tablespoon chia seeds

Preparation:

In a bowl, combine half of the blueberries and all of the orange juice. Cook for about 5 minutes, or until the berries soften. Meanwhile, in a pan over low heat, add the oats, milk, and 450 ml water and mix until creamy. Blueberries, almond butter, chia seeds, sliced almonds, and banana are sprinkled on top.

Nutrition information per serving: Calories: 533 kcal, Protein: 17 g, Total Carbs: 66 g, Dietary Fibers: 13 g, Total Fat: 19 g

11. Greek Omelet

Serves: 1

Total time: 5 minutes

Ingredients:

- 20 g pure egg white protein powder
- 1 whole egg
- ¼ cup tomato
- 1 tablespoon red onion

Optional: basil to garnish, salt, and pepper to taste

Preparation:

Use a fork or an electric mixer to re-constitute pure egg white protein powder with 3 tablespoons water until an egg-white consistency is achieved. Mix whole egg in it and set it aside. In a warm non-stick pan greased with olive oil, cook the onion until translucent, then add the tomatoes and cook until they are soft. Pour in the egg, keeping these ingredients to one side of the plate, and wait until the egg begins to firm up and bubbles appear on top. Add the cheese, fold it in half, and set it aside to melt. If required, flip the egg and season with salt and pepper to taste.

Nutrition information per serving: Calories: 250 kcal, Protein: 15 g, Total Carbs: 9 g, Dietary Fibers: 1 g, Total Fat: 7 g

12. Mini Egg Muffins

Serves: 6

Total time: 25 minutes

Ingredients:

- 6 tablespoons low fat/fat-free cottage cheese
- Chives (optional)
- 6 tablespoons frozen peas
- 4 eggs
- Black pepper

Preparation:

Preheat the oven to 392°F (200°C) and spray or use muffin cases to line a muffin tin. Combine all of the ingredients and divide them into 6 frittatas. Bake for 20 minutes, and cool before withdrawing from the muffin tin.

Nutrition information per serving: Calories: 83 kcal, Protein: 7 g, Total Carbs: 1 g, Dietary Fibers: 1 g, Total Fat: 5 g

13. Baked eggs

Serves: 1

Total time: 20 minutes

Ingredients:

- Spinach (optional)
- 15 g low-fat hard cheese
- 2 medium eggs

Preparation:

Preheat the oven to 356°F (180°C). In a muffin tray or a ramekin, place the spinach. On the spinach, crack an egg. Bake for 15 minutes with the cheese on top.

Nutrition information per serving: Calories: 172 kcal, Protein: 14 g, Total Carbs: 1.5 g, Dietary Fibers: 0.5 g, Total Fat: 10 g

14. Zucchini Fritters

Serves: 4

Total time: 30 minutes

Ingredients:

- ½ cup raw quick oats
- 6 large eggs
- Oil as needed for cooking.
- 1 small zucchini (grated)

Preparation:

In a mixing bowl, whisk together the oats, eggs, and zucchini until well combined. Spray or brush a non-stick pan with a thin layer of oil, then ladle the batter into the pan. Keep an eye on the heat on these. It's possible that you'll need to reduce the heat to medium and cook these for a little longer. Cook the eggs entirely without burning them. Make the required adjustments. When the fritters are done, remove them from the pan and serve with a dollop of hummus.

Nutrition information per serving: Calories: 164 kcal, Protein: 12 g, Total Carbs: 8 g, Dietary Fibers: 1 g, Total Fat: 9 g

15. Blueberry Chia Overnight Oats

Serves: 1

Total time: 10 minutes (Refrigerating time: 4 hours)

Ingredients:

- 2 tablespoons chia seeds
- ¼ cup rolled oats.
- 1 cup unsweetened vanilla almond milk
- ½ cup blueberries
- ½ tablespoons honey (maple syrup, agave, or 1 Stevia packet)

Preparation:

Combine all of the ingredients. Refrigerate for 4 hours before serving.

The blueberries can be added to the overnight oats before or after mixing. Add them just before serving if you're going to have them in the fridge for a couple of nights.

Nutrition information per serving: Calories: 309 kcal, Protein: 9 g, Total Carbs: 43 g, Dietary Fibers: 12 g, Total Fat: 12 g

16. Cottage Cheese Pancakes

Serves: 4

Total time: 20 minutes

Ingredients:

- 1/3 cup all-purpose flour
- ½ teaspoons baking soda
- 1 cup low-fat cottage cheese
- ½ tablespoons canola oil
- 3 eggs, lightly beaten.

Preparation:

In a shallow mixing bowl, combine flour and baking soda. In another wide mixing bowl, combine the remaining ingredients. Stir in the flour mixture until it is thoroughly mixed into the cottage cheese mixture. Spray a large skillet with cooking spray and heat over low heat. Pour 1/3-cup portions of batter onto skillet and cook until surface bubbles emerge. Flip and cook until brown on the other hand. Drizzle with low-calorie syrup before serving.

Nutrition information per serving: Calories: 152 kcal, Protein: 13 g, Total Carbs: 10 g, Dietary Fibers: 2 g, Total Fat: 7 g

17. Carrot Oatmeal

Serves: 2

Total time: 10 minutes

Ingredients:

- ½ cup shredded carrot (about 1 medium carrot)
- ½ teaspoon cinnamon
- dash of nutmeg
- 1 cup quick oats (old fashioned oats work too)
- 1/3 cup raisins
- 1 tablespoon maple syrup
- Optional: pecans or walnuts for topping

Preparation:

Heat a saucepan over medium-high heat. Cook for 1 minute after adding the shredded carrots. In a saucepan, add 3/4 cup water, cinnamon, and nutmeg. Get the water to a boil. Add the oats. Cook for 60-90 seconds. Turn the burner off. Add the raisins and maple syrup. Cover and set aside for 2-3 minutes. Divide into two dishes, top with nuts if desired, and serve!

Nutrition information per serving: Calories: 261 kcal, Protein: 6 g, Total Carbs: 59 g, Dietary Fibers: 6 g, Total Fat: 3 g

18. Pumpkin Pie Bliss Protein Shake

Serves: 2

Total time: 5 minutes

Ingredients:

- 8 oz. non-fat milk
- 1 tablespoon Protein Powder base
- 2 tablespoons Chai Protein Powder
- 2 tablespoons half and half
- 1 tablespoon Sugar-Free Vanilla Syrup
- 1 ½ tablespoon 100% Pumpkin Puree (not pumpkin pie filling)

Preparation:

Combine all ingredients in a shaker and gently stir to properly combine. Pour over ice with a dollop of whipped cream and a pinch of cinnamon or pumpkin pie spice on top. For a frozen protein drink, mix all ingredients in a blender with 4-5 ice cubes and process until thick and smooth.

Nutrition information per serving: Calories: 194 kcal, Protein: 29 g, Total Carbs: 9 g, Dietary Fibers: 5 g, Total Fat: 3 g

19. Apricot Overnight Oatmeal Recipe

Serves: 1

Total time: 20 minutes

Ingredients:

- ½ cup old fashion oats
- 1 teaspoon ground cinnamon
- ¼ teaspoon ground allspice
- ¼ teaspoon ground ginger
- 1 teaspoon pure vanilla extract
- ¼ cup dried, chopped apricots (no sugar added)

Preparation:

For Overnight Oats:

Toss all of the ingredients in a small zip-top baggie and freeze for up to 6 months. Place your oats in a container or covered bowl with 1 cup milk (any kind) the night before you plan to eat them and leave them in the fridge overnight. Warm on the stovetop or in the microwave if desired.

For Cooking Oats:

Toss all of the ingredients in a small zipper-top baggie and freeze for a possible busy morning. When you're ready to prepare, add the bag's contents with 1 cup of milk (any kind) in a small pot and cook according to the oats box instructions.

Nutrition information per serving: Calories: 266 kcal, Protein: 7 g, Total Carbs: 54 g, Dietary Fibers: 9 g, Total Fat: 3 g

20. Soufflé Omelet with Mushrooms

Serves: 1

Total time: 20 minutes

Ingredients:

- 1 teaspoon olive oil
- 1 garlic clove, minced.
- 8 oz. mushrooms, sliced.
- 1 tablespoon parsley, minced.
- 3 large eggs separated.
- ¼ cup cheddar cheese fat-free, shredded.

Preparation:

Heat the olive oil in a skillet over medium heat and sauté the garlic. Sauté for 10 minutes with the mushrooms. Remove the pan from the heat and add the parsley, and set aside. Whisk the egg yolks until they are thickened. The whites can then be whisked until they are white and frothy. (The egg whites can be blended in a blender.) Fold the whites into the yolks, season with salt and pepper, and fold in the cheese. Using a non-stick spray, coat a big skillet. Cover and pour in the egg mixture. Cook until the top and bottom of the layer is set. Carefully loosen it with the aid of a spatula. Fold the omelet over carefully after adding the mushrooms. Serve immediately.

Nutrition information per serving: Calories: 329 kcal, Protein: 31 g, Total Carbs: 10 g, Dietary Fibers: 2 g, Total Fat: 20 g

21. No-Bake Protein Bars

Serves: 12

Total time: 20 minutes

Ingredients:

- ½ cup natural almond butter, peanut butter, or sunflower seed butter
- 1.5 cups rolled oats, gluten-free and blended into the flour.
- ½ cup vegan protein powder: unsweetened/unflavored
- ¼-½ teaspoon fine grain sea salt, to taste
- ½ cup pure maple syrup (or liquid sweetener of choice)
- 1 teaspoon pure vanilla extract
- ½ cup crisp rice cereal
- ½ tablespoon coconut oil
- 3 tablespoons dark chocolate chip

Preparation:

A piece of parchment paper can be used to line an 8-inch square pan. In a wide mixing bowl, combine the oat flour, protein powder, salt, and rice crisp. Add the maple syrup, nut/seed butter, and vanilla to a mixing bowl. Stir all together thoroughly. If a mixture is too dry, add a splash of non-dairy milk and stir to combine. Roll out with a pastry roller until smooth and press into pan. Place the pan in the freezer. In a small pot over low heat, melt the chocolate chips and coconut oil together. Remove from heat when half of the chips have melted and stir until smooth. Remove the mixture from the freezer after around 5-10 minutes and slice into bars. Drizzle with molten chocolate and return to the freezer to set. In an airtight freezer bag or container, store for a week or longer in the freezer.

Nutrition information per serving: Calories: 200 kcal, Protein: 8 g, Total Carbs: 22 g, Dietary Fibers: 2 g, Total Fat: 9 g

22. Strawberry Chia Pudding

Serves: 4

Total time: 10 minutes

Ingredients:

For the glaze:

- 1/8 teaspoon xanthan gum
- 4 teaspoons granulated stevia
- 1 tablespoon lemon juice
- ½ cup fresh or frozen strawberries (sliced)
- 1 tablespoon water

For the chia pudding:

- 100-gram cream cheese
- ½ cup heavy whipping cream
- 1 cup unsweetened original almond milk
- 2 tablespoons granulated stevia
- 1 teaspoon vanilla extract
- 1 cup fresh or frozen strawberries
- ½ cup chia seeds

Preparation

For the glaze:

Mix the stevia blend and xanthan gum in a small saucepan. Slowly drizzle in the lemon juice and water, whisking constantly. Add the strawberries and mix well. Over medium-low heat, get the mixture to a boil. Remove the pan from the heat until the mixture has achieved a boil. If you're using fresh strawberries, allow them to soften and release their color by simmering for a minute or two. Drizzle about half of the strawberry mixture down the sides of four one-cup serving dishes (reserve the remainder for later). For this, you can also use half-pint canning jars, but dessert dishes and wine glasses often serve well. Put the rest of the strawberry mixture aside.

For the chia pudding:

In a processor, combine all of the ingredients for the chia pudding. Cover and mix on low speed for a few minutes until the ingredients are well-blended. Pour the chia pudding over the strawberry glaze for each of the four serving glasses. The remaining strawberry glaze can be drizzled on top. Refrigerate overnight, covered.

Nutrition information per serving: Calories: 346 kcal, Protein: 7 g, Total Carbs: 13 g, Dietary Fibers: 9 g, Total Fat: 30 g

23. Banana Bread Protein Waffles

Serves: 2

Total time: 10 minutes

Ingredients:

- ½ cup oat flour
- ¼ cup vanilla protein powder
- ¼ cup coconut flour
- ¼ teaspoon cinnamon
- Pinch salt
- ½ cup + 2 tablespoons milk
- ½ cup mashed bananas (~2 small bananas or 1 large banana)
- ½ teaspoon vanilla

Topping:
peaches/strawberries/raspberries/bananas/blackberries and Greek yogurt

Preparation:

Preheat the waffle machine to medium. Combine protein powder, oat flour, cinnamon, coconut flour, and salt in a mixing bowl. Add the mashed bananas, milk, and vanilla to a mixing bowl. Stir gently to form batter-like consistency. Use a non-stick spray to coat the waffle maker thoroughly. Since these waffles are prone to sticking, grease them generously. Cook the waffles until they are done on medium heat. Fruit

and yogurt can be added to the top. No worries if the top layer slips away from the bottom layer as you open the waffle maker. Remove the top layer from the waffle maker with a knife and replace it on the waffle's bottom. It also has the same flavor. Lower the waffle maker's heat setting and cook the waffles slower and longer the next time.

Nutrition information per serving: Calories: 190 kcal, Protein: 4.4 g, Total Carbs: 34 g, Dietary Fibers: 1.4 g, Total Fat: 6.3 g

24. Peanut Butter and Jelly Chia Pudding

Serves: 3

Total time: 1 hr. 30 minutes

Ingredients:

Compote:

- 1 cup wild blueberries (frozen or fresh)
- 1 tablespoon orange juice
- 1 tablespoon chia seeds

Chia Pudding:

- 1 cup unsweetened plain almond milk
- ½ cup light coconut milk
- 1 teaspoon vanilla (optional)
- 1-2 tablespoons maple syrup (to taste)
- 3 tablespoons natural salted peanut butter (creamy or crunchy // plus more for serving)
- 1/3 cup chia seeds
- Fresh blueberries (optional // for topping)

Preparation:

Add the blueberries and orange juice to a small skillet or saucepan. Warm over medium-high heat until it begins to bubble. Reduce to medium-low heat and cook for 2 minutes, stirring periodically. Remove the pan from the heat and stir in the chia seeds. To combine them thoroughly, stir all together. Divide the compote into 6 small serving dishes for safe storage in the fridge, and chill until ready to serve.

Meanwhile, combine almond and coconut milk, vanilla (optional), maple syrup, and peanut butter in a blender. To thoroughly combine them, blend on high. Taste and adjust the flavor as desired, adding more maple syrup or peanut butter for sweetness or saltiness, accordingly.

Pulse a few times after adding the chia seeds, being cautious not to blend them because you want the chia seeds to remain whole. Pour them in a liquid measuring cup or container in the fridge for cooling.

Allow the chia compote to cool for 10 minutes. Then, take the chia pudding and compote it out of the fridge. Stir the chia pudding to redistribute the seeds, then split among the three serving dishes directly on top of the compote. Cover tightly and cool for at least 1-2 hours (preferably overnight) or until thoroughly chilled and pudding-like consistency. Cover with additional peanut butter and fresh blueberries to serve (optional). Keep in the refrigerator for 3-4 days covered for later usage.

Nutrition information per serving: Calories: 211 kcal, Protein: 6.1 g, Total Carbs: 19 g, Dietary Fibers: 6 g, Total Fat: 13.3 g

25. Strawberry Buckwheat Pancakes

Serves: 4

Total time: 15 minutes

Ingredients:

- 300 ml almond milk
- 1 teaspoon vanilla extract
- 75 g blanched almonds
- 100 g buckwheat flour
- 100 g rice flour
- olive oil
- 2 level teaspoons baking powder
- 1 ripe banana
- 350 g of seasonal berries, such as blackberries, strawberries, blueberries, raspberries
- maple syrup
- one sprig of fresh rosemary
- 4 tablespoons Greek yogurt

Preparation:

In a mixer, combine the vanilla extract, milk, almonds, flours, and baking powder. Blitz until smooth after adding the banana.

Preheat a wide non-stick frying pan over medium heat. Once the pan is warm, add 1 teaspoon of oil for each portion of two pancakes, along with 3 teaspoons of batter per pancake. Cook for 4 minutes, just until the bottoms are nicely golden (the first pancakes are often a little uncomfortable when you change the temperature control).

Cook for 2 minutes, or until golden on the other side, with a bit of pressure applied with an egg flip, then move to a pan, fruit side up. Repeat the procedure using a ball of kitchen paper to clean out the pan. Place the rosemary sprig in the maple syrup bottle and gently brush the syrup over the hot pancakes. Serve with extra berries on the side and a dollop of yogurt on top of each slice, if desired.

Nutrition information per serving: Calories: 143 kcal, Protein: 5 g, Total Carbs: 24 g, Dietary Fibers: 3 g, Total Fat: 3 g

26. Cleansing Smoothie

Serves: 2

Total time: 10 minutes

Ingredients:

- 1 eating apple
- 1 dessert pear
- 10 g/small handful spinach leaves
- 5 tablespoons low-fat coconut milk
- ¼ ripe avocado, peeled and chopped.
- 150 ml/2/3 cup fresh orange juice

Preparation:

Cut the apple and pear into small chunks after coring. Add the spinach, apple, coconut milk, avocado, pear, and orange juice to a food processor or smoothie maker. Pulse until the mixture is smooth and well combined. To serve, pour into a bottle.

Nutrition information per serving: Calories: 283 kcal, Protein: 3.2 g, Total Carbs: 40.8 g, Dietary Fibers: 6 g, Total Fat: 13 g

27. Protein Banana Cream pie

Serves: 8

Total time: 10 minutes

Ingredients:

- 2 boxes instant pudding - fat-free, sugar-free banana cream
- 1 ½ scoops protein powder - 45 g vanilla or banana
- 2 ½ cups milk substitute - or milk (20 oz.)
- 1 medium banana
- ½ cup whipped topping
- 1 pre-made pie crust - fat-free or reduced-fat

Preparation:

Use a whisk or hand mixer, blend Instant Pudding, Protein, and Milk for 1-2 minutes. Slice banana into slivers and lightly combine them in the mixture. Pour the mixture onto the pie crust and cover it. Refrigerate it for a couple of hours. Spread the Whipped Topping on top for serving (optional).

Nutrition information per serving: Calories: 171 kcal, Protein: 6.2 g, Total Carbs: 24.8 g, Dietary Fibers: 1.2 g, Total Fat: 5.2 g

28. Savory Bread Pudding

Serves: 4

Total time: 30 minutes

Ingredients:

- 4 slices diced wholemeal bread.
- 1 red pepper, diced.
- ½ red onion, diced.
- ½ cup mushrooms, diced.
- 2 cloves garlic, minced.
- 3 eggs
- ½ cup skim milk
- 1 teaspoon cumin
- ½ teaspoons cayenne pepper
- Black pepper, to taste
- 4 oz. low-fat mozzarella cheese

Preparation:

Preheat the oven to 375°F. Collect a medium-sized mixing bowl. Combine the bread, onion, mushroom, peppers, and garlic in a mixing bowl. In a separate bowl, whisk together the eggs and milk until thoroughly mixed. Combine the bread mixture with the egg mixture. Stir in the seasonings thoroughly. Pour the batter into a 4×4 baking pan that has been lightly greased. Add the shredded cheese on top. Bake for 40-50 minutes, or until the eggs are set, at 375°F.

Nutrition information per serving: Calories: 188 kcal, Protein: 18 g, Total Carbs: 19 g, Dietary Fibers: 3 g, Total Fat: 4 g

29. Fresh Apple & Quinoa Breakfast

Serves: 4

Total time: 15 minutes

Ingredients:

- 1 ½ apple, peeled and diced.
- 2 teaspoons ground nutmeg
- 2 tablespoons fresh lemon juice
- 2 cups water
- 1 cup uncooked quinoa
- 4 tablespoons skim milk

Preparation:

In a pot, combine the apples, nutmeg, and lemon juice. Over medium heat, bring the mixture to a boil. Cook until the apples are soft and mildly caramelized, stirring frequently. Remove with a slotted spoon from the pot and put aside. Fill the pot with water and quinoa (without wiping it down). Follow the package instructions for cooking the quinoa.

For serving:

Add quinoa (drained) into 4 bowls. Swirl in 1 tablespoon Milk and top with apples.

Nutrition information per serving: Calories: 192 kcal, Protein: 6 g, Total Carbs: 35 g, Dietary Fibers: 5 g, Total Fat: 3 g

30. Spiced Pumpkin Breakfast Bars

Serves: 4 bars

Total time: 30 minutes

Ingredients:

- ¼ cup canned pumpkin purée.
- ¼ cup plain low-fat yogurt
- 1 egg
- 2 tablespoons smooth peanut butter
- 1 tablespoon honey
- ½ teaspoons nutmeg
- ½ teaspoons vanilla extract
- ½ teaspoons baking soda
- ¼ cup dry rolled oat.

Preparation:

Preheat the oven to 375ºF. Combine the pumpkin, egg, peanut butter, yogurt, and honey in a wide mixing bowl. Stir in the remaining ingredients until well combined. Fill a greased 9x9 pan with the batter and bake for 25-30 minutes.

Nutrition information per serving: Calories: 113 kcal, Protein: 5 g, Total Carbs: 12 g, Dietary Fibers: 2 g, Total Fat: 5 g

31. Banana & Chia Seed Breakfast

Serves: 5

Total time: 10 minutes

Ingredients:

- 2 medium ripe bananas
- 2 cups almond milk
- 1 tablespoon smooth peanut butter
- 2 tablespoons chia seeds
- 2 tablespoons soy protein powder

Preparation:

In a food processor or mixer, combine all of the ingredients. Blend until everything is well mixed. Refrigerate for at least an hour before serving.

Nutrition information per serving: Calories: 162 kcal, Protein: 7 g, Total Carbs: 24 g, Dietary Fibers: 4 g, Total Fat: 5 g

32. Avocado & Berry Breakfast Bowls

Serves: 5

Total time: 6 minutes

Ingredients:

- ½ avocado peeled and diced.
- 1 cup frozen raspberries
- 1 cup low-fat Greek yogurt

Preparation:

In a high-powered processor, combine all of the ingredients. Blend until entirely smooth. Enjoy in chilled serving cups or sundae glasses.

Nutrition information per serving: Calories: 132 kcal, Protein: 12 g, Total Carbs: 13 g, Dietary Fibers: 5 g, Total Fat: 5 g

33. Spiced Sweet Potato Muffins

Serves: 6

Total time: 30 minutes

Ingredients:

- ½ cup cooked, mashed sweet potato.
- 1 egg
- 1/3 cup brown sugar
- 1/3 cup almond milk/skim milk
- 2 tablespoons coconut oil
- ½ teaspoons nutmeg
- 3/4 cup whole wheat flour
- ½ teaspoons baking soda
- ½ cup finely chopped red pepper.
- 1 tablespoon paprika for sprinkling

Preparation:

Preheat the oven to 375°F. Place a large mixing bowl. Combine the potatoes, egg, sugar, milk, oil, and nutmeg in a large mixing bowl. Mix, so it is well blended. Stir in the flour and baking soda until just combined. Add the red pepper and mix well. Scoop into 6 muffin tins lined with paper liners and bake for 20-25 minutes. Hint: When a toothpick stuck in the middle comes out clean, they're done. Allow cooling completely before serving with paprika.

Nutrition information per serving: Calories: 120 kcal, Protein: 3 g, Total Carbs: 22 g, Dietary Fibers: 3 g, Total Fat: 5 g

34. Banana and Honey Muffins

Serves: 6

Total time: 30 minutes

Ingredients:

- 2 tablespoons coconut oil, solid
- 2 tablespoons honey
- 2 tablespoons almond milk (or other milk of choice)
- 1 egg
- ½ cup very ripe mashed bananas
- ½ teaspoons vanilla extract
- 3/4 cup whole wheat flour
- 3/4 cup rolled oats.
- ½ teaspoons nutmeg
- ½ teaspoons baking soda

Preparation:

Preheat the oven to 375°F. In a microwave-safe dish, combine the coconut oil and honey. Microwave about 10 seconds at a time until the coconut oil is melted, stirring occasionally. Mix in the almond milk, egg, banana, and vanilla until thoroughly combined. Stir in the remaining ingredients until they are almost all mixed. Fill 6 muffin tins with batter (to the top) and bake for 22 minutes. Hint: When a toothpick inserted into the middle comes out clean, they're done. Before eating, remove from the oven and cool on a wire rack.

Nutrition information per serving: Calories: 182 kcal, Protein: 4 g, Total Carbs: 29 g, Dietary Fibers: 3 g, Total Fat: 6 g

35. Melting Tuna and Cheese Toasties

Serves: 4

Total time: 25 minutes

Ingredients:

- 6 oz. canned line-caught tuna in water
- 1 teaspoon lemon juice
- ½ tablespoons olive oil
- A pinch of sea salt and black pepper
- ¼ cooked yellow corn.
- 4 slices of wholemeal bread
- ½ cup low-fat cheddar

Preparation:

Preheat the broiler or grill to the highest temperature. Drain and flake the tuna into a bowl. Combine the lemon juice and olive oil in a mixing bowl. Salt and freshly ground black pepper to taste. Add the corn to the mixture. Under the grill, toast the bread until all sides are nicely browned, and spread the tuna mixture on top, right up to the toast's edges. Grate the cheese on top and grill until it is bubbling. Slice in half and serve on a plate.

Nutrition information per serving: Calories: 170 kcal, Protein: 15 g, Total Carbs: 14 g, Dietary Fibers: 2 g, Total Fat: 4 g

36. Vegetarian Spinach Tortillas

Serves: 5

Total time: 20 minutes

Ingredients:

- 3 large eggs
- 2 teaspoons skim milk
- ½ teaspoons salt
- ½ teaspoons garlic powder
- ½ teaspoons dried cilantro
- Olive oil cooking spray
- 1 cup fresh spinach roughly chopped.
- 1 cup canned kidney beans rinsed and drained.
- 5 small whole wheat tortillas

- 6 oz. low-fat cheese (mozzarella or cheddar)

Preparation:

In a large mixing bowl, whisk together the eggs, milk, and seasonings. Over medium heat, warm a big skillet sprayed with cooking oil. Allow the spinach for 1 minute to wilt. Then add beans, followed by the eggs. Cook, occasionally stirring, until the mixture is set. Season to taste with salt and pepper. Switch off the heat. Sprinkle 1/5 of the melted cheese on each tortilla, leaving a thin border around the side. Then add 1/5 of the egg mixture on top, then fold in half. Rep for the remaining tortillas. To serve, wipe the skillet clean, re-spray it with cooking spray, and heat it over medium heat. Cook the quesadillas until golden brown on all sides and the cheese is melted, around 5-6 minutes overall. Serve warm, cut into triangles.

Nutrition information per serving: Calories: 1247 kcal, Protein: 18 g, Total Carbs: 32 g, Dietary Fibers: 4 g, Total Fat: 5 g

37. Rustic Bean & Mushroom Hash

Serves: 4

Total time: 15 minutes

Ingredients:

- 16 oz. canned kidney beans
- Olive oil cooking spray
- 1 cup mushrooms, sliced.
- 4 tablespoons shallots, chopped
- 1 avocado peeled and sliced.
- A pinch of pepper to taste

Preparation:

The liquid from the kidney beans should be drained. Cook the beans for 10 minutes in a pot over medium heat (do not boil). In a different skillet, spray oil and add mushroom. Toss in the shallots. Cook until golden brown, for around 5 minutes. Remove the pot from the heat and add the bean. Remove the beans mixture from the hot pan and place them on a plate to cool. Serve the bean mixture with a slice of avocado on top. Season with salt and pepper to taste.

Nutrition information per serving: Calories: 156 kcal, Protein: 8 g, Total Carbs: 21 g, Dietary Fibers: 8 g, Total Fat: 5 g

38. Golden French Toast

Serves: 4

Total time: 15 minutes

Ingredients:

- 4 egg whites
- ½ cup fat-free soft/cream cheese
- Salt, a pinch
- ½ teaspoon nutmeg
- 1 teaspoon vanilla extract
- 4 slices of whole wheat bread
- Olive oil cooking spray

Preparation:

With a fork, beat the egg whites. Mix in the cheese, salt, and nutmeg. Add vanilla extract until the egg whites are almost smooth. Cover all sides of the bread with the egg mixture. Cook for 3-4 minutes on each side in a non-stick skillet sprayed with cooking oil. Serve warm.

Nutrition information per serving: Calories: 24 cal, Protein: 12 g, Total Carbs: 15 g, Dietary Fibers: 2 g, Total Fat: 2 g

39. Berry Wrap

Serves: 4

Total time: 5 minutes

Ingredients:

- 3 tablespoons fat-free soft/cream cheese
- 3 tablespoons reduced-sugar strawberry jelly.
- 1 cup fresh, halved raspberries
- 4 small whole wheat tortillas

Preparation:

On each tortilla, spread cheese and jelly. On top, sprinkle sliced raspberries. Enjoy the rolled-up tortillas.

Nutrition information per serving: Calories: 162 kcal, Protein: 6 g, Total Carbs: 27 g, Dietary Fibers: 6 g, Total Fat: 4 g

40. Cherry Vanilla Baked Oatmeal

Serves: 6

Total time: 55 minutes

Ingredients:

- Non-stick cooking spray
- 1 cup old fashioned oats
- ½ teaspoon ground cinnamon
- ¾ teaspoon baking powder
- 1 tablespoon ground flaxseed
- 3 eggs
- 1 cup low-fat milk
- ½ cup low-fat plain Greek yogurt
- 1 teaspoon vanilla extract
- 1 teaspoon liquid stevia (optional)
- 1 cup fresh pitted cherries
- 1 apple peeled, cored, and chopped.

Preparation:

Preheat oven to 375ºF. Cover an 8-by-8-inch baking dish lightly with cooking spray. In a medium mixing dish, combine the oats, cinnamon, baking powder, and flaxseed. Gently whisk the eggs, milk, yogurt, vanilla, and stevia together in a separate wide mixing bowl. Combine the dry and wet ingredients in a mixing bowl and stir to combine. Fold in the cherries and apples gently. Bake for 45 minutes, or until the edges of the pan begin to fall away from the sides and the oatmeal feels soft when touched. Fill airtight glass containers with extra oatmeal. For a quick and straightforward meal, refrigerate for up to a week.

Nutrition information per serving: Calories: 149 kcal, Protein: 8 g, Total Carbs: 21 g, Dietary Fibers: 4 g, Total Fat: 4 g

41. Andreas Hangry Eggs with Cauliflower

Serves: 2

Total time: 10 minutes

Ingredients:

- 2 large eggs
- Non-stick cooking spray
- 4 thin slices of deli ham (nitrate-free)
- ½ (10 oz.) bag of frozen cauliflower florets

Preparation:

In a microwave-safe bowl or steamer, combine the cauliflower and 2 tablespoons of water. Cook for 4 minutes on high, or until vegetables are soft. Add the ham during the last 30 seconds to thoroughly heat it. After cooking, drain any remaining water. Place a small skillet over medium heat and coat it with cooking spray. In a small dish, crack two eggs and put them aside. Carefully add the eggs into the heated skillet. Reduce the heat to a low setting. Enable eggs to cook for 2-3 minutes, or until the white becomes opaque and the yolk begins to cook but is still soft in the middle, flipping the pan slightly. Place the cauliflower on a plate and cover it with the ham. Pour in the eggs, allowing the yolk to run all over the plate. Enjoy it.

Nutrition information per serving: Calories: 109 kcal, Protein: 11 g, Total Carbs: 4 g, Dietary Fibers: 2 g, Total Fat: 6 g

42. Deviled Eggs

Serves: 3

Total time: 15 minutes

Ingredients:

- ½ teaspoon dill
- 2 tablespoons creamy horseradish sauce or Greek yogurt
- ¼ teaspoon spicy mustard (Use Dijon for mild deviled eggs.)
- Dash of black pepper and paprika
- 6 hard-boiled eggs (You will not use three of the yolks in this recipe.)
- ⅛ teaspoon salt

Preparation:

Cut the eggs in half lengthwise after peeling them. Put aside the whites and place three yolks in a mixing dish. (Reserve the remaining three yolks for another recipe.) Use creamy horseradish sauce or Greek yogurt, dill, mustard, and salt to mash with yolks. Fill egg white halves with yolk filling by spooning or piping. Season with pepper and paprika.

Nutrition information per serving: Calories: 131 kcal, Protein: 10 g, Total Carbs: 1 g, Dietary Fibers: 0 g, Total Fat: 8.7 g

43. High-Protein Pumpkin Pie Oatmeal

Serves: 1

Total time: 5 minutes

Ingredients:

- ½ cup canned pumpkin,
- ⅓ cup (30 grams) of old-fashioned oats
- ⅛ teaspoon cinnamon
- 1 teaspoon the baking blend
- Dash ground cloves
- ½ cup cottage cheese: no salt added.

- Dash ground ginger

Preparation:

In a microwave-safe bowl, combine the spices, pumpkin, oats, and sweetener. Microwave for about 90 seconds on high. Add cottage cheese and mix well. Microwave for about 60 seconds on high. Allow it to sit for a few minutes before consuming.

Nutrition information per serving: Calories: 205 kcal, Protein: 14 g, Total Carbs: 34 g, Dietary Fibers: 6 g, Total Fat: 3 g

44. Mixed Bean Purée

Serves: 2

Total time: 5 minutes

Ingredients:

- 1 oz. canned white beans
- ¼ cup canned chickpeas
- 1 tablespoon water/soy milk

Preparation:

Heat a skillet over low heat. Bring the beans, peas, and water to a simmer. Reduce the heat to low and cook for 5 minutes (do not cause the beans to boil). Remove from the heat, cool slightly, and blend until smooth in a food processor or with a hand blender.

Nutrition information per serving: Calories: 91 kcal, Protein: 6 g, Total Carbs: 15 g, Dietary Fibers: 4 g, Total Fat: 1 g

45. Protein Turkey and Brown Rice Purée

Serves: 4

Total time: 20 minutes

Ingredients:

- ½ cup carrots, washed, peeled, and sliced.
- 1 cup brown rice
- ½ cup cooked turkey cubes/slices

Preparation:

Cook rice as directed on the package. Place carrots in a steaming basket in the bottom of a pan with an inch or two of water. Remove from heat and drain after steaming or boiling for 10-15 minutes till soft. If you're steaming, keep an eye on the water level because you may need to replenish it in the process to avoid drying out. In a food processor, combine the ingredients, adding water if required to achieve the desired consistency. Serve warm.

Nutrition information per serving: Calories: 98 kcal, Protein: 5 g, Total Carbs: 13 g, Dietary Fibers: 1 g, Total Fat: 3 g

46. Homemade Low-Fat Yogurt

Serves: 5

Total time: 9 hrs.

Ingredients:

- 1 tablespoon yogurt starter (alternatively, look for unflavored natural yogurt in the store) must contain active cultures.
- ½-liter skim milk

Preparation:

Place a large saucepan of water (with a lid) over high heat and bring to a boil for 5 minutes. To sterilize the thermometer and a spoon, add them. Replace the water with the milk and heat over medium heat until the temperature exceeds 185°F (this would destroy any potentially harmful bacteria). To keep an eye on the milk, leave the lid off when doing this. Don't let the milk boil. Remove the pan from the heat and set it aside to cool until the temperature reaches 110-115°F. If the milk has reached the desired temperature, whisk the yogurt into it until it is perfectly combined, then cover the container with the lid. Place the pan in a warm location (wrapped in a thick towel or the airing cupboard works well). Check on it for a minimum of 9 hours, at a constant temperature. The longer it is left, the heavier it can get. Allow cooling thoroughly before transferring to airtight containers and freezing for up to 3-4 days in the refrigerator.

Nutrition information per cup: Calories: 137 kcal, Protein: 14 g, Total Carbs: 19 g, Dietary Fibers: 0 g, Total Fat: 0 g

47. Puréed Banana Oats

Serves: 2

Total time: 5 minutes

Ingredients:

- ½ banana
- ¼ cup ground oats
- 8 oz. boiling water

Preparation:

Peel and cut the banana into slices. Steam bananas for 10 minutes. Mix boiling water and oatmeal in a separate bowl. Blend oatmeal and banana until you have a smooth consistency. You may add more water or oatmeal, depending on your preferred consistency. Serve warm.

Nutrition information per serving: Calories: 59 kcal, Protein: 1 g, Total Carbs: 14 g, Dietary Fibers: 2 g, Total Fat: 0 g

48. Scrambled Eggs

Serves: 2

Total time: 20 minutes

Ingredients:

- Non-stick cooking spray
- 2 large eggs
- 1 tablespoon low-fat milk
- ½ teaspoon dried thyme

- Freshly ground black pepper to taste

Preparation:

Place a small skillet over medium heat and coat with the cooking spray on the bottom. Lightly beat the eggs in a shallow bowl with a fork or whisk. Combine the milk and thyme in a mixing bowl. Reduce the flame to medium-low and add the egg mixture to the skillet. With a rubber spatula, gently stir the eggs for 10 to 15 minutes until fluffy and thoroughly fried. Sprinkle the black pepper on top of the eggs and serve.

Nutrition information per serving: Calories: 87 kcal, Protein: 7 g, Total Carbs: 1 g, Dietary Fibers: 0 g, Total Fat: 6 g

49. Cinnamon Oatmeal

Serves: 10

Total time: 7 to 8 hours

Ingredients:

- 8 cups water
- 2 cup steel-cut oats
- 2 teaspoons ground cinnamon
- 1 teaspoon ground nutmeg

For Protein add-ins (per serving)

- ½ cup low-fat milk (add before serving or while reheating)
- 2 tablespoons unflavored or vanilla protein powder
- 2 tablespoons nonfat powdered milk or egg white powder
- 2 tablespoons powdered peanut butter.

For flavor (per serving)

- ½ cup fresh or frozen berries
- ½ apple, pear, peach, or banana peeled and sliced.
- ¼ cup pumpkin puree
- 1/8 cup chopped pecans, walnuts, or almonds.

Preparation:

Combine the water, oats, cinnamon, and nutmeg in a slow cooker. Cook on low for 7 to 8 hours, covered. Before serving, select and add one of your favorite protein and flavor add-ins.

Nutrition information per serving: Calories: 136 kcal, Protein: 6 g, Total Carbs: 23 g, Dietary Fibers: 4 g, Total Fat: 2 g

50. Wisconsin Scrambler with Aged Cheddar Cheese

Serves: 6

Total time: 20 minutes

Ingredients:

- Non-stick cooking spray
- 8 oz. extra-lean Turkey sausage(nitrate-free)
- 6 large eggs, beaten.
- ¼ cup fat-free milk
- ½ teaspoon onion powder
- ½ teaspoon garlic powder
- 3 oz. extra-sharp Wisconsin cheddar cheese, shredded.

Preparation:

Over medium-high heat, warm a wide skillet coated with cooking oil. Brown the turkey sausages, breaking them up with a wooden spoon into small pieces cook them for 7 minutes until no longer pink.

Whisk together the eggs and milk in a medium mixing bowl. Combine the onion and garlic powder in the same mixing bowl. In the same skillet, add the eggs. Reduce the heat to medium-low, stir the eggs softly and continuously with a rubber spatula for 5 minutes, or until fluffy and cooked through. Serve with the cheese on top.

Nutrition information per serving: Calories: 169 kcal, Protein: 15 g, Total Carbs: 2 g, Dietary Fibers: 0 g, Total Fat: 11 g

Chapter 6: Soups and Salads

1. Chicken Salad

Serves: 2

Total time: 5 minutes

Ingredients:

- 1 cup Lettuce, romaine, fresh, chopped,
- ¼ cup green bell peppers, chopped
- ¼ cup grated carrots
- 4 oz. Chicken, broiler/fryer, breast, w/o skin
- 2 tablespoons low-fat Cheddar Cheese, shredded
- 1 teaspoon olive oil
- 1 tablespoon balsamic vinegar
- ¼ teaspoons black pepper
- ¼ teaspoons ground oregano

Preparation:

Place the lettuce and vegetables on 2 plates. Top with equally divided chicken and cheese. Sprinkle with olive oil, vinegar, and seasonings. Make sure to consume the chicken first, followed by the vegetables. Chew each bite thoroughly and stop eating at the first sign of fullness. Refrain from drinking during meals. It is best to stop taking in liquids at least 30 minutes before and after each meal. This will allow you to consume adequate amounts of food/protein before getting full.

Nutrition information per serving: Calories: 140 kcal, Protein: 18.9 g, Total Carbs: 4.9 g, Dietary Fibers: 1.4 g, Total Fat: 4.6 g

2. Barbecued Chicken Salad

Serves: 2

Total time: 25 minutes

Ingredients:

- 8 oz. Chicken breast, w/o skin
- ½ cup BBQ Sauce,
- 2 cup fresh Romaine Lettuce, chopped
- 1 Tomato
- ½ cup Onion, chopped
- ½ cup chopped cucumber
- 4 teaspoons olive oil
- ¼ cup cider vinegar

Preparation:

Preheat oven to 350°F. Place chicken in a small baking pan and cover with barbecue sauce. Bake until done, about 20 minutes. Place the lettuce and fresh vegetables in a large salad bowl. Place the chicken on top and sprinkle salad with olive oil and vinegar.

Nutrition information per serving: Calories: 168.1 kcal, Protein: 12.4 g, Total Carbs: 15.1 g, Dietary Fibers: 1.7 g, Total Fat: 6.1 g

3. Parmesan-Basil Chicken Salad

Serves: 1

Total time: 10 minutes

Ingredients:

- 2 oz. chicken breast, w/o skin
- 1 celery stalk
- 1 tablespoon mayonnaise, fat-free
- 1 ½ teaspoons lemon Juice
- 2 fresh basil leaves
- ½ fresh garlic cloves
- 1 tablespoon parmesan cheese, fat-free
- 2 cups romaine lettuce, chopped

Preparation:

Cut chicken into thin crosswise strips and place in a small bowl. Wash, trim and finely chop celery. Add to chicken and toss. In a food processor or blender, puree the lemon juice, mayonnaise, garlic (minced), basil (chopped), and Parmesan cheese. Add this mixture to the chicken mixture and toss again. Chill until ready to serve. When ready to serve, place on a bed of washed and chopped lettuce.

Nutrition information per serving: Calories: 145 kcal, Protein: 20.0 g, Total Carbs: 9.2 g, Dietary Fibers: 3.8 g, Total Fat: 2.5 g

4. Greek Chicken Salad

Serves: 3

Total time: 10 minutes

Ingredients:

- 3 cups romaine lettuce
- ½ cup pared cucumber, w/o skin.
- ¼ cup chopped onion.
- 12 oz. chicken breast w/o skin

- 1 cup lentil beans
- 2 tablespoons lemon juice
- 1 teaspoon olive oil
- 1 tablespoon red wine vinegar
- ¼ teaspoons black pepper
- ¼ cup oregano
- 1 teaspoon spices

Preparation:

Toss lettuce, cucumbers, and onions in a large salad bowl. Top with chicken and lentils. Refrigerate until ready to serve. Toss with lemon juice, oil, vinegar, and seasonings at service time.

Nutrition information per serving: Calories: 143 kcal, Protein: 20.0 g, Total Carbs: 9.2 g, Dietary Fibers: 3.5 g, Total Fat: 2.8 g

5. Creamy Cauliflower Soup

Serves: 3

Total time: 30 minutes

Ingredients:

- ¼ cup raw cashews
- 2 tablespoons olive oil
- ½ small white onion, diced
- 2 cloves garlic, minced
- 1 medium cauliflower, cut into 2-inch chunks
- 2 tablespoons tahini (sesame paste)
- salt and pepper to taste

Preparation:

Soak raw cashews covered in water for 8 hours or overnight, then drain well. Heat oil in a Dutch oven over medium heat, and sauté onions and garlic until softened for about 5 minutes. Add 4 cups of water to a pot, chopped cauliflower, soaked and drained cashews, bring to a boil; reduce heat, and let simmer until cauliflower fork-tender, about 15-20 minutes. Remove soup from heat and let cool for 10 minutes. Stir in tahini. Transfer soup to a blender or, using a handheld immersion blender, puree until soup. Season with salt and pepper to taste. Optional: dollop plain Greek yogurt on top and sprinkle fresh chopped parsley. Serve with high fiber crackers

Nutrition information per serving: Calories: 146 kcal, Protein: 7 g, Total Carbs: 10 g, Dietary Fibers: 2 g, Total Fat: 8 g

6. Protein Egg Drop Soup

Serves: 1

Total time: 10 minutes

Ingredients:

- 1 scoop chicken soup
- 1 medium egg
- 1 cup water

Preparation:

First, whisk the egg in a bowl to mix and then set the bowl aside. Heat the water in a mug in the microwave for 2 ½ minutes. Take the mug out of the microwave. Using a fork, add the beaten egg to the water slowly, constantly stirring. When the egg has formed shreds or ribbons, let the mug sit and cool to 140°F (checking with a kitchen thermometer). When the soup is 140°F or below, add 1 scoop of Chicken Soup and whisk well.

Nutrition information per serving: Calories: 160 kcal, Protein: 28 g, Total Carbs: 2 g, Dietary Fibers: 2 g, Total Fat: 4 g

7. Tuna Spinach Salad

Serves: 3

Total time: 6 minutes

Ingredients:

- 6 cups baby spinach,
- 1 cup canned white beans, rinsed, and drained,
- 4 oz. sliced mushrooms
- 1 15-ounce can artichoke hearts, drained and halved,
- 2 7-ounce packs chunk white tuna,
- 1 tablespoon extra-virgin olive oil
- 2 tablespoons white wine vinegar,
- 1 tablespoon lemon juice,
- 1 tablespoon water

Preparation:

Wash and dry baby spinach leaves. Place in a large bowl with tomatoes, white beans, mushrooms, artichoke hearts, and tuna. Whisk oil, vinegar, lemon juice and water or place in a small screw-top jar and shake vigorously. Drizzle over Salad and toss well.

Nutrition information per serving: Calories: 408 kcal, Protein: 31 g, Total Carbs: 19 g, Dietary Fibers: 12 g, Total Fat: 26 g

8. Tomato Mozzarella Salad

Serves: 3

Total time: 10 minutes

Ingredients:

- ½ cup Italian dressing,
- 1 15-ounce can black beans, organic,
- 1 15-ounce can Great Northern beans, organic
- 1 small cucumber, quartered lengthwise and sliced (1 cup)
- 8 oz. round- or log-shaped fresh part-skim mozzarella, thinly sliced,
- 2 red and yellow tomatoes, thinly sliced
- 4 green onions, thinly sliced (½ cup),
- Fresh basil sprigs (optional)

Preparation:

Drain thoroughly and rinse beans. Mix beans, cucumber, and dressing in a large bowl: toss. Divide them into four plates. Assemble cheese and tomato slices alternately, and on top, place bean mixture. Garnish with sliced green onion and basil sprigs, if required.

Nutrition information per serving: Calories: 199 kcal, Protein: 10 g, Total Carbs: 6.2 g, Dietary Fibers: 1.1 g, Total Fat: 15.2 g

9. Black Bean Salad

Serves: 6

Total time: 5 minutes

Ingredients:

- 2 (15 oz.) cans black beans – rinsed and drained,
- 1 (2 ¼ ounce) can slice ripe olives drained
- 1/3 cup shredded cheddar cheese
- ¼ cup chopped green onions (2 to 3 medium),
- 1 ½ cups seeded and chopped tomatoes (2 medium),
- ¼ cup chopped fresh cilantro,
- 2 tablespoons lime juice
- 1 teaspoon ground cumin,
- ¼ teaspoon pepper,
- 4 cups chopped salad greens (about 6 oz.)

Preparation:

Mix olives, beans, tomatoes, green onions, cheese, and cilantro. Mix lime juice, cumin and pepper in a small bowl and toss it with bean mixture. Serve with chopped salad greens.

Nutrition information per serving: Calories: 195 kcal, Protein: 4 g, Total Carbs: 17 g, Dietary Fibers: 5 g, Total Fat: 13 g

10. Crab Salad

Serves: 6

Total time: 10 minutes

Ingredients:

- 1 pack (1 lb.) imitation crab,
- ½ cup light mayo or ½ cup plain Greek yogurt,
- 1 medium cucumber
- 1 small tomato,
- 3 green onions,
- 1 cup parmesan cheese
- 1 package Ranch dressing mix,
- 1 tablespoon Salt,
- 1 tablespoon black pepper

Preparation:

Chop crab meat, cucumber, tomato, and green onion. Add remaining ingredients. Start with ½ package of ranch mix. Add more for the desired flavor. Mix all ingredients with hands until evenly distributed. Serve with veggies or wheat crackers.

Nutrition information per serving: Calories: 146 kcal, Protein: 9.5 g, Total Carbs: 6 g, Dietary Fibers: 0.2 g, Total Fat: 7.7 g

11. Fish Stock

Serves: 8

Total time: 1 hr.

Ingredients:

- 3 lb. fish bones, including heads.
- 3 pt. water
- 1 large carrot, chopped.
- 2 leeks, chopped.
- 2 onions, chopped.
- 1 tablespoon black peppercorns

Preparation:

Place the fish bones and water in a large stockpot, and bring to a boil. Reduce the heat, and simmer for 20 minutes. Strain the stock through a muslin cloth and ensure that all the bones are removed. Return the stock to the pot, and add in the carrot, leeks, onions, and peppercorns. Bring to the boil again, and simmer for 40 minutes. Remove the vegetables from the stock, and strain again through the muslin cloth. Transfer to containers and allow the stock to cool completely before storing.

Nutrition information per serving: Calories: 5 kcal, Protein: 1 g, Total Carbs: 0 g, Dietary Fibers: 0 g, Total Fat: 0 g

12. Collard Greens Soup Topped with Sage Mushrooms

Serves: 2

Total time: 45 minutes

Ingredients:

- 1 teaspoon olive oil
- 1 teaspoon smoked paprika
- 1 teaspoon cumin
- 2 medium carrots, sliced.
- 2 cups water
- ½ cup cherry tomatoes
- 3 tablespoons lemon juice
- A pinch of freshly ground black pepper to taste.
- 2 cups collard greens, loosely packed, big stems removed.

For the sage mushrooms

- Olive oil cooking spray
- ½ cup shiitake mushrooms
- 1 teaspoon dried sage

Preparation:

Heat the olive oil in a nonstick soup pot over low heat and gently fry the paprika and cumin. Increase to medium heat and add the carrots and ¼ cup water. Cover and cook for 10 minutes, stirring occasionally. Add in the rest of the soup's ingredients and increase to medium-high heat to let the soup come to a boil. Reduce the heat to medium, and let the soup simmer uncovered for 30-35 minutes, or until the vegetables are tender. While the soup is simmering, sauté the shiitake mushrooms.

To make the shiitake mushrooms:

Lightly spray a nonstick frying pan with olive oil cooking spray. Allow the pan to get very hot before adding the mushrooms as this will prevent the mushrooms from releasing their liquids when the mushrooms are wilted, season with the dried sage. Serve the soup with a sprinkling of sage mushrooms.

Nutrition information per serving: Calories: 101 kcal, Protein: 3 g, Total Carbs: 16 g, Dietary Fibers: 4 g, Total Fat: 3 g

13. Carrot and Potato Soup

Serves: 2

Total time: 25 minutes

Ingredients:

- 1 cup reduced-sodium vegetable stock.
- ½ cup scallions (green tips only), sliced
- 2 medium potatoes, diced.
- 2 large carrots, diced.
- 1 ½ tablespoon fresh cilantro, chopped, plus more for garnishing.
- ¼ cup almond milk

Preparation:

Bring 2 tablespoons of Stock to the boil in a deep pot. Add the scallions and stir gently for 1 to 2 minutes. Add the potatoes and carrots to the pot, and cook over low heat for 5 minutes, stirring occasionally. Add the remaining stock to the saucepan and turn up the heat to bring the soup to a rolling boil. Reduce the heat, cover, and simmer for 10 to 15 minutes until the vegetables are softened. Remove the soup from the heat, and add in the fresh cilantro. Set the soup aside to cool. When the soup is cool enough to handle, blend with a handheld blender until the soup reaches your desired consistency. Return the soup to low heat and stir in the almond milk. Serve warm topped with fresh cilantro.

Nutrition information per serving: Calories: 145 kcal, Protein: 6 g, Total Carbs: 28 g, Dietary Fibers: 4 g, Total Fat: 2 g

14. Red Pepper and Tomato Soup

Serves: 4

Total time: 35 minutes

Ingredients:

- 2 red peppers, deseeded & cut into strips.
- 2 large carrots peeled & chopped.
- 1 tablespoon rice bran oil
- Freshly ground black pepper, to taste
- 1 cup low-fat vegetable stock
- 1 cup canned tomatoes, chopped.
- 3 tablespoons fresh parsley

Preparation:

Preheat the oven to 400°F. Toss the peppers and carrots with the rice bran oil, and arrange them across an oven tray. Season well with freshly ground black pepper. Roast the vegetables for 20 to 25 minutes, being sure to stir the vegetables halfway through cooking. Transfer the vegetables with their juices into a deep soup pot. Add the vegetable stock and the canned tomatoes to the pot. Blend with a handheld blender. Bring the soup to a gentle boil to blend the flavors, and serve warm topped with fresh parsley.

Nutrition information per serving: Calories: 54 kcal, Protein: 6 g, Total Carbs: 8 g, Dietary Fibers: 3 g, Total Fat: 1 g

15. Slow Cooker Chicken Soup with Baby Spinach Leaves

Serves: 2

Total time: 6-7 hours slow cooker, 10 minutes

Ingredients:

- 2 cups low fat chicken stock
- 6 oz. skinless chicken breasts thickly sliced.
- 2 large carrots peeled and diced.
- ½ cup scallions (green tips only), chopped.
- ½ teaspoons dried thyme
- ½ teaspoons dried rosemary
- 2 bay leaves
- 1 tablespoon lemon juice
- Freshly ground black pepper, to taste
- 1 cup baby spinach leaves

Preparation:

Pour the chicken stock into the slow cooker. Arrange the remaining ingredients except for the baby spinach leaves into the slow cooker. Cook for 6 to 7 hours on LOW. To serve, top the soup with the baby spinach leaves.

Nutrition information per serving: Calories: 172 kcal, Protein: 23 g, Total Carbs: 9 g, Dietary Fibers: 4 g, Total Fat: 5 g

16. Thai Chicken Soup

Serves: 2

Total time: 30 minutes

Ingredients:

- 1 cup low fat chicken stock
- 1 cup water
- 6 oz. skinless chicken breasts, sliced.
- Freshly ground black pepper, to taste
- ½ teaspoons turmeric
- ½ tablespoons galangal, sliced.
- 1 clove garlic, crushed.
- 1 tablespoon sliced scallions - green ends only
- 1 large tomato, diced.
- 1/3 cup baby corn
- 1/3 cup snow peas
- Juice of 1 lime

Preparation:

Combine the chicken stock and water in a soup pot and boil over high heat. Reduce the heat, and add all the remaining ingredients, except for the snow peas and lime juice. Bring to a boil again, then reduce the heat so that the soup is simmering for about 20 to 25 minutes. Add the snow peas in the last 10 minutes of the cooking time. The soup is ready when the chicken is cooked through. Stir in the lime juice, and serve warm.

Nutrition information per serving: Calories: 166 kcal, Protein: 23 g, Total Carbs: 13 g, Dietary Fibers: 3 g, Total Fat: 4 g

17. Cherry Tomato Soup

Serves: 4

Total time: 30 minutes

Ingredients:

- Olive oil cooking spray
- 1 large onion, chopped.
- 1 ½ lb. sun sugar tomatoes
- 1 ½ lb. cherry tomatoes
- 1 bay leaf
- 1 teaspoon dried thyme
- Freshly ground black pepper, as desired

Preparation:

Lightly spray a large soup pot and heat it over medium heat. Add the onions and sauté until the onions have released their flavor and are translucent. Add the tomatoes and herbs to the pot. Cover the pot with a lid, and simmer the tomatoes on low heat for 20 minutes. Allow resting for 10 minutes. Remove the bay leaf from the pot,

and blend the soup with a handheld mixer. Strain the soup, and season with black pepper to serve.

Nutrition information per serving: Calories: 116 kcal, Protein: 6 g, Total Carbs: 19 g, Dietary Fibers: 7 g, Total Fat: 0 g

18. Curried Zucchini Soup

Serves: 2

Total time: 40 minutes

Ingredients:

- Olive oil cooking spray
- 1 white onion, chopped.
- 2 zucchinis, chopped.
- ½ teaspoons curry powder
- 2 cups reduced-sodium vegetable stock.

Preparation:

Lightly spray a nonstick pot with the olive oil cooking spray and heat over medium heat. Add the onion, zucchinis, and curry powder to the pan, and sauté for 5 to 8 minutes until the onions are translucent and the zucchinis are soft. Add the vegetable stock, cover the pot with a fitting lid, and simmer for 30 minutes. Blend with a handheld blender, and serve warm.

Nutrition information per serving: Calories: 77 kcal, Protein: 3 g, Total Carbs: 14 g, Dietary Fibers: 4 g, Total Fat: 1 g

19. Rutabaga and Sweet Potato Soup

Serves: 2

Total time: 40 minutes

Ingredients:

- Olive oil cooking spray
- ½ onion peeled and chopped.
- ½ lb. rutabaga peeled and chopped.
- ¼ lb. sweet potatoes peeled and chopped.
- 2 cups reduced-sodium chicken stock.

Preparation:

Preheat the oven to 350°F. Lightly spray a baking dish with the olive oil cooking spray, and arrange the onions, rutabaga, and sweet potatoes in the dish. Bake for 20 to 25 minutes until the roots are slightly tender. Now bring the chicken stock to a slow simmer in a soup pot over medium-high heat. Add the root vegetables to the stock and bring to a boil. Reduce the heat, and simmer for 15 minutes, or until the roots are completely softened. Remove from the heat and allow the soup to cool. When cool enough to handle, blend with a handheld blender, and serve warm.

Nutrition information per serving: Calories: 147 kcal, Protein: 8 g, Total Carbs: 31 g, Dietary Fibers: 6 g, Total Fat: 0 g

20. High Protein Chickpea and Garden Pea Stew

Serves: 8

Total time: 30 minutes

Ingredients:

- ½ cup reduced-sodium chicken stock.
- 2 teaspoons paprika
- Freshly ground black pepper, to taste
- 1 cup canned chickpeas drained and rinsed.
- 1 cup frozen green peas, defrosted.
- 1 tablespoon fresh cilantro, chopped.
- ½ tablespoons lemon juice

Preparation:

Combine the chicken stock, paprika, and black pepper in a soup pot and bring to a boil. Reduce the heat and add the chickpeas. Simmer covered for 15 minutes or until the chickpeas are softened. Add the green peas and cilantro, and heat through for 5 minutes. Serve hot, and drizzle over the lemon juice.

Nutrition information per serving: Calories: 168 kcal, Protein: 11 g, Total Carbs: 31 g, Dietary Fibers: 11 g, Total Fat: 2 g

21. Greens Soup

Serves: 2

Total time: 30 minutes

Ingredients:

- Olive oil cooking spray
- ½ white onion finely diced.
- 1 garlic clove, minced.
- 2 cups reduced-sodium beef stock.
- 4 cups baby spinach leaves
- 4 cups watercress
- 2 cups frozen garden peas, defrosted.
- 1 cup water
- 1 tablespoon fresh parsley, chopped.

Preparation:

Spray the cooking spray in a soup pot, and heat over medium heat. Add the onions and garlic and sauté for 5 minutes until soft. Add the stock and water and bring to a rolling boil. Add the spinach leaves and watercress and turn down to a simmer for 20 minutes.

Add the peas in the last 5 minutes. Remove from the heat and allow the soup to cool slightly before blending with a handheld blender. Serve warm, topped with the chopped fresh parsley.

Nutrition information per serving: Calories: 116 kcal, Protein: 10 g, Total Carbs: 14 g, Dietary Fibers: 5 g, Total Fat: 1 g

22. Cumin and Turmeric Fish Stew

Serves: 2

Total time: 30 minutes

Ingredients:

- Olive oil cooking spray
- 1 teaspoon grated fresh ginger
- 1 teaspoon ground cumin
- 1 teaspoon turmeric
- 1 teaspoon cayenne pepper
- 1 cup cherry tomatoes
- 9 oz. water
- 6 oz. firm white fish fillets (cod, snapper, or ling), cut into chunks.
- Freshly ground black pepper
- 1 tablespoon fresh cilantro leaves

Preparation:

Lightly spray a large heavy-based pot with the cooking spray, and heat over medium heat. Gently fry the ginger, cumin, and turmeric for about 2 minutes until the flavors are released. Add the cayenne pepper, tomatoes, and water to the pot, and bring to a boil. Reduce the heat, and simmer for 10 to 15 minutes. Add the fish chunks to the soup and simmer for 5 minutes, or until the fish is almost cooked through and tender. Season to taste with freshly ground black pepper and garnish with fresh cilantro leaves.

Nutrition information per serving: Calories: 128 kcal, Protein: 16 g, Total Carbs: 10 g, Dietary Fibers: 5 g, Total Fat: 4 g

23. Cabbage Soup with Arugula Leaves

Serves: 2

Total time: 45 minutes

Ingredients:

- Olive oil cooking spray
- ¼ large onion, diced.
- ½ clove garlic, minced.
- 1 cup reduced-sodium chicken stock.
- 1 head of cabbage, chopped.
- 1 cup cherry tomatoes
- 7 oz. canned cannellini beans
- 2 cups arugula leaves

Preparation:

Lightly spray a large soup pot with cooking spray and heat over medium heat. Add the onions and garlic to the pot, and sauté until their fragrances are released. Add the chicken stock, cabbage, and tomatoes to the pot. Add more water if necessary to just about cover the cabbage. Bring to a boil, reduce the heat, and simmer until the cabbage is tender for 30 minutes. Add the cannellini beans, and simmer for another 10 minutes. Serve topped with fresh arugula leaves.

Nutrition information per serving: Calories: 128 kcal, Protein: 8 g, Total Carbs: 17 g, Dietary Fibers: 10 g, Total Fat: 0 g

24. Turkey Goulash with Baby Spinach Leaves

Serves: 2

Total time: 35 minutes

Ingredients:

- Olive oil cooking spray
- 6 oz. skinless turkey breast, cubed.
- 1 carrot, diced.
- ½ cup green pepper, chopped.
- 4 beef tomatoes, chopped.
- 1 teaspoon paprika
- Freshly ground black pepper
- 1 tablespoon reduced-sodium tomato paste.
- 1 cup reduced-sodium chicken stock.
- 1 cup organic baby spinach leaves
- 1 tablespoon chives snipped.

Preparation:

Lightly spray a nonstick frying pan with the olive oil cooking spray and heat on medium heat. Add the turkey pieces and sear until they are evenly browned. Add the carrot, pepper, tomatoes, paprika, and freshly ground black pepper. Cook for 2 minutes and add the tomato paste and stock to the pan. Bring to a boil, and then reduce the heat. Cover the goulash with a lid, and simmer for 20 minutes until the sauce is thick and the flavors are well blended. Stir occasionally to prevent the sauce from sticking to the pan. Serve hot topped with the baby spinach leaves and freshly snipped chives.

Nutrition information per serving: Calories: 210 kcal, Protein: 30 g, Total Carbs: 20 g, Dietary Fibers: 3 g, Total Fat: 4 g

25. Carrot and Turkey Soup

Serves: 2

Total time: 35 minutes

Ingredients:

- 2 cups reduced-sodium chicken stock.
- 6 oz. turkey breast, cubed.
- 1 carrot, diced.
- 1 cob of corn, cut into 2-inch-thick pieces.
- 1 tablespoon fresh parsley roughly chopped.

Preparation:

Bring the chicken stock to a boil in a soup pot over high heat. Reduce the heat, and add the turkey, carrots, and corn pieces to the pot. Ensure that the ingredients are submerged in the stock, and add some water to the pot if necessary. Bring to a boil again, then reduce the heat, and simmer for 15 to 20 minutes until the turkey is cooked through. Remove the turkey from the soup and set it aside to cool. When the turkey is cool enough to handle, shred the meat and return to pot with all its released juices. Stir through. Serve the soup warm, topped with fresh parsley.

Nutrition information per serving: Calories: 177 kcal, Protein: 23 g, Total Carbs: 15 g, Dietary Fibers: 1 g, Total Fat: 4 g

26. Fennel and Ginger Chicken soup with Asparagus Tips

Serves: 2

Total time: 3 Hours Slow Cooker

Ingredients:

- 2 small skinless chicken breasts, diced.
- ¼ teaspoons ground black pepper
- 1 bulb fennel, cored and cut into thin wedges.
- 1 red bell pepper, de-seeded, and diced.
- 1 teaspoon dried rosemary
- 1 teaspoon ground ginger
- ½ cup reduced-sodium chicken stock.
- ½ cup water
- 1 tablespoon dried oregano
- 7 oz. asparagus tips (not stalks)

Preparation:

Season the chicken pieces with ground pepper and place them in the slow cooker pot. Add the remaining ingredients to the pot. Cover and cook on High for 2 ½ to 3 hours.

Nutrition information per serving: Calories: 121 kcal, Protein: 19 g, Total Carbs: 7 g, Dietary Fibers: 3 g, Total Fat: 5 g

27. Slow Cooker Chicken and Lemon Rice Stew

Serves: 2

Total time: 6-7 Hours Slow Cooker

Ingredients:

- Olive oil cooking spray
- 2 small, skinless chicken breasts, cubed.
- 1 cup reduced-sodium chicken stock.
- 1 cup water
- 1 teaspoon dried oregano
- A pinch of black pepper
- ½ cup uncooked brown rice, rinsed.
- 1 lemon, juice, and grated zest
- 1 cucumber washed and sliced.

Preparation:

Lightly spray a nonstick frying pan with olive oil cooking spray. Add the chicken cubes and sear until they are browned. Transfer the chicken to the slow cooker pot. Add the chicken stock, water, dried oregano, black pepper, uncooked brown rice, lemon juice, and lemon zest to the pot. Mix well, and set the cooker at LOW for 6-7 hours. Serve with fresh cucumbers.

Nutrition information per serving: Calories: 194 kcal, Protein: 21 g, Total Carbs: 25 g, Dietary Fibers: 2 g, Total Fat: 4 g

28. Roast Turkey Breasts with Brussels Sprouts

Serves: 2

Total time: 45 minutes

Ingredients:

- 2 small skinless turkey breasts
- Freshly ground black pepper to taste
- ½ teaspoon dried oregano
- ½ teaspoon Dried thyme
- ½ teaspoon dried sage
- ½ cup reduced-sodium chicken stock.
- 1 cup water
- 1 carrot peeled and chopped.
- 5 oz. Brussels sprouts

Preparation:

Preheat the oven to 450°F. Rub the turkey breasts with the combined black pepper, dried oregano, dried thyme, and dried sage. Pour the chicken stock and water into an ovenproof dish, and arrange the turkey in the dish. Add the carrots to the dish, bake for 30 to 40 minutes, or wait until the turkey is cooked through. Meanwhile, blanch the Brussels sprouts in boiling water for 5 minutes. Serve the turkey with the carrots and Brussels sprouts, and drizzle over with the dish's released juices.

Nutrition information per serving: Calories: 107 kcal, Protein: 16 g, Total Carbs: 10 g, Dietary Fibers: 4 g, Total Fat: 5 g

29. Slow Cooker Chicken Chili

Serves: 2

Total time: slow cooker 4-5 hours

Ingredients:

- ½ chopped onion.
- ½ clove garlic, minced.
- 1 cup bell peppers
- 1 cup reduced-sodium chicken broth.
- ½ teaspoons cumin
- 4 oz. ground chicken
- ¼ cup canned black beans, drained and rinsed.

Preparation:

Place all the ingredients except the black beans into the slow cooker pot. Set the slow cooker at low for 4-5 hours. An hour before the chili is done, add the black beans to the slow cooker and mix well to blend the flavors.

Nutrition information per serving: Calories: 113 kcal, Protein: 16 g, Total Carbs: 10 g, Dietary Fibers: 4 g, Total Fat: 4 g

30. Split Pea Soup

Serves: 2

Total time: slow cooker 8 hours

Ingredients:

- 8 cups water
- 1 lb. bag dry split peas
- 1 ham bone
- 2 cups diced ham.
- 2 cups diced onions.
- 2 cups diced carrots.
- 1 tablespoon butter
- 2 tablespoons olive oil
- 1 ½ tablespoon onion powder

- 1 tablespoon minced garlic
- 2 bay leaves
- 2 sprigs thyme
- 1 diced russet potato

Preparation:

Wash peas and in a large slow cooker, add all the ingredients. Cook it on low for 8 hours or on high for 6 hours. When the peas are soft, they are ready to serve, and the soup has reached the amount of thickness you want. Remove the stalks of ham bone/hawk, bay leaf, and thyme and serve.

Nutrition information per serving: Calories: 343 kcal, Protein: 19 g, Total Carbs: 33 g, Dietary Fibers: 9 g, Total Fat: 15 g

31. French Onion Soup

Serves: 3

Total time: 1 hr.

Ingredients:

- 6 cups thinly sliced sweet onions, red onions, yellow onions, single variety, or mixed.
- 2 garlic cloves, sliced.
- 2 tablespoons butter
- 1 cup white wine
- 4 cups chicken broth - Chicken Stock is a good choice.
- 2 cups beef broth - Beef Stock is a good choice.
- Freshly grated nutmeg

Preparation:

Sauté onions and garlic in the butter until browned and caramelized, 25 to 30 minutes, take plenty of time for this step. Add white wine, chicken, and beef broth, and cook for 30 to 45 minutes. Add ¼ teaspoon of the nutmeg, or to taste - season with salt and pepper.

Nutrition information per serving: Calories: 290 kcal, Protein: 16.8 g, Total Carbs: 33.4 g, Dietary Fibers: 3.1 g, Total Fat: 9.6 g

32. Classic Tuna Salad

Serves: 3

Total time: 10 minutes

Ingredients:

- 1 (5-oz.) can of water-packed tuna
- 1 tablespoon freshly squeezed lemon juice
- 1 tablespoon olive oil-based mayonnaise
- 1 tablespoon low-fat plain Greek yogurt
- ½ teaspoon Dijon mustard
- 1 tablespoon finely chopped red onion.
- 1 teaspoon pickle relish or finely chopped pickles
- ½ teaspoon freshly ground black pepper.

Preparation:

In a fine-mesh sieve, drain the tuna over the sink. Transfer it to a small bowl. Add the lemon juice, mayonnaise, Greek yogurt, Dijon mustard, red onion, pickle relish, and black pepper, and mix with the tuna until well combined. Serve right away or cover and refrigerate overnight to improve the flavors.

Nutrition information per serving: Calories: 73 kcal, Protein: 11 g, Total Carbs: 3 g, Dietary Fibers: 0 g, Total Fat: 2 g

Chapter 7: Side Dishes and Snacks

1. Hummus

Serves: 6

Total time: 10 minutes

Ingredients:

- 1 15-ounce can of chickpeas and rinsed.
- 1 clove smashed and peeled garlic,
- 3 tablespoons fresh lemon juice
- 1 tablespoon tahini
- 3 tablespoons extra-virgin olive oil
- ½ teaspoon salt

Preparation:

In a food mixer, chop the garlic to finely mince it. Clean the food mixer's sides and add lemon juice, chickpeas, tahini, oil, and salt. Process until completely smooth, scraping down sides as necessary (1-2 minutes).

Nutrition information per serving: Calories: 72 kcal, Protein: 1.5 g, Total Carbs: 7.5 g, Dietary Fibers: 3 g, Total Fat: 4.5 g

2. Snaxican

Serves: 2

Total time: 8 minutes

Ingredients:

- ½ cup Fat-free refried beans,
- Light Laughing Cow cheese, 1 portion
- 1 tablespoon Salsa,
- 2 teaspoons Corn,

Preparation:

In a microwaveable bowl, layer the refried beans and Laughing Cow cheese. Swirl the cheese into the beans. Heat in the microwave on medium power until it's hot. Spread salsa and sprinkle the corn grains on top of the bean and cheese mixture.

Nutrition information per serving: Calories: 50 kcal, Protein: 5 g, Total Carbs: 2 g, Dietary Fibers: 0 g, Total Fat: 2.5 g

3. Thai 'Rice Noodle' Salad

Serves: 2

Total time: 25 minutes

Ingredients:

- 2 tablespoons fish sauce
- 1 tablespoon white vinegar
- 2 tablespoons fresh lime, juiced
- 2 zucchinis
- ½ cup carrot peeled and grated.
- ¼ cup peeled, diced, seeded cucumber.
- ¼ cup scallions, sliced.
- 1 tablespoon fresh cilantro leaves are finely chopped.
- 1 tablespoon fresh mint leaves finely chopped.

Preparation:

Whisk dressing ingredients in a small bowl and set aside until ready to serve. Use a julienne peeler to make zucchini noodles with the zucchinis. Mix the zucchini noodles with the salad dressing, and top with the grated carrot, sliced scallions, diced cucumber, fresh cilantro, and fresh mint leaves. Use a mix of green and yellow zucchinis to add more color and flavor to the dish. Stop peeling when you reach the seeds of the zucchinis, as they will not hold their shape.

Nutrition information per serving: Calories: 79 kcal, Protein: 4 g, Total Carbs: 13 g, Dietary Fibers: 3 g, Total Fat: 0 g

4. Cucumber and Sundried Tomatoes

Serves: 2

Total time: 5 minutes

Ingredients:

- 4 oz. Sundried tomatoes finely chopped.
- 1 cup cucumbers peeled and chopped.
- 1 teaspoon olive oil
- 1 lime, juiced
- Freshly ground black pepper

Preparation:

Combine the sundried tomatoes, cucumbers, olive oil, and lime juice in a serving bowl. Serve immediately.

Nutrition information per serving: Calories: 134 kcal, Protein: 2 g, Total Carbs: 9 g, Dietary Fibers: 2 g, Total Fat: 3 g

5. Spiced Lentils on a Baby Spinach Bed

Serves: 2

Total time: 25 minutes

Ingredients:

- 1 cup canned red lentils, drained.
- 1 bay leaf
- 1 teaspoon cumin
- 1 teaspoon turmeric
- 1 cup baby spinach leaves, washed.

Preparation:

In a soup pot, submerge the lentils in 2 ¼ cups water. Add a bay leaf to the pot, and bring to a boil. Lower the heat and cook for 20 to 30 minutes or until the lentils are softened. Drain the lentils and transfer them to a bowl. Season the lentils with cumin and turmeric. Arrange the baby spinach leaves on a serving plate and top them with the cooked lentils.

Nutrition information per serving: Calories: 126 kcal, Protein: 8 g, Total Carbs: 22 g, Dietary Fibers: 5 g, Total Fat: 1 g

6. Edamame and Avocado Dip

Serves: 4

Total time: 5 minutes

Ingredients:

- 1 small avocado
- 12 oz. cooked edamame beans
- ½ onion, chopped.
- ½ cup low-fat Greek yogurt
- 1 lemon, juiced

Preparation:

Mash the avocado and edamame beans with a fork until smooth. Stir in the onions, Greek yogurt, and lemon juice. Serve immediately.

Nutrition information per serving: Calories: 120 kcal, Protein: 9 g, Total Carbs: 11 g, Dietary Fibers: 4 g, Total Fat: 5 g

7. Chicken and Spinach Salad

Serves: 2

Total time: 25 minutes

Ingredients:

- 1 oz. dry, white wine
- 2 tablespoons ginger
- 1 scallion stem finely chopped.
- 6 oz. skinless, chicken breasts
- 1 cup baby spinach leaves, washed.

Preparation:

To make the marinade:

Combine the wine, ginger, and scallions in a small bowl. Make incisions in the chicken breasts and rub well with the marinade. Place the chicken breasts in a heatproof dish and steam for 15 to 20 minutes, or until the chicken is cooked through.

To Serves:

Arrange the baby spinach leaves on two serving plates. Slice the chicken breasts and arrange the slices on the spinach beds. Drizzle the released juices from the dish over the chicken and enjoy. Pour the released juices from the dish into a small saucepan and some chicken stock. Season well with pepper, simmer to reduce the stock into a thickened sauce.

Nutrition information per serving: Calories: 135 kcal, Protein: 18 g, Total Carbs: 2 g, Dietary Fibers: 1 g, Total Fat: 5 g

8. Ginger Quinoa with Balsamic-Roasted Brussels

Serves: 2

Total time: 25 minutes

Ingredients:

- 1 cup Brussels sprouts, halved.
- 1 teaspoon balsamic vinegar
- Freshly ground black pepper
- 2 oz. quinoa
- 4 oz. water
- 1 teaspoon finely grated ginger
- 1 teaspoon ground cumin
- 1 teaspoon ground coriander seeds
- ½ teaspoons salt

Preparation:

Preheat the oven to 350°F. To make the balsamic-roasted Brussels sprouts, combine the Brussels sprouts with the balsamic vinegar, and season well with freshly ground black pepper. Bake in the oven for 20 to 25 minutes, or until the Brussels sprouts are softened. Meanwhile, rinse the quinoa well in cold water and drain. Boil the quinoa with the water, ginger, cumin, ground coriander, and salt for 10 to 15 minutes, or until nearly all the water has been absorbed. Serve hot, topped with the roasted Brussels sprouts, and spoon over with the baking dish's juices.

Nutrition information per serving: Calories: 134 kcal, Protein: 5 g, Total Carbs: 24 g, Dietary Fibers: 4 g, Total Fat: 2 g

9. Cucumber Bites Stuffed with Lemon-Dill Cottage Cheese

Serves: 2

Total time: 25 minutes

Ingredients:

- 1 small cucumber, cut into 1-inch-thick slices.
- 3/4 cup low fat cottage cheese

- 1 teaspoon fresh dill, chopped.
- 1 teaspoon fresh parsley, chopped.
- 1 scallion stem, sliced.
- ½ lemon, juiced
- Freshly ground black pepper

Preparation:

For each cucumber slice, use a cookie cutter to core the center, resembling a doughnut ring. Combine the cottage cheese, dill, parsley, scallions, lemon juice in a bowl, and season well with freshly ground black pepper. Stuff each cucumber with the cottage cheese filling, and chill until ready to serve.

Nutrition information per serving: Calories: 77 kcal, Protein: 9 g, Total Carbs: 6 g, Dietary Fibers: 4 g, Total Fat: 2 g

10. Nutella Protein Bars

Serves: 8 Bars

Total time: 25 minutes

Ingredients:

- 1 cup wholegrain rolled oats
- ¼ cup chocolate protein powder
- ½ tablespoons ground flax
- ½ tablespoons oat bran
- ½ teaspoons ground cinnamon
- ¼ teaspoons sea salt
- 1 tablespoon Nutella
- 1/8 cup coconut oil
- 1/8 cup honey
- ¼ cup chocolate skim milk

Preparation:

Preheat the oven to 350°F, and lightly spray a 4x5-inch baking tray with cooking spray. Combine the wholegrain rolled oats, chocolate protein powder, ground flax, oat bran, ground cinnamon, and salt in a large bowl. Set aside. Whisk together the Nutella, coconut oil, honey, and chocolate skim milk in a medium bowl until well combined. Add the wet ingredients to the dry ingredients and stir until well combined. Pour the mixture into the prepared

baking pan, and use a spatula to spread the mixture evenly in the pan. Press down firmly. Bake for 15 to 20 minutes, or until the edges begin to turn golden brown. Remove the pan from the oven and cool for 20 minutes before slicing into 8 equal pieces.

Nutrition information per serving: Calories: 114 kcal, Protein: 7 g, Total Carbs: 15 g, Dietary Fibers: 2 g, Total Fat: 5 g

11. Zucchini Bread

Serves: 8

Total time: 1 hr.

Ingredients:

- Roasted walnut oil spray.
- 1 ½ cups whole wheat flour
- ½ teaspoons baking soda
- ½ teaspoons baking powder
- ½ teaspoons salt
- ½ teaspoons ground cinnamon
- ¼ teaspoons ground nutmeg
- ½ cup stevia
- 1 ½ cups shredded zucchini
- 3 tablespoons unsweetened applesauce
- ½ cup plain low-fat Greek yogurt
- 1 large egg
- 1 teaspoon vanilla extract

Preparation:

Preheat the oven to 350°F, and lightly coat a 9x5-inch baking pan with the roasted walnut oil spray. Whisk together the whole wheat flour, baking soda, baking powder, salt, ground cinnamon, and ground nutmeg in a large bowl. Set aside. In another bowl, combine shredded zucchini, stevia, unsweetened apple-sauce, low-fat yogurt, egg, and vanilla extract. Add the wet ingredients to the dry ingredients and mix until well combined. Pour the batter into the prepared pan, and bake for 50 to 60 minutes, or until a toothpick inserted into the center comes out clean. Remove from the oven, and let the zucchini bread cool in the pan for 10 minutes before transferring onto a wire rack. Allow the bread to cool completely before slicing to let it reabsorb the juices released during cooking.

Nutrition information per serving: Calories: 162 kcal, Protein: 6 g, Total Carbs: 33 g, Dietary Fibers: 6 g, Total Fat: 2 g

12. Rice Cooker Quinoa

Serves: 2

Total time: 25 minutes

Ingredients:

- 2 oz. quinoa
- 4 oz. water
- 2 bunches of green onions, chopped.
- 2 teaspoons shredded ginger
- 1 teaspoon freshly ground black pepper.
- 1 teaspoon ginger-infused olive oil
- 1 tablespoon shredded lemon zest

Preparation:

Wash the quinoa thoroughly and drain. This will remove the bitterness. Combine the quinoa, the water, and all the remaining ingredients in a rice cooker pot, and set to cook. Serve it when done.

Nutrition information per serving: Calories: 134 kcal, Protein: 5 g, Total Carbs: 21 g, Dietary Fibers: 3 g, Total Fat: 4 g

13. Parsley Sautéed Mushrooms

Serves: 2

Total time: 15 minutes

Ingredients:

- Olive oil cooking spray
- 4 cups button mushrooms, sliced.
- 1 cup fresh parsley, chopped.
- 1 teaspoon grated lemon zest
- 1 lemon, juiced

Preparation:

Heat a nonstick frying pan over high heat until very hot. Lightly spray the pan with cooking spray, and add the button mushrooms to the pan. The mushrooms will shrivel against the heat of the pan. When the mushrooms are all shriveled, add the fresh parsley and lemon zest, and cook for another 3 to 5 minutes. Remove from the heat, and drizzle over with the lemon juice.

Nutrition information per serving: Calories: 77 kcal, Protein: 9 g, Total Carbs: 12 g, Dietary Fibers: 4 g, Total Fat: 1 g

14. Bean Sause with Eggs

Serves: 3

Total time: 30 minutes

Ingredients:

- 2 cloves garlic
- ½ green onion
- Olive oil cooking spray
- 14.5 oz. canned whole peeled tomatoes
- A pinch of smoked paprika
- ½ teaspoons ground cumin
- ½ teaspoon dried oregano
- ¼ teaspoon cayenne pepper
- 2 tablespoons soy protein powder
- A pinch of salt and pepper to taste
- 6 oz. can of mixed beans
- 3 large eggs
- A handful of fresh parsley, chopped.

Preparation:

Garlic should be minced, and onion should be finely chopped. Cook until smooth and clear in a large deep skillet sprayed with olive oil cooking spray over medium heat (for about 5 minutes). Add the canned tomatoes and their juices. Before you add the tomatoes to the skillet, crush them. Add cumin, smoked paprika, oregano, protein powder, cayenne, salt, and pepper. To mix, stir all together. Allow the sauce to come to a boil for 5-7 minutes, stirring regularly. At this stage, the sauce should be thickened. Drain and add the beans to the skillet. To mix, stir all together. Reduce the heat to a low simmer. Continue to cook for another 2-3 minutes.

Into skillet, crack eggs. Cover with a lid. Cook for 5 minutes, or until the whites are all set (the yolks should be soft). To serve, sprinkle sliced parsley on top of the skillet.

Nutrition information per serving: Calories: 337 kcal, Protein: 27 g, Total Carbs: 47 g, Dietary Fibers: 12 g, Total Fat: 5 g

15. Spinach Dip

Serves: 6

Total time: 10 minutes

Ingredients:

- 1 cup plain nonfat Greek yogurt
- 4 oz. Neufchatel cheese
- ½ cup olive oil-based mayonnaise
- 2 teaspoons minced garlic
- 1 ½ teaspoons onion powder
- 1 teaspoon smoked paprika.
- ¾ teaspoon freshly ground black pepper.
- ¼ teaspoon red pepper flakes
- 2 teaspoons Worcestershire sauce
- 1 (8-ounce can water chestnuts, drained, and finely chopped
- ½ cup chopped scallions.
- 1 (10-ounce) package frozen chopped spinach thawed and squeezed of excess moisture

Preparation:

In a large bowl, use a hand mixer on low speed to mix yogurt, Neufchatel cheese, mayonnaise, garlic, onion powder, paprika, black pepper, red pepper flakes, and Worcestershire sauce. Add the water, chestnuts, scallions, and spinach and stir by hand until well combined. Cover and refrigerate for at least 2 hours before serving or overnight. Serve with raw vegetables or whole-grain crackers.

Nutrition information per serving: Calories: 71 kcal, Protein: 3 g, Total Carbs: 5 g, Dietary Fibers: 1 g, Total Fat: 4 g

16. Pickle Rollups

Serves: 6

Total time: 20 minutes

Ingredients:

- ¼ pound deli ham (nitrate-free), thinly slice, 8 slices.
- 8-ounce Neufchatel cheese, at room temperature
- 1 teaspoon dried dill
- 1 teaspoon onion powder
- 8 whole kosher dill pickle spears

Preparation:

Get a large cutting board or clean counter space to assemble your roll-ups. Lay the ham slices on the work surface and carefully spread them on the Neufchatel cheese. Season each lightly with dill and onion powder. Place an entire pickle on the end of the ham and carefully roll. Slice each pickle roll-up into rounds, about ½ to 1 inch wide. Skew each with a toothpick for easier serving.

Nutrition information per serving: Calories: 86 kcal, Protein: 4 g, Total Carbs: 4 g, Dietary Fibers: 0 g, Total Fat: 7 g

17. Baked Zucchini fries

Serves: 6

Total time: 40 minutes

Ingredients:

- 3 large Zucchini
- 2 large eggs
- 1 cup whole-wheat breadcrumbs
- ¼ cup shredded Parmigiano-Reggiano cheese
- 1 teaspoon garlic powder
- 1 teaspoon onion powder

Preparation:

Preheat the oven to 425°F. Use aluminum foil to line a rimmed baking sheet. Halve each zucchini lengthwise and continue slicing each piece into fries about ½ inch in diameter. You will have about 8 strips per zucchini. In a small bowl, crack the eggs and beat lightly. In a medium bowl, combine the bread crumbs, Parmigiano-Reggiano cheese, garlic powder, and onion powder. One by one, dip each zucchini strip into an egg, roll in the bread crumbs mixture, Place on the prepared baking dish. Roast for 30 minutes, stirring the fries halfway through. Zucchini fries are done once browned and crispy. Serve immediately.

Nutrition information per serving: Calories: 89 kcal, Protein: 5 g, Total Carbs: 10 g, Dietary Fibers: 1 g, Total Fat: 3 g

18. Spicy Mango Chutney

Serves: 4

Total time: 30 minutes

Ingredients:

- ½ teaspoons olive oil
- ¼ cup onion finely diced.
- 1 teaspoon ginger root, minced.
- ¼ cup mango finely diced.
- 1 teaspoon mustard seeds
- 1 teaspoon chia seeds

Preparation:

Heat the olive oil in a nonstick frying pan and sauté the onions until they soften and become translucent for about 5 minutes. Add the ginger and stir-fry for another 2 minutes. Add the diced mangoes, mustard seeds, and chia seeds to the pan. Cover and simmer for 10 to 15 minutes until the flavors and fragrances are released. Remove from the heat and allow the chutney to cool completely in the pan before transferring to an airtight container.

Nutrition information per serving: Calories: 73 kcal, Protein: 2 g, Total Carbs: 7 g, Dietary Fibers: 2 g, Total Fat: 5 g

19. Tomato, Basil and Cucumber Salad

Serves: 4

Total time: 40 minutes

Ingredients:

- 1 large cucumber seeded and sliced.
- 4 medium tomatoes, quartered.
- 1 medium red onion thinly sliced.
- ½ cup chopped fresh basil.
- 3 tablespoons vinegar
- 1 tablespoon extra-virgin olive oil
- ½ teaspoon Dijon mustard
- ½ teaspoon freshly ground black pepper.

Preparation:

In a medium bowl, mix cucumber, tomatoes, red onion, and basil. Ina small bowl, whisk together the vinegar, olive oil, mustard, and pepper. Pour the dressing over the vegetables and gently stir until well combined. Cover and chill for at least 30 minutes before serving.

Nutrition information per serving: Calories: 72 kcal, Protein: 1 g, Total Carbs: 8 g, Dietary Fibers: 1 g, Total Fat: 4 g

20. Cauliflower Rice

Serves: 4

Total time: 10 minutes

Ingredients:

- 1 Cauliflower head
- 1 teaspoon extra-virgin olive oil

Preparation:

Prepare the Cauliflower head by removing the stems and leaves. Cut it into four large sections. Put the cauliflower in a food processor and pulse until it breaks down into pieces the rice size. You may need to remove any leftover pieces of stem. Alternatively, you can use a box grater to shred the cauliflower. Transfer the riced cauliflower to a plate or bowl and pat it dry with a paper towel. Place a small skillet over medium heat and add the olive oil. When the oil is hot, add cauliflower. Sauté for 5 to 6 minutes or until tender. Alternatively, steam the cauliflower rice and drain off any excess liquid before serving.

Nutrition information per serving: Calories: 12 kcal, Protein: 1 g, Total Carbs: 2 g, Dietary Fibers: 1 g, Total Fat: 0 g

Chapter 8: Dressings, Sauces, and Seasonings

1. Greek Salad Dressing

Serves: 1 cup

Total time: 10 minutes

Ingredients:

- 1/3 cup extra virgin olive oil
- 1 lemon, juiced
- 4 teaspoons minced garlic
- 1 tablespoon dried oregano
- 1 teaspoon dried basil
- ½ teaspoon freshly ground black pepper.
- ½ teaspoon Dijon mustard
- ½ cup vinegar

Preparation:

In a medium bowl, whisk together olive oil, lemon juice, garlic, oregano, basil, pepper, and mustard. Whisk in vinegar until well emulsified. Serve immediately. Refrigerate any leftovers in an airtight container. When ready to use, let the dressing sit for 10 to 15 minutes at room temperature before serving if the oil is solidified. Give it a whisk or shake before dressing your salad.

Nutrition information per serving: Calories: 89 kcal, Protein: 0 g, Total Carbs: 1 g, Dietary Fibers: 0 g, Total Fat: 9 g

2. Creamy Peppercorn Ranch Dressing

Serves: 1 cup

Total time: 10 minutes

Ingredients:

- ¾ cup low-fat plain Greek yogurt
- 1/3 cup grated Parmigiano-Reggiano Cheese.
- ¼ cup low-fat buttermilk
- 1 lemon, juiced
- 2 teaspoons freshly ground black pepper.
- ½ teaspoon onion flakes
- ¼ teaspoon salt

Preparation:

In a blender or food processor, puree the yogurt, cheese, buttermilk, lemon juice, pepper, onion flakes, and salt on medium-high speed until the dressing is completely smooth and creamy.

Nutrition information per serving: Calories: 35 kcal, Protein: 4 g, Total Carbs: 2 g, Dietary Fibers: 0 g, Total Fat: 1 g

3. Seafood Sauce

Serves: 2 cups

Total time: 10 minutes

Ingredients:

- 1 ½ cups catsup (free of high-fructose corn syrup)
- 2 tablespoons grated horseradish
- 1 lemon, juiced
- 1 tablespoon Worcestershire sauce
- 1 teaspoon chili powder
- ¼ teaspoon freshly ground black pepper.

Preparation:

In a small bowl, combine the catsup, grated horseradish, lemon juices, Worcestershire sauce, chili powder, and black pepper. Refrigerate and cover for at least 30 minutes or overnight to let the flavors meld. Serve with shrimp cocktail, oysters, grilled scallops, or other seafood.

Nutrition information per serving: Calories: 56 kcal, Protein: 0 g, Total Carbs: 14 g, Dietary Fibers: 0 g, Total Fat: 0 g

4. Homemade Enchilada Sauce

Serves: 2 cups

Total time: 15 minutes

Ingredients:

- 1 tablespoon extra-virgin olive oil
- ¼ cup chopped onion.
- 1 teaspoon minced garlic
- 2 tablespoons whole wheat pastry flour
- 1 tablespoon chili powder
- ½ teaspoon dried oregano
- ½ teaspoon smoked paprika 1 teaspoon ground cumin.
- 1 cup low sodium vegetable or chicken broth
- ½ cup water

- 1 medium tomato seeded and chopped.

Preparation:

Place a small saucepan on the stove over medium heat. Add the oil, onion, and garlic. Sauté for 1 to 2 minutes or until tender. Add the flour. Continue stirring until the onion and garlic are evenly coated. Mix in the chili powder, oregano, paprika, and cumin. Gradually whisk in the broth and water, constantly whisking to prevent lumps from forming. Add the tomatoes. Cook for 8 to 10 minutes, stirring frequently or until the mixture has thickened. Use an immersion blender to puree the tomato chunks until smooth. Alternatively, transfer the sauce to a blender and puree until smooth. Serve immediately or refrigerate in an airtight container for up to 1 week. You can also freeze and use it at a later date.

Nutrition information per serving: Calories: 37 kcal, Protein: 0 g, Total Carbs: 7 g, Dietary Fibers: 2 g, Total Fat: 0 g

5. Mango Salsa

Serves: 2 cups

Total time: 15 minutes

Ingredients:

- 1 large mango peeled and diced.
- ¼ cup fresh cilantro, finely chopped.
- 2 limes, juiced
- 1 Jalapeño pepper, stemmed, seeded, and diced.
- ¼ large red onion, finely diced (about ¼ cup)

Preparation:

In a medium bowl, mix the mango, cilantro, lime juice, jalapeno pepper, and red onion. Enjoy immediately or refrigerate in an airtight container for up to 3 days.

Nutrition information per serving: Calories: 27 kcal, Protein: 0 g, Total Carbs: 7 g, Dietary Fibers: 1 g, Total Fat: 0 g

6. Basil Pesto

Serves: 5 tablespoons

Total time: 5 minutes

Ingredients:

- 1 cup fresh basil leaves
- ¼ cup Parmigiano-Reggiano Cheese
- 2 ½ tablespoons extra virgin olive oil
- 2 tablespoons pine-nuts
- 2 tablespoons water

Preparation:

Place all ingredients in a food processor or blender. Pulse until smooth. Serve immediately or keep in an airtight container before serving.

Nutrition information per serving: Calories: 99 kcal, Protein: 2 g, Total Carbs: 1 g, Dietary Fibers: 0 g, Total Fat: 10 g

7. Marinara Sauce with Italian herbs

Serves: 3 cups

Total time: 40 minutes

Ingredients:

- 1 teaspoon extra-virgin olive oil
- 2 teaspoons minced garlic
- ½ large yellow onion, finely diced.
- 1 medium red bell pepper, washed, seeded, and finely diced.
- 10 to 12 fresh whole tomatoes chopped or 1 (28-ounce) can crushed tomatoes.
- 1 teaspoon dried oregano
- ¼ teaspoon red pepper flakes
- 1 teaspoon dried basil
- 2 bay leaves

Preparation:

Place a saucepan over medium heat. Heat the olive oil and garlic for 1 minute. Add the onion and red bell pepper. Cook for 1 to 2 minutes, stirring frequently or until tender. Add the tomatoes, oregano, red pepper flakes, and basil. Gently stir to combine. Add bay leaves. Cover and reduce the heat to medium-low. Let simmer for 30 minutes. Remove the cover and discard bay leaves. Use an immersion blender to puree the marinara to your desired consistency. Alternatively, transfer the sauce to the blender and pulse to achieve the preferred consistency.

Nutrition information per serving: Calories: 37 kcal, Protein: 0 g, Total Carbs: 7 g, Dietary Fibers: 2 g, Total Fat: 0 g

8. Baba Ghanoush Dip

Serves: 4

Total time: 45 minutes

Ingredients:

- 1 medium eggplant (about 1 lb.), halved.
- 1 teaspoon olive oil
- 2 tablespoons lightly roasted tahini
- ½ teaspoons cumin
- ½ lemon, juiced
- ½ teaspoons cayenne pepper
- 1 clove garlic, minced.
- 1 tablespoon fresh parsley, chopped.

Preparation:

Prick the eggplant in several places with a fork and lay it on an oven tray. Broil the eggplants on the top oven rack under medium-low heat for 45 minutes, turning every 10 minutes or so, until the eggplant is charred all over. Remove from the oven and cover very loosely with foil to allow to sweat. When cool, remove the skin and transfer the pulp to a blender or food processor. Add all remaining ingredients except the fresh parsley and blend until very smooth. Transfer to a serving bowl and sprinkle with the parsley.

Nutrition information per serving: Calories: 87 kcal, Protein: 1 g, Total Carbs: 8 g, Dietary Fibers: 4 g, Total Fat: 5 g

9. Homemade BBQ Sauce

Serves: 2

Total time: 10 minutes

Ingredients:

- 1 ½ cup reduced-sodium tomato paste.
- ¼ cup apple cider vinegar
- 1 tablespoon finely chopped onions
- 1 teaspoon garlic, minced
- Freshly ground black pepper
- A dash of hot sauce
- 1 tablespoon stevia

Preparation:

Combine the tomato paste and apple cider vinegar in a bowl. Heat a small saucepan over low heat, and gradually add the tomato paste mixture a tablespoon to simmer until the sauce starts to thicken. Add the onions, garlic, pepper, sauce to the pot, and simmer for 2 minutes. Stir in the stevia and remove from the heat.

Nutrition information per serving: Calories: 37 kcal, Protein: 1 g, Total Carbs: 9 g, Dietary Fibers: 2 g, Total Fat: 0 g

10. Mixed Bean Salsa

Serves: 2

Total time: 35 minutes

Ingredients:

- 3 tablespoons canned mixed beans
- 1 beef tomato finely diced.
- ¼ red onion finely diced.
- ½ tablespoons olive oil
- 1 teaspoon red wine vinegar
- ½ lemon, juiced
- Freshly ground black pepper

Preparation:

Combine all the ingredients in a serving bowl, and chill for at least 30 minutes before serving.

Nutrition information per serving: Calories: 82 kcal, Protein: 3 g, Total Carbs: 8 g, Dietary Fibers: 2 g, Total Fat: 4 g

11. Spicy Lentils

Serves: 2

Total time: 1 hr. 5 minutes

Ingredients:

- ½ cup lentils
- ½ cup water
- ¼ cup onion, chopped.
- 1 teaspoon cumin
- 1 teaspoon curry powder

Preparation:

Combine all the ingredients in a nonstick pot and bring to a boil. Reduce the heat to a simmer and leave to cook, covered, for an hour until the lentils are softened.

Nutrition information per serving: Calories: 52 kcal, Protein: 3 g, Total Carbs: 9 g, Dietary Fibers: 1 g, Total Fat: 0 g

12. Parsley Hummus

Serves: 2

Total time: 5 minutes

Ingredients:

- ¼ cup reduced-sodium canned chickpeas, juice reserved.
- 1 lemon, juiced
- Freshly ground black pepper

- 1 clove garlic, crushed.
- ¼ cup fresh parsley, chopped.
- 2 tablespoons low-fat Greek yogurt

Preparation:

Combine all the ingredients in a food processor and blend until it reaches your desired consistency (use the reserved juice from the chickpeas or use olive oil to adjust the hummus consistency.)

Nutrition information per serving: Calories: 58 kcal, Protein: 3 g, Total Carbs: 10 g, Dietary Fibers: 2 g, Total Fat: 1 g

13. White Cheese Sauce

Serves: 5

Total time: 15 minutes

Ingredients:

- 1 tablespoon low-fat butter
- ¼ cup low carb all-purpose flour
- 3/4 cup skim milk
- 4 oz. low-fat soft cheese
- ¼ teaspoons white pepper

Preparation:

Melt the butter over low heat in a nonstick frying pan. Add the flour to the butter, stirring consistently to get a paste. Slowly add in the skim milk and cream cheese, and stir continuously until the sauce thickens. Season with the white pepper, and use with the desired recipe.

Nutrition information per serving: Calories: 85 kcal, Protein: 7 g, Total Carbs: 6 g, Dietary Fibers: 1 g, Total Fat: 4 g

Chapter 9: Poultry and Meat Recipes

1. One-Tray Chicken and Kale Bake

Serves: 2

Total time: 45 minutes

Ingredients:

- Canola oil cooking spray
- ½ onion, cut into wedges.
- 2 small chicken breasts, boneless and skinless
- 1 cup reduced-sodium chicken stock.
- 1 tablespoon chopped fresh thyme.
- 2 cups chopped kale.

Preparation:

Preheat the oven to 350°F. Lightly spray an ovenproof dish with the canola oil spray and arrange the onions and chicken breasts in the dish. Pour in the chicken stock and add the chopped fresh thyme. Bake for 25 minutes in the oven. Flip the chicken breasts over and arrange the kale in the dish. Bake for another 20 minutes until the chicken is cooked through and the kale is tender. Serve hot.

Nutrition information per serving: Calories: 174 kcal, Protein: 28 g, Total Carbs: 8 g, Dietary Fibers: 2 g, Total Fat: 4 g

2. Zucchini Pasta with Ground Turkey and Fresh Peaches

Serves: 2

Total time: 10 minutes

Ingredients:

- Canola oil cooking spray
- 1 onion, chopped.
- 1 garlic clove, minced.
- 4 oz. lean ground turkey
- 3 cups zucchini noodles
- 1 medium carrot peeled and grated.
- 1 cup sliced peaches.

Preparation:

Lightly spray a non-stick pan with the canola cooking spray, and heat over medium heat. Add the onions, garlic, ground turkey, and sauté until the turkey is cooked for 10-12 minutes. Toss the zucchini noodles with the ground turkey, grated carrots, and sliced peaches. Allow to heat through or serve immediately. For a vegetarian take, toss zucchini noodles with grated carrots, juicy peaches, juicy nectarines, and some blueberries.

Nutrition information per serving: Calories: 144 kcal, Protein: 12 g, Total Carbs: 15 g, Dietary Fibers: 3 g, Total Fat: 5 g

3. Slow Cooker Polenta and Turkey Curry

Serves: 2

Total time: 7-8 hours

Ingredients:

- 6 oz. skinless and boneless turkey breasts, cubed.
- ½ cup canned tomatoes
- 1 medium onion, chopped.
- 2 teaspoons fresh garlic, crushed.
- 2 teaspoons fresh ginger, crushed.
- 3 teaspoons cumin powder
- 3 tablespoons water
- 1 teaspoon Garam Masala
- 1 tablespoon coriander seeds
- ½ cup pre-cooked polenta/cornmeal, cubed.
- 2 tablespoons chopped fresh cilantro.

Preparation:

Place all the ingredients, except the polenta and cilantro, into the slow cooker pot, and set on LOW for 6-7 hours. About 30 minutes before serving, add the cubed polenta into the slow cooker. Garnish with fresh cilantro to serve. If desired, precooked polenta can be air-fried and then topped over with the curry. The crispy texture with curry is delicious.

Nutrition information per serving: Calories: 237 kcal, Protein: 22 g, Total Carbs: 33 g, Dietary Fibers: 5 g, Total Fat: 5 g

4. Salt and Peppered Grilled Chicken

Serves: 2

Total time: 25 minutes

Ingredients:

- 1 cup sliced pears.
- 1 cup arugula leaves, shredded.
- 2 small skinless, boneless chicken breasts
- A pinch of sea salt and pepper to season
- Olive oil cooking spray
- 2 tablespoons lemon juice

Preparation:

To make the arugula fruit salad: Combine the pears and arugula leaves in a small salad bowl, and chill until ready to serve. Generously season the chicken breasts with sea salt and black pepper. Lightly spray a non-stick grill pan with the cooking spray and heat on medium-high. Place the chicken breasts in the grill pan, and sear on both sides until lightly browned. Cover the pan with a fitting lid and reduce the heat to medium-low. Let the chicken cook for 10 to 15 minutes more, or until cooked through. To serve, drizzle the lemon juice over the grilled chicken alongside the arugula salad.

Nutrition information per serving: Calories: 170 kcal, Protein: 23 g, Total Carbs: 13 g, Dietary Fibers: 3 g, Total Fat: 3 g

5. Grilled Chicken and Caprese Sandwich

Serves: 2

Total time: 5 minutes

Ingredients:

- 2 small grilled chicken breasts, thickly sliced.
- 2 beef tomatoes thinly sliced.
- 3 oz. firm pre-cooked tofu, thinly sliced.
- 2 tablespoons fresh basil, torn.
- 2 teaspoons balsamic vinegar

Preparation:

Assemble sandwiches by using the chicken slices as the sandwich' bread'. Begin with a thick slice of chicken, add some tomatoes and tofu, top with some fresh basil, and drizzle over a little balsamic vinegar. Top with another slice of chicken, and secure with a toothpick if necessary.

Nutrition information per serving: Calories: 187 kcal, Protein: 28 g, Total Carbs: 9 g, Dietary Fibers: 3 g, Total Fat: 5 g

6. Air fried Chicken Satay with Cucumber Salsa

Serves: 2

Total time: 25 minutes

Ingredients:

- Olive oil cooking spray
- 6 oz. skinless, boneless chicken breasts, cubed.
- ½ tablespoons smooth peanut butter
- 1 cucumber, diced.
- 2 tablespoons chopped shallots.
- 1 tablespoon apple cider vinegar

Preparation:

Preheat the Air fryer to 350°F, and lightly coat the Air Fryer Baking Pan with the cooking spray. Coat the chicken cubes with the peanut butter and arrange them in the Air Fryer Baking Pan. Place the pan in the Air Fryer Basket, set the timer for 15 minutes, or until the chicken is cooked through, giving the pan a shake halfway through the cooking time to allow for even cooking. While the chicken is cooking, make the cucumber salsa by combining the cucumber, shallots, and apple cider vinegar in a small bowl. Keep chilled until ready to serve.

Nutrition information per serving: Calories: 181 kcal, Protein: 27 g, Total Carbs: 5 g, Dietary Fibers: 1 g, Total Fat: 6 g

7. Hoisin Chicken Cabbage Wraps

Serves: 2

Total time: 25 minutes

Ingredients:

- Canola oil cooking spray
- 4 oz. canned bamboo shoots drained and sliced.
- 1 teaspoon ginger, minced
- 2 garlic cloves, minced.
- 6 oz. lean ground chicken breast
- 1 teaspoon hoisin sauce
- 1 teaspoon reduced-sodium soy sauce
- ½ teaspoons toasted sesame oil
- 1 teaspoon cooking wine
- ¼ cup scallions, chopped.
- ½ cup (4 oz.) canned water chestnuts, drained and diced.
- 2 large iceberg lettuce leaves, washed and patted dry.

Preparation:

Lightly spray a non-stick wok with the cooking spray, sauté the bamboo shoots, minced ginger, minced garlic, and ground chicken for 10-15 minutes or until the chicken is cooked through. Season with the hoisin sauce, soy sauce, sesame oil, and cooking wine.

Add the scallions to the wok. Stir well to combine, bring to a boil, and remove from the heat. Stir in the water chestnuts. Divide the chicken between the iceberg lettuce leaves. Roll the lettuce leaves to form wraps so that the chicken is enclosed, and secure with a toothpick.

Nutrition information per serving: Calories: 206 kcal, Protein: 27 g, Total Carbs: 11 g, Dietary Fibers: 2 g, Total Fat: 6 g

8. Air fried Chicken Kebabs

Serves: 2

Total time: 35 minutes

Ingredients:

- 6 oz. chicken breasts, cubed.
- ½ teaspoons brown sugar
- 1 teaspoon grated lime zest
- ½ lime, juiced
- ½ onion, cut into wedges.
- 2 beef tomatoes, cut into wedges.

Preparation:

Marinate the chicken cubes with sugar, lime zest, and lime juice for at least 20 minutes. Preheat the Air fryer to 350°F. Skewer the chicken, onions, and tomatoes on the Air fryer skewers, and place the rack into the Air fryer basket. Set the timer for 15 minutes or until the chicken is cooked through.

Nutrition information per serving: Calories: 185 kcal, Protein: 27 g, Total Carbs: 12 g, Dietary Fibers: 3 g, Total Fat: 4 g

9. Shredded Chicken and Berry Salad

Serves: 2

Total time: 5 minutes

Ingredients:

- 6 oz. Grilled chicken, shredded.
- 1 cup peeled and grated carrot.
- ½ cup shredded cucumbers
- ½ cup blueberries
- ½ cup strawberries, stems removed and halved.

Preparation:

Combine the chicken, carrots, cucumbers, and berries in a salad bowl. Chill until ready to serve.

Nutrition information per serving: Calories: 193 kcal, Protein: 27 g, Total Carbs: 14 g, Dietary Fibers: 3 g, Total Fat: 4 g

10. Marinated Paprika Chicken

Serves: 2

Total time: 20 minutes

Ingredients:

- 2 small skinless chicken breasts
- 2 teaspoons smoked paprika
- 1 teaspoon ground cumin
- 1 teaspoon ground ginger
- 1 lemon, juiced
- A pinch of salt and pepper, to taste

Preparation:

Score 2-3 slits into the chicken breasts. Combine the smoked paprika, ground cumin, ground ginger, lemon juice, salt, and pepper, and rub the chicken evenly with the mixture, being sure to rub it into the incisions. Refrigerate in an airtight container overnight. Preheat the broiler or barbecue to medium-high when ready to cook. Place chicken breasts on an ovenproof sheet and broil for 6-8 minutes on each side. Ensure the chicken is thoroughly cooked through its thickest part by inserting a sharp knife and ensuring liquids come out clear and there is no pink meat in the center. Serve with your choice of side salad.

Nutrition information per serving: Calories: 139 kcal, Protein: 23 g, Total Carbs: 4 g, Dietary Fibers: 1 g, Total Fat: 3 g

11. Baked Parmesan & Herb Coated Chicken Strips

Serves: 2

Total time: 20 minutes

Ingredients:

- 1 oz. low-fat parmesan cheese, grated.
- ¼ cup whole wheat bread-crumbs
- 1 teaspoon dried basil
- 1 teaspoon dried oregano
- 1 teaspoon dried thyme
- ½ teaspoons paprika

- ¼ teaspoons sea salt
- 1 large egg, white only
- 6 oz. Skinless chicken breasts, sliced into the 1-inch-thick strip.

Preparation:

Preheat the oven to 400°F and line a baking sheet with parchment paper. Combine the grated parmesan cheese with bread crumbs, dried herbs, paprika, and sea salt. Spread over a shallow dish. Whisk the egg white and pour into another shallow dish. Dredge the chicken strips in the whisked egg white, and then coat them evenly in the bread crumbs. Arrange the chicken strips onto the baking sheet and bake for 15 to 20 minutes, or until the chicken is cooked through. Serve with a crispy lettuce salad.

Nutrition information per serving: Calories: 236 kcal, Protein: 35 g, Total Carbs: 13 g, Dietary Fibers: 2 g, Total Fat: 5 g

12. Chicken Simmered with Black Beans

Serves: 2

Total time: 30 minutes

Ingredients:

- ½ teaspoons olive oil
- 6 oz. Skinless chicken breasts, cubed.
- 1 teaspoon curry powder
- ½ teaspoons ground cumin
- ½ teaspoons garlic powder
- ½ teaspoons paprika
- ¼ teaspoons red pepper flakes
- ¼ teaspoons freshly ground black pepper.
- 2 tablespoons low sodium chicken stock
- Juice of 1 lime
- ¼ cup canned black beans, drained and rinsed.

Preparation:

Heat the olive oil in a large non-stick pan over medium heat and sear the chicken cubes until browned on all sides. Add the curry powder, ground cumin, garlic powder, paprika, red pepper flakes, black pepper, chicken stock, and lime juice to the pan. Cover the pan with a lid, cook over medium-low heat for another 10 to 15 minutes or until the chicken is cooked through. Add the black beans to the pan, and simmer covered for 5 minutes until the beans are heated through.

Nutrition information per serving: Calories: 144 kcal, Protein: 22 g, Total Carbs: 8 g, Dietary Fibers: 3 g, Total Fat: 5 g

13. Greek Baked Chicken

Serves: 2

Total time: 45 minutes

Ingredients:

- Olive oil cooking spray
- 2 ripe beef tomatoes finely chopped.
- 1 tablespoon balsamic vinegar
- 2 small skinless chicken breasts
- 2 teaspoons minced garlic
- 1 tablespoon dried oregano
- 1 teaspoon chopped chives
- ½ cup reduced-sodium chicken stock.
- ¼ cup reduced-sodium green olives stuffed with pimiento, thickly sliced.

Preparation:

Preheat the oven to 400°F. Spray an ovenproof dish with cooking spray. Marinate the tomatoes with balsamic vinegar and set them aside. Rub the chicken breasts with minced garlic, dried oregano, and chives. Pour the chicken stock into the oven dish and arrange the chicken breasts in the dish. Bake for 20 minutes. Remove the dish from the oven and reduce the temperature to 350°F. Flip over the chicken breasts and add the marinated tomatoes and olives to the dish. Return to the oven for another 20 to 25 minutes, or until the chicken is cooked through and the tomatoes are softened.

Nutrition information per serving: Calories: 177 kcal, Protein: 23 g, Total Carbs: 13 g, Dietary Fibers: 1 g, Total Fat: 4 g

14. Sweet and Tangy Chicken with Pumpkin Purée

Serves: 2

Total time: 45 minutes

Ingredients:

- 1 lime, zest and juice
- 1 tablespoon bacon root syrup
- 2 tablespoons chopped lemongrass, and 1 stalk lemongrass, bruised.
- 2 x small skinless chicken breasts
- 1 tablespoon oil
- ½ cup canned pumpkin purée.

Preparation:

To make the marinade: Mix the lime zest, lime juice, bacon root syrup, chopped lemongrass in a bowl, and set aside. Make a few scores on each chicken breast with a sharp knife. Rub the marinade onto the chicken breasts, taking care to also rub it into the scores. This will help the meat absorb more of the flavor. Set aside to rest for 15 minutes. Meantime, preheat the grill/broiler, and line the grill tray with foil. Grill the chicken breasts for 10 to 15 minutes or until they are cooked through. Remove from the grill and set aside for the meat to rest. To make the pumpkin purée: Heat the oil in a small frying pan over low heat, and lightly fry the lemongrass stalk until its fragrance is released. Stir in the pumpkin purée and allow to cook for a few minutes until the purée is heated through. Discard the lemongrass stalk. Divide the pumpkin purée between 2 plates and arrange the chicken breasts on the top to serve.

Nutrition information per serving: Calories: 171 kcal, Protein: 20 g, Total Carbs: 8 g, Dietary Fibers: 2 g, Total Fat: 5 g

15. Low-Carb Chicken Tortillas

Serves: 2

Total time: 20 minutes

Ingredients:

- Olive oil cooking spray
- ¼ red pepper deseeded and sliced thinly.
- ¼ yellow pepper deseeded and sliced thinly.
- 6 oz. skinless chicken breasts, cut into thin strips.
- ¼ teaspoons paprika
- ¼ teaspoons cumin
- ¼ teaspoons dried oregano
- 2 low-carb tortillas
- 2 cups iceberg lettuce, finely shredded

Preparation:

Preheat the oven to 325°F. Lightly spray a non-stick frying pan with the cooking spray, and heat over medium heat. Add the peppers and sauté until they are softened. Add the chicken, paprika, cumin, and dried oregano to the peppers. Continue cooking for 15 minutes or until the chicken is cooked through. When the chicken is cooking, the tortillas can be wrapped in foil and warmed for 5 minutes. To assemble: Spoon half of the chicken into the center of each tortilla and top with a cup of shredded lettuce. Roll the tortilla and serve warm.

Nutrition information per serving: Calories: 196 kcal, Protein: 26 g, Total Carbs: 3 g, Dietary Fibers: 1 g, Total Fat: 4 g

16. Stuffed Chicken

Serves: 2

Total time: 60 minutes

Ingredients:

- ½ cup fresh green beans, trimmed, blanched, and cooled.
- ½ cup cherry tomatoes, halved.
- ¼ red onion finely chopped.
- ½ clove garlic, minced.
- 1 teaspoon balsamic vinegar
- Freshly ground black pepper, to taste
- 2 small skinless chicken breasts
- 2 tablespoons low-fat spreadable cheese

Preparation:

To make the green bean and tomato salad: Combine the green beans, cherry tomatoes, onions, garlic, and balsamic vinegar in a bowl. Season well with freshly ground black pepper. Set aside to chill for an hour. Preheat the oven to 400°F and line a baking tray with parchment paper. Cut a slit in the chicken breasts to form a pocket. Season well with black pepper and stuff 1 tablespoon Cheese into each cavity. Secure with a toothpick if needed. Bake for 35 to 40 minutes, or until the chicken is cooked through. Serve with the green bean and tomato salad.

Nutrition information per serving: Calories: 140 kcal, Protein: 20 g, Total Carbs: 7 g, Dietary Fibers: 2 g, Total Fat: 4 g

17. Cheesy Chicken and Cauliflower Bake

Serves: 2

Total time: 50 minutes

Ingredients:

- Olive oil cooking spray
- 6 oz. skinless chicken breast(s), cubed.
- 1/3 cup purple cauliflower florets
- 1/3 cup orange or yellow cauliflower florets
- 1/3 cup white or green cauliflower florets
- ¼ cup low-fat parmesan cheese, grated.

Preparation:

Preheat the oven to 350°F. Spray a skillet with non-stick cooking spray and heat over medium heat. Add the chicken cubes and sear for 15 minutes until the chicken is lightly browned. Add the cauliflower florets to the chicken and top with the grated parmesan cheese. Place the skillet in the oven and bake for 30 minutes. Colored cauliflower can also be pulsed into a rice-like texture and used as a colorful and healthy substitute for fried 'rice' or pizza 'crust.'

Nutrition information per serving: Calories: 162 kcal, Protein: 27 g, Total Carbs: 3 g, Dietary Fibers: 1 g, Total Fat: 5 g

18. Chicken and Lotus Root Soup

Serves: 1

Total time: slow cooker: 5 to 7 hours

Ingredients:

- 3 ½ oz. lotus roots
- 3 oz. skinless chicken breast
- 1 cup reduced-sodium chicken stock.
- 1 cup water
- ½ carrot, diced.

Preparation:

Combine the ingredients in a slow cooker. Set on LOW for 6-7 hours. Serve piping hot.

Nutrition information per serving: Calories: 212 kcal, Protein: 26 g, Total Carbs: 26 g, Dietary Fibers: 6 g, Total Fat: 2 g

19. Stuffed Cubanelle Peppers

Serves: 2

Total time: slow cooker: 6 to 8 hours

Ingredients:

- 6 oz. lean ground turkey
- 1 teaspoon dried rosemary
- ½ teaspoons garlic-infused oil.

- 1 tablespoon onions, chopped.
- 2 beef tomatoes finely diced.
- 1 tablespoon chives finely chopped.
- Freshly ground black pepper
- 2 large cubanelle peppers

Preparation:

In a medium bowl, mix the ground turkey, dried rosemary, garlic-infused oil, chopped onions, diced tomatoes, chives, and season well with freshly ground black pepper. Set aside to marinate for 15 minutes. Make an incision across the length of the cubanelle peppers and remove any seeds and membranes. Divide the marinated ground turkey between the peppers. Place the peppers in a heatproof dish that will fit the slow cooker snugly. Cook on LOW for 6 to 8 hours. During cooking, spoon the released juices over the peppers for extra flavor.

Nutrition information per serving: Calories: 191 kcal, Protein: 22 g, Total Carbs: 18 g, Dietary Fibers: 4 g, Total Fat: 5 g

20. Air fried Herbed Chicken Breasts with Balsamic Cherry Tomato Salad

Serves: 2

Total time: 60 minutes

Ingredients:

- 2 small skinless chicken breasts
- ½ teaspoons ground ginger
- ½ teaspoons cumin
- ½ teaspoons coriander seeds, ground
- ½ teaspoons dried parsley flakes
- 1 teaspoon freshly ground black pepper.
- 1 cup cherry tomatoes, halved.
- 1 teaspoon balsamic vinegar

Preparation:

Make incisions into the chicken breasts using a sharp knife. Rub generously with the combined ground ginger, cumin, coriander seeds, dried parsley flakes, and black pepper. Set aside to rest for 30

minutes. Preheat the Air fryer to 350ºF. Arrange the chicken breasts in the Air Fryer Basket and set the time for 30 minutes. Halfway through the cooking time, flip the chicken breasts to allow even cooking. While the chicken is cooking, combine the cherry tomatoes and balsamic vinegar, and chill until ready to serve.

Nutrition information per serving: Calories: 122 kcal, Protein: 20 g, Total Carbs: 5 g, Dietary Fibers: 2 g, Total Fat: 4 g

21. Cajun Chicken Stuffed with Pepper Jack Cheese and Spinach

Serves: 4

Total time: 50 minutes

Ingredients:

- 1-pound boneless, skinless chicken breasts
- 3 oz. reduced-fat pepper jack cheese (shredded)
- 1 cup frozen spinach thawed and drained (or fresh cooked)
- 2 tablespoons Cajun seasoning
- 1 tablespoon bread-crumbs
- Toothpicks

Cajun Seasoning (makes approximately 2 tablespoons)

- 3/4 tablespoon paprika
- 3/4 teaspoon onion powder
- 3/4 teaspoon garlic powder
- ¼ teaspoon black pepper
- ½ teaspoon cayenne pepper
- ¼ teaspoon white pepper
- ¼ teaspoon cumin
- ¼ teaspoon thyme
- ¼ teaspoon oregano

Preparation:

Set an oven at 350ºF. Level chicken to a thickness of ¼ inch. Combine the salt, spinach, pepper jack cheese, and pepper in a medium mixing dish. In a mixing dish, mix bread crumbs and Cajun seasoning.

Use ¼ cup of the spinach mixture to spread on each chicken breast. Each chicken breast should be tightly rolled and the seams secured with toothpicks. Olive oil must be brushed on each chicken breast. Evenly distribute the Cajun seasoning mixture in the dish. Any leftover spinach and cheese can be sprinkled on top of the chicken (optional). Place the chicken on a baking sheet lined with tin foil, seam side up (for easy cleanup), and bake for 35–40 minutes or until the chicken is cooked through. Before serving, remove the toothpicks. Cut into medallions or serve whole.

Nutrition information per serving: Calories: 241 kcal, Protein: 32 g, Total Carbs: 2 g, Dietary Fibers: 1 g, Total Fat: 9.7 g

22. Cheesy Stuffed Acorn Squash

Serves: 4

Total time: 30 minutes

Ingredients:

- 2 acorn squash halved and seeded.
- 1-pound extra-lean ground turkey breast
- 1 cup diced celery.
- 1 cup finely chopped onion
- 1 cup fresh mushrooms, sliced.
- 1 teaspoon basil
- 1 teaspoon oregano
- 1 teaspoon garlic powder
- 1/8 teaspoon salt
- 1 pinch ground black pepper
- 1 8-ounce can tomato sauce.
- 1 cup reduced-fat shredded cheddar cheese.

Preparation:

Preheat oven to 350°F. Place squash cut side down in a glass dish. Cook in the microwave for 20 minutes on high, until almost tender. In a non-stick saucepan over medium heat, brown ground turkey. Add celery and onion, sauté until transparent. Stir in mushrooms; cook 2 to 3 minutes more. Add in tomato sauce and dry seasonings. Divide mixture into quarters, spoon into the squash and cover. Cook 15 minutes in the preheated 350°F oven. Uncover,

sprinkle with cheese, and put back in the oven until the cheese bubbles.

Nutrition information per serving: Calories: 299 kcal, Protein: 30 g, Total Carbs: 38 g, Dietary Fibers: 6 g, Total Fat: 4 g

23. Lean Spring Stew

Serves: 4

Total time: 20 minutes

Ingredients:

- 1 lb. diced fire-roasted tomatoes
- 4 boneless & skinless chicken thighs
- 1 tablespoon dried basil
- 8 oz. chicken stock
- Salt & pepper to taste
- 4 oz. tomato paste
- 3 chopped celery stalks
- 3 chopped carrots
- 2 chili peppers finely chopped.
- 2 tablespoons olive oil
- 1 finely chopped onion
- 2 garlic cloves, crushed.
- ½ container mushrooms
- Sour cream

Preparation:

Warm the olive oil over medium-high temperature. Add the celery, onions, and carrots and stir-fry for 5 to 10 minutes. Transfer to a deep pot and add tomato paste, basil, garlic, mushrooms, and seasoning. Keep stirring the vegetables until they are entirely covered by tomato sauce. At the same time, cut the chicken into small cubes to make it easier to eat. Put the chicken in a deep pot, pour the chicken stock over it and throw in the tomatoes. Stir the chicken in to ensure the ingredients and vegetables are mixed adequately with it. Turn the heat to low and cook for about an hour. The vegetables and chicken should be cooked before you turn the heat off. Top with sour cream and serve.

Nutrition information per serving: Calories: 277 kcal, Protein: 25.6 g, Total Carbs:

19 g, Dietary Fibers: 5.3 g, Total Fat: 11.9 g

24. Orange Arugula Salad with Smoked Turkey

Serves: 4

Total time: 10-15 minutes

Ingredients:

- 3.5 oz. arugula, torn.
- 3.5 oz. lamb's lettuce, torn.
- 3.5 oz. lettuce, torn.
- 8 oz. smoked turkey breast, chopped into bite-sized pieces.
- 2 large oranges, peeled and sliced.

For dressing:

- ¼ cup Greek yogurt
- 3 tablespoons lemon juice
- 1 teaspoon apple cider vinegar
- ¼ cup olive oil

Preparation:

Combine arugula, lamb's lettuce, and lettuce in a large colander. Wash thoroughly under cold running water and drain well. Tear into small pieces and set aside. Now, combine vegetables in a large bowl. Add turkey breast and toss well. Then add sliced oranges and set aside. Place Greek yogurt in a small bowl. Add lemon juice, apple cider, and olive oil. Whisk together until thoroughly combined. Drizzle over salad and serve.

Nutrition information per serving: Calories: 231 kcal, Protein: 13.5 g, Total Carbs: 16.4 g, Dietary Fibers: 3.1 g, Total Fat: 15.1 g

25. Pureed Chicken Breast Salad

Serves: 1

Total time: 5 minutes

Ingredients:

- 1 cooked chicken breast
- 2 tablespoons Greek yogurt (sugar-free)
- 2 tablespoons fat-free mayonnaise
- 1/8 teaspoons onion powder
- Salt and black pepper as per taste

Preparation:

Place the cooked chicken breast in the food mixer-grinder. Grind chicken breast till it achieves a baby food consistency. Stir the contents in Greek yogurt and mayonnaise. Add onion powder, salt, and pepper, and stir again.

Nutrition information per serving: Calories: 435 kcal, Protein: 30 g, Total Carbs: 1 g, Dietary Fibers: 0.5 g, Total Fat: 33 g

26. Avocado Eggs with Dried Rosemary

Serves: 6

Total time: 10 minutes

Ingredients:

- 3 medium ripe avocados, cut in half, and pit removed.
- 6 large eggs
- 1 medium tomato finely chopped.
- 3 tablespoons olive oil
- 2 teaspoons dried rosemary
- ¼ teaspoon salt
- ¼ teaspoon black pepper, ground

Preparation:

Preheat oven to 350°F. Cut avocado in half and remove the center's pit and flesh. Place one boiled egg and chopped tomato in each avocado half and sprinkle with rosemary, salt, and pepper. Grease the baking pan with olive oil and place the avocados on top. You will want to use a small baking pan so your avocados can fit tightly. Place in the oven for about

15-20 minutes. Remove from the oven and let it cool for a while before serving.

Nutrition information per serving: Calories: 185 kcal, Protein: 7.1 g, Total Carbs: 4 g, Dietary Fibers: 2.4 g, Total Fat: 16.5 g

27. Sweet Potatoes with Egg Whites

Serves: 4

Total time: 15 minutes

Ingredients:

- 4 medium sweet potatoes, peeled.
- 6 large eggs
- 2 medium onions, peeled.
- 1 tablespoon ground garlic
- 4 tablespoons olive oil
- ½ teaspoon sea salt
- ¼ teaspoon ground pepper

Preparation:

Preheat your oven to 350°F. Spread 2 tablespoons of olive oil over a medium-sized baking sheet. Place the potatoes on the baking sheet. Bake for about 20 minutes. Remove from the oven and allow it to cool for a while. Lower the oven heat to 200°F. Meanwhile, chop the onions into small pieces. Separate egg whites from yolks. Cut the potatoes into thick slices and place them in a bowl. Add chopped onions, two tablespoons of olive oil, egg whites, ground garlic, sea salt, and pepper. Mix well. Spread this mixture over a baking sheet and bake for another 15-20 minutes.

Nutrition information per serving: Calories: 285 kcal, Protein: 10.8 g, Total Carbs: 14.2 g, Dietary Fibers: 2 g, Total Fat: 21.6 g

28. Chicken Thighs

Serves: 6

Total time: 20 minutes

Ingredients:

- 2 lbs. chicken thighs
- 2 medium onions, chopped.

- 2 small chili peppers
- 1 cup chicken broth
- ¼ cup freshly squeezed orange juice, unsweetened
- 1 teaspoon orange extract, sugar-free
- 2 tablespoons olive oil
- 1 teaspoon barbecue seasoning mix
- 1 small red onion, chopped.

Preparation:

Warm olive oil in a large saucepan. Add chopped onions and fry for several minutes over a medium temperature until golden color. Combine chili peppers, orange juice, and orange extract. Mix well in a food processor for 20-30 seconds. Add this mixture into a saucepan and stir well. Reduce heat to simmer. Coat the chicken with a barbecue seasoning mix and put it into a saucepan. Add chicken broth and bring it to a boil. Cook over a medium temperature until the water evaporates. Remove from the heat. Preheat the oven to 350°F. Place the chicken into a large baking dish. Bake for about 15 minutes to get a nice crispy, golden brown color.

Nutrition information per serving: Calories: 357 kcal, Protein: 45 g, Total Carbs: 5.2 g, Dietary Fibers: 0.9 g, Total Fat: 16.2

29. Slow cooker White Chicken Chili

Serves: 4

Total time: 30 minutes

Ingredients:

- 1 lb. boneless, skinless chicken breasts,
- 1 medium onion, chopped.
- 2 cloves garlic, minced.
- 1 ¾ cup chicken broth,
- 1 teaspoon ground cumin,
- 1 teaspoon dried oregano leaves,
- ½ teaspoons salt
- ¼ teaspoons red pepper sauce,
- 2 cans (15.8 oz.) great northern beans

- 1 can (15.25 oz.) corn (chickpeas may be substituted),
- 2 tablespoons fresh cilantro, chopped.

Preparation:

Place chicken, onion, garlic, broth, cumin, oregano, salt, and red pepper sauce in a large pot. Add water to cover the chicken. Cook on medium heat until the chicken is done. Use a meat thermometer in the largest part of the breast to ensure a safe temperature of 180° F is reached. Remove chicken from the pan, shred and return to the pot. Add beans, cilantro, and additional water if needed. Cook for an additional 20 minutes and serve.

Nutrition information per serving: Calories: 152 kcal, Protein: 3 g, Total Carbs: 6 g, Dietary Fibers: 5.2 g, Total Fat: 1 g

30. Turkey Tacos

Serves: 4

Total time: 30 minutes

Ingredients:

- 1 lb. pack lean ground turkey meat,
- 1 envelope low sodium taco seasoning,
- 1 can black beans, any size
- 1 can tomatoes, any size,
- 1 sweet onion,
- 1 red bell pepper,
- 2 cups water

Preparation:

Heat skillet to medium and sauté onion and bell pepper until tender. Add turkey meat and stir into veggies, breaking up the meat as much as possible. Combine canned tomatoes and black beans into a meat mixture. Add taco seasoning, then water to desired consistency. Simmer for 15 to 20 minutes or until sauce has thickened. Serve with a baked tostada or wrap with an iceberg lettuce leaf. Top with fat-free sour cream and fat-free cheddar.

Nutrition information per serving: Calories: 150 kcal, Protein: 17.6 g, Total Carbs: 4.8 g, Dietary Fibers: 1.5 g, Total Fat: 7.2 g

31. Kung Pao Chicken

Serves: 4

Total time: 20 minutes

Ingredients:

- ¼ cup (divided 2 tablespoons + 2 tablespoons) reduced-sodium soy sauce.
- ¼ cup (divided 2 tablespoons + 2 tablespoons) rice wine or sake.
- 2 clove garlic, minced.
- 2 tablespoons sesame oil
- 1 teaspoon + 1 teaspoon cornstarch
- 1 lb. boneless, skinless chicken breast (or firm tofu), cut into bite-sized pieces.
- 1 teaspoon dark brown sugar
- ¼ teaspoon red pepper flakes
- 2 tablespoons neutral, high heat oil (canola oil, avocado oil)
- 2 stalks celery, chopped.
- 1 red bell pepper, chopped.
- ½ cup salted, roasted peanuts.
- 1 green onion, minced.

Preparation:

In a bowl, mix 2 tablespoons of soy sauce, 2 tablespoons of sake, garlic, and 1 teaspoon of cornstarch. Toss with the chicken (or tofu). Set aside. In another bowl, mix 2 tablespoons of soy sauce, 2 tablespoons of sake, 2 tablespoons Sesame oil, 1 teaspoon of cornstarch, sugar, and pepper flakes, with 2 tablespoons of water. In a large non-stick pan, heat the neutral oil over high heat until the pan is hot but not smoking. Stir-fry the chicken until almost cooked, 1-2 minutes (4-5 minutes if using tofu). Push the chicken (or tofu) to the side. Add celery, bell pepper, and peanuts to the pan. Sauté until veggies are crisp-tender. Pour the soy sauce mixture into the pan. Stir to coat everything with the sauce and heat through. Remove from the heat. Sprinkle with the scallion.

Nutrition information per serving: Calories: 306 kcal, Protein: 26 g, Total Carbs: 11 g, Dietary Fibers: 2 g, Total Fat: 17 g

32. Noodle- less lasagna with Ricotta Cheese

Serves: 8

Total time: 30 minutes

Ingredients:

- Non-stick cooking spray
- 1 (15-ounce) container part-skim ricotta cheese
- ¼ cup grated Parmigiano-Reggiano cheese.
- 1 large egg, lightly beaten.
- ½ cup Marinara Sauce along with Italian herbs or ½ cup jarred low-sugar marinara sauce.
- ½ cup shredded part-skim mozzarella cheese

Preparation:

Preheat the oven to 375ºF. Coat an 8x8-inch baking dish with the cooking spray. In a small bowl, combine ricotta cheese, Parmigiano-Reggiano cheese, and egg. Spread the cheese mixture over the bottom of the baking dish. Layer the marinara sauce over the ricotta mixture and top it with mozzarella cheese. Bake for 15 to 20 minutes or until the mozzarella cheese is bubbly.

Nutrition information per serving: Calories: 121 kcal, Protein: 9 g, Total Carbs: 6 g, Dietary Fibers: 0 g, Total Fat: 7 g

33. Slow-cooker Barbecue Shredded Chicken

Serves: 4

Total time: 6 ½ to 8 ½ hours

Ingredients:

- 4 (4-oz.) boneless, skinless chicken breasts
- 1 cup catsup (free of high-fructose corn syrup)
- ½ cup water
- 1 tablespoon freshly squeezed lemon juice
- 1 tablespoon dried onions
- ½ teaspoon dried mustard
- ¼ teaspoon red pepper flakes
- 3 tablespoons Worcestershire sauce
- 1 tablespoon white vinegar

Preparation:

Place the chicken breasts in a slow cooker. In a small bowl, whisk together the catsup, water, lemon juice, dried onions, dried mustard, red pepper flakes, Worcestershire sauce, and white vinegar. Pour the mixture over the chicken. Cover the slow cooker and turn on low to cook for 6 to 8 hours. Transfer the chicken to a plate and shred it with a fork. Return it to the slow cooker and cook on low for 30 minutes more before serving, allowing the chicken to absorb some of the liquid.

Nutrition information per serving: Calories: 188 kcal, Protein: 22 g, Total Carbs: 16 g, Dietary Fibers: 0 g, Total Fat: 3 g

34. Whole Herb Roasted Chicken in the slow cooker

Serves: 6

Total time: 7 hours, 15 minutes

Ingredients:

- 1 teaspoon garlic powder
- 1 teaspoon smoked paprika.
- 2 lemon wedges
- ½ teaspoon dried sage
- 1 teaspoon onion powder
- 2 sprigs fresh rosemary
- 1 teaspoon dried thyme
- 1 (4-pound) whole chicken
- ½ teaspoon freshly ground black pepper.

Preparation:

In a small bowl, mix the garlic powder, paprika, onion powder, thyme, black pepper, and sage. Remove any giblets from the chicken cavity. Rinse the chicken's outside and inner cavity under the cold water and use a paper towel to pat dry. Place the chicken in the slow cooker. Rub the chicken with the herb mixture, getting as much as possible under the skin. Stuff the inside of the chicken with rosemary and lemon wedges. Cover the slow cooker and turn on low to cook for 7 hours, or until the temperature of the innermost part of a thigh and thickest part of the breast has reached 165°F.

Nutrition information per serving: Calories: 191 kcal, Protein: 29 g, Total Carbs: 0 g, Dietary Fibers: 0 g, Total Fat: 8 g

35. Mediterranean Turkey Meatloaf

Serves: 4

Total time: 1 hour, 5 minutes

Ingredients:

For the meatloaf

- Non-stick cooking spray
- 1-pound extra-lean ground turkey
- 1 large egg, lightly beaten.
- ¼ cup whole-wheat bread-crumbs
- ¼ fat-free feta cheese
- ¼ cup kalamata olives pitted and halved.
- ¼ cup chopped fresh parsley.
- ¼ cup minced red onion.
- ¼ cup plus 2 tablespoons hummus, such as lantana Cucumber Hummus, divided
- ¼ teaspoon dried oregano
- 2 teaspoons minced garlic
- ½ teaspoon dried basil

For the topping

- ½ small cucumber, peeled, seeded, and chopped.
- 1 large tomato, chopped.
- 2 to 3 tablespoons minced fresh basil.
- ½ lemon, juiced
- 1 teaspoon extra-virgin olive oil

Preparation:

Preheat the oven to 350°F. Coat an 8x4-inch loaf pan with the cooking spray. In a large bowl, combine the ground turkey, egg, bread-crumbs, feta cheese, olives, parsley, onion, 2 tablespoons of hummus, garlic, basil, and oregano. Using clean hands, mix until just combined. Place the meatloaf mixture evenly in the loaf pan. Spread the remaining ¼ cup of hummus over the top of the meatloaf. In a small bowl, mix the cucumber, tomato, basil, lemon juice, and olive oil for topping. Refrigerate until ready to serve. The meatloaf is done when it reaches an internal temperature of 165°F. Let it sit for 5 minutes before serving, then slice and garnish with the topping.

Nutrition information per serving: Calories: 232 kcal, Protein: 22 g, Total Carbs: 10 g, Dietary Fibers: 2 g, Total Fat: 8 g

36. Creamy Chicken Soup with Cauliflower

Serves: 8

Total time: 55 minutes

Ingredients:

- 1 teaspoon minced garlic
- 1 teaspoon extra-virgin olive oil
- ½ yellow onion
- 1 carrot diced.
- 1 celery stalk, diced.
- 1 ½ pound (3 or 4 medium) cooked chicken breast, diced.
- 2 cups low-sodium chicken broth
- 2 cups water
- 1 teaspoon freshly ground black pepper.
- 1 teaspoon diced thyme
- 2 ½ cups fresh cauliflower florets
- 1 cup fresh spinach, chopped.
- 2 cups nonfat or 1 % milk

Preparation:

Place a large soup pot over medium-high heat. Sauté the garlic in olive oil for 1 minute. Add the onions, carrot, and celery and sauté until tender, 3 to 5 minutes. Add the chicken breast, broth, water, black pepper, thyme, and cauliflower. Bring to a simmer, reduce the heat medium-low, and cook, uncovered for 30 minutes. Add the fresh spinach and stir until wilted for about 5 minutes. Stir in the milk, then serve immediately.

Nutrition information per serving: Calories: 164 kcal, Protein: 25 g, Total Carbs: 5 g, Dietary Fibers: 1 g, Total Fat: 3 g

37. Slow cooker Turkey Chili

Serves: 16

Total time: 8 hours

Ingredients:

- Non-stick Cooking spray
- 2 lb. extra- lean ground turkey
- 2 (14.5 oz.) cans of (drained and rinsed) kidney beans
- 1 (8-oz.) can of tomato puree
- 1 (28-ounce) can of tomatoes (diced) with green chilies
- 1 large onion finely chopped.
- 1 green bell pepper finely chopped.
- 2 celery stalks are finely chopped.
- 4 teaspoons minced garlic
- 1 teaspoon dried oregano
- 2 tablespoons ground cumin
- 3 tablespoons chili powder
- 1 (8-ounce) can tomato juice

Preparation:

Place a large skillet over medium-high heat and coat it with cooking spray. Add the ground turkey. Using a wooden spoon, break it into smaller pieces and cook until browned, 7 to 9 minutes. While the turkey browns, place the beans, tomatoes, tomato puree, onion, bell pepper, celery, garlic, oregano, cumin, chili powder, and tomato juice in the slow cooker. Stir in the cooked ground turkey and mix well. Cover the slow cooker and turn on low to cook for 8 hours. Serve garnished with Greek yogurt, shredded cheese, and chopped scallions (if using).

Nutrition information per serving: Calories: 140 kcal, Protein: 14 g, Total Carbs: 12 g, Dietary Fibers: 4 g, Total Fat: 4 g

38. Baked fried Chicken Thighs

Serves: 4

Total time: 45 minutes

Ingredients:

- Non-stick cooking spray
- ½ teaspoon cayenne pepper
- 1 teaspoon smoked paprika.
- 4 (5-ounce) boneless, skinless chicken thighs
- ½ teaspoon garlic powder
- 1 teaspoon Dijon mustard
- ½ teaspoon freshly ground black pepper.
- 2 large eggs
- ½ teaspoon dried oregano
- 1 tablespoon water
- 2 ½ cups bran flakes

Preparation:

Preheat the oven to 400°F. Use an aluminum foil to line a large, rimmed baking sheet and place it in the oven below a clean oven rack. Spray the clean rack with the cooking spray. In a large zip-top bag, combine the paprika, garlic powder, black pepper, cayenne pepper, and oregano. Add the chicken thighs to the bag, seal the bag and shake to coat the thighs with the seasonings. Set aside. In a small bowl, lightly whisk together the eggs, water, and mustard. Crush the bran flakes in another large plastic bag. To bake the chicken, dredge the seasoned chicken thighs in the egg mixture and then put them in a crushed cereal bag. Shake to coat well. Place the chicken thighs on the clean oven rack, making sure the baking sheet is directly under the chicken to catch any drippings. Bake for 35 minutes or until the thighs are crispy and reach an internal temperature of 165°F and serve.

Nutrition information per serving: Calories: 272 kcal, Protein: 35 g, Total Carbs: 15 g, Dietary Fibers: 3 g, Total Fat: 8 g

39. Chicken, barley, and Vegetable Soup

Serves: 8

Total time: 60 minutes

Ingredients:

- 1 tablespoon extra-virgin olive oil
- 1 teaspoon minced garlic
- 1 large onion, diced.
- 2 large carrots, chopped.
- 3 celery stalks, chopped.
- 1 (14.5 oz.) can diced tomatoes
- ¾ cup pearl barley
- 2 ½ cups diced cooked chicken.
- 4 cups low sodium chicken broth
- 2 cups water
- ½ teaspoon dried thyme
- ½ teaspoon dried sage
- ¼ teaspoon dried rosemary
- 2 bay leaves

Preparation:

Place a large soup pot over medium-high heat. Sauté the olive oil and garlic for 1 minute. Add the onion, carrots, and celery and sauté until tender, 3 to 5 minutes. Add the tomatoes, barley, chicken, broth, water, thyme, sage, rosemary, and bay leaves. Bring to a simmer, then reduce the heat to medium-low and cook uncovered for about 45 minutes. The soup is done when the barley is tender. Remove and discard bay leaves before serving.

Nutrition information per serving: Calories: 198 kcal, Protein: 16 g, Total Carbs: 9 g, Dietary Fibers: 2 g, Total Fat: 3 g

40. Mexican Taco skillet with red peppers and zucchini

Serves: 6

Total time: 30 minutes

Ingredients:

- 2 teaspoons extra virgin olive oil
- 1 large onion, finely chopped.
- 1 tablespoon garlic, minced
- 1 Jalapeño pepper, seeded and finely chopped.
- 2 medium red bell peppers, diced.
- 1-pound boneless, skinless chicken breast, cut into 1-inch cubes
- 1 tablespoon ground cumin
- 1 teaspoon low sodium taco seasoning
- 1(14.5 oz.) can diced tomatoes
- 1 large zucchini halved lengthwise and diced.
- ½ cup shredded mild cheddar cheese.
- 1 cup chopped fresh cilantro.
- ½ cup chopped scallions.

Preparation:

In a large skillet over medium heat, heat the olive oil. Add the onions, garlic, jalapeno, and red bell peppers. Sauté the vegetables for 5 minutes or until tender. Add the chicken, cumin, and taco seasoning and stir until the chicken and vegetables are well coated. Stir in the tomatoes. Bring the mixture to a boil. Cover the skillet reduce the heat to medium-low, and cook for 10 minutes. Add the zucchini and mix well. Cook for 7 minutes more or until the zucchini is tender. Remove the skillet from the heat. Mix in the cheese, cilantro, and scallions and serve.

Nutrition information per serving: Calories: 162 kcal, Protein: 18 g, Total Carbs: 8 g, Dietary Fibers: 2 g, Total Fat: 7 g

41. Zoodles with Turkey Meatballs

Serves: 4

Total time: 15 minutes

Ingredients:

- Non-stick cooking spray
- 1 large egg
- ½ cup whole-wheat bread-crumbs
- ½ cup chopped onion.
- ½ teaspoon freshly ground black pepper.
- 1 lb. extra-lean ground turkey
- 1 lb. zucchini

- 1 teaspoon extra-virgin olive oil
- 2 cups Marinara sauce with Italian herbs

Preparation:

Preheat the oven to 400°F. Coat the bottom of a shallow baking pan with the cooking spray. In a large bowl, combine egg, bread-crumbs, onion, and pepper. Add the ground turkey, and using clean hands, mix well until the mixture is evenly distributed. Shape the meat mixture into 2-inch balls and place in the baking pan. Bake uncovered for 15 minutes. Cut off the ends of the zucchini. Use a mandolin, spiralizer, or the side of a box grater to the sliced zucchini into long thin strips. In a medium skillet over medium heat, heat the olive oil. Add the zucchini strips and sauté for about 5 minutes or until tender. Transfer to a serving bowl. Serve the meatballs over the noodles and top with the marinara sauce.

Nutrition information per serving: Calories: 191 kcal, Protein: 22 g, Total Carbs: 15 g, Dietary Fibers: 3 g, Total Fat: 5 g

42. Chicken Cordon Bleu

Serves: 6

Total time: 45 minutes

Ingredients:

- Non-stick cooking spray
- 6 boneless, skinless chicken breasts (about 3 oz. each) thinly sliced.
- 6 slices (nitrate-free) lean deli ham
- 2 large eggs
- 6 slices Swiss cheese reduced-fat (3 oz. total) halved.
- 1 tablespoon water
- ¼ cup whole-wheat bread-crumbs
- 2 tablespoons grated Parmigiano-Reggiano Cheese

Preparation:

Preheat the oven to 450°F. Spray a baking sheet with the cooking spray. Pound the chicken breasts to ¼ inch thickness. Layer 1 slice of ham and 1 slice (2

halves) of cheese on each chicken breast. Carefully roll the chicken. Place it seam-side down on the baking sheet. In a small bowl, lightly whisk the eggs. In a second small bowl, mix the bread-crumbs and Parmigiano-Reggiano cheese. Using a pastry brush, lightly brush each chicken roll with the egg wash and then sprinkle on the bread-crumb mixture. Bake for 30 minutes, or until the chicken is cooked thoroughly and lightly browned on top.

Nutrition information per serving: Calories: 174 kcal, Protein: 24 g, Total Carbs: 3 g, Dietary Fibers: 0 g, Total Fat: 7 g

43. Chicken Nachos with sweet bell pepper

Serves: 16 nachos

Total time: 35 minutes

Ingredients:

- Non-stick cooking spray
- 1 (1 pound) package bell peppers, stemmed, seeded, and halved
- 2 teaspoons extra virgin olive oil
- ½ onion, minced.
- 2 cups cooked shredded chicken breast.
- 1 large tomato diced.
- 1 teaspoon garlic powder
- 1 teaspoon ground cumin
- ½ teaspoon smoked paprika.
- 1 cup shredded Colby Jack Cheese
- ¼ cup sliced black olives.
- 3 scallions are finely sliced.
- 1 Jalapeño pepper, seeded, thinly sliced.

Preparation:

Preheat the oven to 400°F. Line a baking sheet with aluminum foil and coat the foil with the cooking spray. Arrange the bell pepper halves on the baking sheet cut-side up. Heat the olive oil over medium heat in a large skillet. Add the onion and cook for 1 to 2 minutes or until tender Add the chicken, tomato, garlic powder, cumin, and paprika and cook for 5 minutes or until the tomato has softened and the chicken is heated through. Spoon 1 heaping tablespoon of the chicken mixture into each bell pepper half. Top each with the cheese, black olives, scallions, and jalapeno (if using). Bake for 15 minutes or until cheese has melted and browned. Enjoy immediately.

Nutrition information per serving: Calories: 189 kcal, Protein: 29 g, Total Carbs: 9 g, Dietary Fibers: 2 g, Total Fat: 3 g

44. Buffalo Chicken Wrap

Serves: 5 wraps

Total time: 15 minutes

Ingredients:

- 3 cups cooked, grilled, canned, or rotisserie chicken breast.
- 2 cups chopped romaine lettuce.
- 1 tomato, diced.
- ½ red onion, finely sliced.
- ½ red onion, finely sliced.
- ¼ cup buffalo wing sauce, such as Franks Red-hot
- ¼ cup ranch dressing
- Chopped raw cereal (optional)
- 5 small 100 % whole grain low carb wraps

Preparation:

In a large mixing bowl, combine the chicken, lettuce, tomato, onion, wing sauce, dressing, and celery. Place about 1 cup of the mixture onto each wrap. Fold the wrap over the top of the salad, close in the side, and then lightly roll the wrap closed. Use a toothpick to secure the wrap, if needed, and serve.

Nutrition information per serving: Calories: 200 kcal, Protein: 28 g, Total Carbs: 14 g, Dietary Fibers: 8 g, Total Fat: 7 g

45. Jerk Chicken with Mango salsa

Serves: 4

Total time: 1 hour

Ingredients:

- 2 tablespoons extra virgin olive oil
- 1 lime, juiced
- 1 tablespoon garlic, minced
- 1 teaspoon ground ginger
- ½ teaspoon dried thyme
- ½ teaspoon cinnamon
- ½ teaspoon ground all spices.
- ½ teaspoon ground nutmeg
- ¼ teaspoon cayenne pepper
- 1 teaspoon finely ground black pepper.
- ¼ teaspoon ground cloves
- 4 boneless, skinless chicken breasts about 1 pound
- 1 cup mango salsa

Preparation:

In a gallon-sized zip-top freezer bag, put the olive oil, lime juice, garlic, ginger thyme, cinnamon, allspice, nutmeg, cayenne, cloves, and black pepper. Tightly seal the bag and gently mix the marinade. Add the chicken breasts to the marinade. Tightly seal the bag and shake to coat the chicken in the marinade. Refrigerate for at least 30 minutes or overnight. Preheat the grill to medium-high heat. Place the chicken on the grill and discard the marinade. Cook the chicken for about 6 minutes on each side or until the breasts are no longer pink in the middle and reach an internal temperature of 165°F or bake the chicken for 25 minutes in preheated oven at 400°F. Let the chicken rest for 5 minutes before slicing. Top the chicken slices with the mango salsa.

Nutrition information per serving: Calories: 206 kcal, Protein: 25 g, Total Carbs: 11 g, Dietary Fibers: 1 g, Total Fat: 9 g

46. Baked Potato Soup

Serves: 6

Total time: 40 minutes

Ingredients:

- 4 slices turkey bacon (nitrate-free)
- 2 tablespoons extra-virgin Olive oil
- 3 tablespoons whole-wheat flour
- 1 ½ cup 1 % milk
- 1 ½ cup vegetable or chicken broth
- 3 medium unpeeled russet potatoes, cut into 1-inch chunks.
- ½ cup low fat plain Greek yogurt
- ½ cup shredded sharp cheddar cheese.
- 4 tablespoons chopped chives.

Preparation:

Place a stockpot over medium heat. Add the bacon and cook until crispy on both sides, turning once for about 5 minutes. Transfer to a paper towel-lined plate to absorb any excess grease. Once cooled, chop finely and set aside. Heat olive oil in the stockpot over medium heat. Add the flour and cook, constantly stirring until browned, 2 to 3 minutes. Add the milk and constantly whisk until it starts to thicken. Whisk in the broth. Add the potatoes. Bring to a boil, reduce the heat to low, and let the soup simmer for about 20 minutes or until the potatoes are tender. Add the Greek yogurt and stir to combine. Serve garnished with the turkey bacon, cheese, chives, and an additional dollop of plain Greek yogurt.

Nutrition information per serving: Calories: 181 kcal, Protein: 9 g, Total Carbs: 18 g, Dietary Fibers: 3 g, Total Fat: 9 g

47. Egg roll

Serves: 6

Total time: 30 minutes

Ingredients:

- 2 teaspoons sesame oil, divided.
- 1 teaspoon minced garlic
- 1 onion finely diced.
- 1 lb. extra-lean ground chicken or turkey
- 1 ½ tablespoon low-sodium soy sauce
- ½ cup low sodium beef broth
- 2 teaspoons ground ginger
- ½ teaspoon freshly ground black pepper.
- 4 cups green cabbage chopped or shredded into 1-inch ribbons.
- 1 ½ cups shredded carrots.
- 1 cup fresh bean sprouts
- 2 scallions finely chopped.

Preparation:

Place a large skillet over medium-high heat. Add 1 teaspoon of sesame oil and garlic. Stir for 1 minute. Add the onion and cook until tender, 1 to 2 minutes. Add the ground chicken. Cook until browned, breaking up the meat into smaller pieces for 7 to 9 minutes. While the meat is browning, mix the remaining 1 teaspoon of the sesame oil, soy sauce, broth, ginger, and black pepper in a small bowl. When the chicken is cooked, stir the sauce into the skillet. Add the cabbage, carrots, and bean sprouts. Stir to combine. Cover the skillet and simmer until the cabbage is tender for 5 to 7 minutes. Serve in a bowl and garnish with the scallions and additional soy sauce to taste.

Nutrition information per serving: Calories: 133 kcal, Protein: 19 g, Total Carbs: 7 g, Dietary Fibers: 2 g, Total Fat: 3 g

48. Cauliflower Pizza with caramelized Onions and Chicken Sausage

Serves: 1 pizza

Total time: 55 minutes

Ingredients:

- 1 large head cauliflower steamed with leaves removed.
- 2 large eggs, lightly beaten.
- 2 cups shredded part-skim mozzarella cheese, divided.

- ½ cup shredded Parmigiano-Reggiano cheese
- ½ teaspoon dried oregano
- ¼ teaspoon dried basil
- ½ teaspoon garlic powder
- 2 teaspoons extra virgin olive oil
- 2 red onions thinly sliced.
- 2 links pre-cooked chicken sausage (nitrate-free) cut into ¼ inch rounds.

Preparation:

Cut the cauliflower head into 3 or 4 large pieces. Place in a food processor and pulse for 1 to 2 seconds at a time until all the pieces are the size of rice. Remove any large pieces that won't break down. Transfer the riced cauliflower to a bowl and pat dry with a paper towel. Place a small pot over medium heat and add ½ cup water. Put the riced cauliflower directly in the pot and bring the water to a boil. Cover the pot and steam the cauliflower for 3 to 5 minutes or until tender. Remove the pan from the heat and let cool. Place the steamed cauliflower on a paper towel to soak up any moisture and pat dry. In a medium bowl, combine the eggs, 1 cup of mozzarella, Parmigiano-Reggiano cheese, oregano, basil, and garlic powder. Add the cauliflower and mix well. Spread the cauliflower mixture onto a 12-inch pizza pan and press it into an even layer like a pizza crust. Press until it is less than 1 inch thick. Bake for 20 minutes. While the crust bakes, place a large skillet over medium heat. Heat the olive oil, add the onions, and occasionally cook, stirring until caramelized for about 20 minutes. Spread the caramelized onions and chicken sausage evenly across the cauliflower crust. Top with the remaining 1 cup of mozzarella cheese. Bake the pizza for 10 minutes more or until the cheese is bubbly.

Nutrition information per serving: Calories: 121 kcal, Protein: 10 g, Total Carbs: 8 g, Dietary Fibers: 4 g, Total Fat: 7 g

49. Chipotle Shredded Pork

Serves: 8

Total time: 6 hours 10 minutes

Ingredients:

- 1 (7.5 oz.) can chipotle peppers in adobo sauce
- 1 ½ tablespoon apple cider vinegar
- 1 tablespoon ground cumin
- 1 tablespoon dried oregano
- 1 lime, juiced
- 2 lb. pork shoulder trimmed excess fat.

Preparation:

In a blender or a food processor, puree the chipotle peppers and adobo sauce, apple cider vinegar, cumin, oregano, and lime juice. Place the pork shoulder in the slow cooker and pour the sauce over it. Cover the slow cooker and cook on low for 6 hours. The finished pork should shred easily. Use two forks to shred the pork in the slow cooker. If there is any additional sauce, allow the pork to cook on low for 20 minutes to absorb the remaining liquid. Serve warm.

Nutrition information per serving: Calories: 260 kcal, Protein: 20 g, Total Carbs: 5 g, Dietary Fibers: 2 g, Total Fat: 11 g

50. Slow-cooker Pork with peppers and pineapple

Serves: 4

Total time: 5 hours 10 minutes

Ingredients:

- ¼ cup low-sodium soy sauce
- ½ lemon, juiced
- 1 teaspoon garlic powder
- 1 teaspoon ground cumin
- ½ teaspoon cayenne pepper
- 1 ½ pound boneless pork tenderloin
- ¼ teaspoon ground coriander
- 2 red bell peppers thinly sliced.

- 2 (20-ounce) cans pineapple chunks in 100% natural juice

Preparation:

In a small bowl, mix the soy sauce, lemon juice, garlic powder, cumin, cayenne pepper, and coriander. Place the pork tenderloin in the slow cooker and add the red bell pepper slices. Cover with pineapple chunks and their juices. Pour the soya sauce mixture on top. Cover the slow cooker and turn on low for about 5 hours. Shred the pork with a fork and tongs and continue to cook on slow for 20 minutes more or until juices are well absorbed. Serve and enjoy.

Nutrition information per serving: Calories: 131 kcal, Protein: 17 g, Total Carbs: 11 g, Dietary Fibers: 2 g, Total Fat: 2 g

51. Pork, White bean, and Spinach Soup

Serves: 4

Total time: 50 minutes

Ingredients:

- 1 teaspoon extra virgin olive oil
- 1 medium onion chopped.
- 2 (4-ounce) boneless pork chops, cut into 1-inch cubes
- 1 (14.5 oz.) can diced tomatoes
- 3 cups low sodium chicken broth
- ½ teaspoon dried thyme
- ¼ teaspoon crushed red pepper flakes.
- 1 (15 oz.) can great northern beans, drained and rinsed
- 8 oz. fresh spinach leaves

Preparation:

Place a large soup pot or Dutch oven over medium heat and heat the olive oil. Add the onion and sauté for 2 to 3 minutes or until tender. Add the pork and brown it for 4 to 5 minutes on each side. Mix in the tomatoes, broth, thyme, red pepper flakes, and beans. Bring to a boil and then reduce the heat to low to simmer covered for 30 minutes. Add the spinach and stir until wilted, about 5 minutes and serve immediately.

Nutrition information per serving: Calories: 156 kcal, Protein: 17 g, Total Carbs: 17 g, Dietary Fibers: 4 g, Total Fat: 4 g

52. Italian Beef Sandwiches

Serves: 6

Total time: 7 hours

Ingredients:

- 1 cup water
- 1 tablespoon balsamic vinegar
- ¾ teaspoon garlic powder
- ¾ teaspoon onion powder
- 1 ½ teaspoons dried parsley
- ¾ teaspoon dried oregano
- ¼ teaspoon dried thyme
- ½ teaspoon dried basil
- 1 ½ pound boneless beef chuck roast, fat trimmed.
- ¼ teaspoon freshly ground black pepper.
- 1 medium onion, sliced.
- 1 red bell pepper cut into strips.
- 6-sprouted grain hot dog buns or sandwich thins
- 1 (16-ounce) jar pepperoncini (optional)

Preparation:

In a small bowl, mix the water, vinegar, garlic powder, onion powder, parsley, oregano, thyme, basil, and black pepper. Place the beef in the slow cooker and add the onions and bell pepper. Pour the sauce over the roast. Cover the slow cooker and cook on low for 7 hours. The meat should be tender and cooked through. Carefully transfer the roast to a cutting board. Thinly sliced the roast. Toast the buns or sandwich thins. Layer each bun with the beef and top with the au jus, pepper, and onion. Serve warm with pepperoncini.

Nutrition information per serving: Calories: 351 kcal, Protein: 31 g, Total Carbs: 30 g, Dietary Fibers: 5 g, Total Fat: 9 g

53. Sloppy Joes

Serves: 8

Total time: 40 minutes

Ingredients:

- non-stick cooking spray
- 1 ½ pound supreme lean ground beef
- 1 cup chopped onion.
- 1 cup chopped celery.
- 1 (8-ounce) can tomato sauce
- 1/3 cup catsup (free of high fructose)
- 2 tablespoons white vinegar
- 2 tablespoons Worcestershire sauce
- 2 tablespoons Dijon mustard
- 1 tablespoon brown sugar

Preparation:

Spray a large skillet with the cooking spray and place it over medium heat. Add the beef and brown until it is no longer pink, about 10 minutes. Drain off any grease. Mix in the onion and celery and cook for 2 to 3 minutes. Stir in the tomato sauce, catsup, vinegar, Worcestershire sauce, mustard, and brown sugar. Bring the liquid to a simmer and reduce the heat to low. Cook for 15 minutes or until the sauce has thickened. Spoon about ¾ cup of the sloppy joe mixture onto each plate and serve.

Nutrition information per serving: Calories: 269 kcal, Protein: 24 g, Total Carbs: 32 g, Dietary Fibers: 6 g, Total Fat: 5 g

54. Creamy Beef with Mushrooms

Serves: 6

Total time: 40 minutes

Ingredients:

- Non-stick cooking spray
- 1 ½ pound extra-lean beef sirloin, cut into ½ inch strips.
- 1 teaspoon extra virgin olive oil
- 1 medium onion, chopped.
- ½ pound mushroom sliced.
- 2 tablespoons whole wheat flour
- 1 cup low sodium beef broth
- 1 cup water
- 1 teaspoon Worcestershire sauce
- ½ teaspoon dried thyme
- ½ teaspoon dried dill
- ½ cup low-fat Greek plain yogurt
- 2 tablespoons finely chopped fresh parsley for garnish.

Preparation:

Coat a medium pan with the cooking spray and place over medium-high heat. Add the beef. Cook frequently, stirring until browned for about 15 minutes. Transfer to a bowl and set aside. In the Same pan, heat the olive oil over medium-high heat. Add the onion and cook until tender for 1 to 2 minutes. Add the mushrooms and cook until tender for about 3 minutes. Mix in the flour and stir to coat the onion and mushrooms. Stir in the broth, water, Worcestershire sauce, thyme, dill. Bring to a boil, cover the pan and cook for about 10 minutes, stirring frequently. Stir in the yogurt. Mix in the beef. Serve garnished with parsley.

Nutrition information per serving: Calories: 351 kcal, Protein: 31 g, Total Carbs: 30 g, Dietary Fibers: 5 g, Total Fat: 9 g

55. Ranch seasoned Crispy Chicken Tenders

Serves: 6

Total time: 30 minutes

Ingredients:

- Non-stick cooking spray
- 6 chicken tenderloin pieces
- 2 tablespoons whole wheat pastry flour
- 1 egg lightly beaten.
- ½ cup whole wheat bread-crumbs
- 2 tablespoons grated Parmigiano-Reggiano cheese
- 2 teaspoons dried parsley

- ¾ teaspoon dried dill
- ¼ teaspoon garlic powder
- ¼ teaspoon onion powder
- ¼ teaspoon freshly ground black pepper.

Preparation:

Preheat the oven to 425°F. Spray a baking sheet with the cooking spray. Prepare the three small dishes for coating the chicken. Place the flour in the first dish, egg in the second, and in the last dish, mix cheese, bread-crumbs, dill, garlic powder, onion powder, black pepper, and basil. Working one at a time, dip each tenderloin into the flour. Shake off any excess, then dip the chicken into the egg. Finally, place the tenderloin in the bread crumbs and press to coat in the mixture. Place on the baking sheet. Bake for about 20 minutes or until crispy, brown, and cooked through. Serve warm.

Nutrition information per serving: Calories: 163 kcal, Protein: 25 g, Total Carbs: 8 g, Dietary Fibers: 1 g, Total Fat: 2 g

56. Grilled Chicken Wings

Serves: 8

Total time: 35 minutes

Ingredients:

- 1 ½ pound frozen chicken wings
- Freshly ground black pepper
- 1 teaspoon garlic powder
- 1 cup buffalo wing sauce
- 1 teaspoon extra virgin olive oil

Preparation:

Preheat the grill to 350°F. Season the wings with black pepper and garlic powder. Grill the wings for 15 minutes on each side until they are browned and crispy. Toss the wings with sauce and olive oil and serve warm.

Nutrition information per serving: Calories: 82 kcal, Protein: 7 g, Total Carbs: 1 g, Dietary Fibers: 0 g, Total Fat: 6 g

57. Spaghetti Squash Casserole with ground beef

Serves: 8

Total time: 1 hour 30 minutes

Ingredients:

- Non-stick cooking spray
- 2 medium spaghetti squash
- 1-pound supreme lean ground beef
- 2 teaspoons minced garlic
- 1 (8-ounce) can tomato sauce
- 1 large onion minced
- 1 (10-ounce) can diced tomatoes
- 1 teaspoon dried basil
- 1 teaspoon dried oregano
- 1 cup shredded mozzarella cheese
- ½ cup shredded Parmigiano-Reggiano cheese

Preparation:

Preheat the oven to 350°F. Coat a baking sheet with the cooking spray. Halve the spaghetti squash, remove, and discard the stem, pulp, and seeds and place halves cut-side down on the baking sheet. Bake for about 35 minutes or until tender. While the squash bakes, spray a large skillet with the cooking spray, and over medium heat, place it. Add ground beef, onion, and garlic and sauté for about 10 minutes or until the beef is no longer pink and the onion is tender. Add the tomato sauce, diced tomatoes, basil, oregano, and stir to combine well. Remove the pan from heat and set it aside. When the spaghetti squash is cool enough to handle carefully, use a fork, pull the flesh from the outer skin and make spaghetti. Set aside in a bowl. In a 9 by 13-inch baking dish, layer one-third of the meat and tomato mixture in the bottom of the dish. Evenly spread half of the squash over the meat layer. Assemble another layer in the same pattern over it. In last, sprinkle cheese over the top. Cover with aluminum foil and bake for 30 minutes. Remove the foil and bake for more than 10 minutes or until cheese begins to brown. Serve warm.

Nutrition information per serving: Calories: 229 kcal, Protein: 20 g, Total Carbs: 16 g, Dietary Fibers: 3 g, Total Fat: 10 g

58. Pork chops with Apples and red onion

Serves: 4

Total time: 40 minutes

Ingredients:

- 2 teaspoons extra virgin olive oil, divided.
- 4 boneless center-cut thin pork chops
- 2 small apples thinly sliced.
- 1 small red onion thinly sliced.
- 1 cup low sodium chicken broth
- 1 teaspoon Dijon mustard
- 1 teaspoon dried sage
- 1 teaspoon dried thyme

Preparation:

Place a large non-stick frying pan over high heat and add 1 teaspoon of olive oil. When oil is hot, add the pork chops and reduce the heat to medium. Sear the chops for 3 minutes on one side, flip and sear the other side for 3 minutes, 6 minutes in total. Transfer the chops to a plate and set them aside. In the same pan, add the remaining 1 teaspoon of olive oil. Add the apples and onion. Cook for 5 minutes or until tender. While the apples and onion cook, mix the broth and Dijon mustard in a small bowl. Add the sage and thyme to the pan and stir to coat the onions and apples. Stir in the broth mixture and return the pork chops to the pan. Cover the pan and simmer for 10 to 15 minutes. Let pork chops rest for 2 minutes before cutting.

Nutrition information per serving: Calories: 234 kcal, Protein: 20 g, Total Carbs: 13 g, Dietary Fibers: 3 g, Total Fat: 11 g

59. Greek Yogurt Chicken

Serves: 4

Total time: 45 minutes

Ingredients:

- 4 boneless skinless chicken breasts (4 oz. each)
- 1 cup plain Greek yogurt
- ½ cup grated Parmesan cheese.
- 1 teaspoon garlic powder
- 1 ½ teaspoons seasoning salt
- ½ teaspoon pepper

Preparation:

Preheat oven to 375°F. Combine Greek yogurt, cheese, and seasonings in a bowl. Line baking sheet with foil and spray with cooking spray. Coat each chicken breast in a Greek yogurt mixture and place on a foiled baking sheet. Bake for 45 minutes.

Nutrition information per serving: Calories: 266 kcal, Protein: 46 g, Total Carbs: 3 g, Dietary Fibers: 0 g, Total Fat: 4 g

Chapter 10: Vegetarian Recipes

1. Provençal Ratatouille

Serves: 2

Total time: 40 minutes

Ingredients:

- Olive oil cooking spray
- 2 tablespoons onions, chopped.
- 1 clove garlic, minced.
- ½ cup pumpkin, diced.
- 2 medium carrots, diced.
- 1 large turnip, diced.
- 1 cup zucchinis, sliced.
- 2 beef tomatoes, chopped.
- 1 teaspoon dried Herbs de Provence
- 1 cup water
- 1 cup baby spinach leaves

Preparation:

Spray a large pan with the cooking spray and heat over medium heat. Add the onions, garlic, pumpkin, carrots, turnip, and zucchini, and cook for 5 minutes or until the vegetables start to soften. Add in the chopped tomatoes and dried herbs, and simmer until thickened, frequently stirring to prevent the vegetables from burning, for about 15 minutes. Add the water, and simmer for another 15 to 20 minutes until the sauce is reduced and the vegetables are cooked. Top with the baby spinach leaves to serve.

Nutrition information per serving: Calories: 133 kcal, Protein: 7 g, Total Carbs: 29 g, Dietary Fibers: 9 g, Total Fat: 1 g

2. Mix Veggies

Serves: 4

Total time: 40 minutes

Ingredients:

- Olive oil cooking spray
- 2 tablespoons chopped onions.
- 1 cup diced red peppers.
- 1 clove garlic, minced.
- ½ cup diced winter squash.
- 1 cup cherry tomatoes, halved.
- 1 cup reduced-sodium canned tomatoes.
- ½ cup dark red, reduced-sodium canned kidney beans (liquid reserved)

- 1 cup reduced-sodium canned black beans (liquid reserved)
- 1 jalapeño pepper, sliced.
- 2 teaspoons lime juice

Preparation:

Spray the cooking spray into a non-stick pan, and heat on medium heat. Add the onions, red peppers, garlic, and squash to the pan. Cover the pan, reduce the heat to low, and cook for 10 minutes. Mix in the cherry tomatoes, canned tomatoes, beans, jalapeño pepper, and lime juice. Simmer for 20 minutes. Serve hot.

Nutrition information per serving: Calories: 133 kcal, Protein: 6 g, Total Carbs: 24 g, Dietary Fibers: 5 g, Total Fat: 0 g

3. Crunchy Super Salad

Serves: 2

Total time: 10 minutes

Ingredients:

- 1 teaspoon dry mustard
- 1 tablespoon lemon juice
- ¼ cup apple cider vinegar
- 2 tablespoons mint leaves
- 5 cherry tomatoes, stems removed.
- 2 cups zucchini noodles
- ½ carrot peeled and grated
- ½ yellow pepper thinly sliced
- ¼ cup cooked red quinoa
- Freshly ground black pepper

Preparation:

Blend the mustard, lemon juice, apple cider vinegar, mint leaves, and cherry tomatoes in a food processor to make the dressing. Transfer to a bowl and keep chilled until ready to serve. Toss together the zucchini noodles, carrots, and pepper with the dressing. **To Serve:** Top the zucchini noodles with the cooked quinoa, and season with freshly ground black pepper.

Nutrition information per serving: Calories: 118 kcal, Protein: 4 g, Total Carbs: 23 g, Dietary Fibers: 2 g, Total Fat: 1 g

4. Refreshing Zucchini and Parsley Noodles

Serves: 2

Total time: 10 minutes

Ingredients:

- 1 lemon, juiced
- 2 beef tomatoes, diced.
- 1 cup fresh parsley, chopped.
- 1 clove garlic, minced.
- 1 tablespoon chopped shallots.
- 3 cups zucchini noodles

Preparation:

To make the dressing, mix the lemon juice, beef tomatoes, fresh parsley, garlic, and shallots in a bowl and rest for at least 30 minutes for the flavors to blend. Toss in the cold zucchini noodles and serve.

Nutrition information per serving: Calories: 91 kcal, Protein: 7 g, Total Carbs: 18 g, Dietary Fibers: 3 g, Total Fat: 1 g

5. Air fried Carrot and Zucchini Fritters

Serves: 2

Total time: 25 minutes

Ingredients:

- 1 teaspoon salt
- 1 large zucchini, grated.
- 1 tablespoon flax meal
- 2 ½ tablespoons water
- 1 large clove of garlic, minced.
- 1 cup grated carrots.

Preparation:

Add the salt to the grated zucchinis and rest for 5 to 10 minutes so that the salt can draw out the excess water from the zucchinis. Rinse well and drain from the water. Pat them dry with a kitchen towel and set them aside. Preheat the Air fryer to 350°F. To make the flax egg, mix the flax meal with water and rest until it thickens. Combine the zucchini, carrots, garlic, and flax egg and form the desired size patties. Arrange the patties in the Air Fryer Basket and set the timer for 10 minutes. Halfway through the cooking time, flip the fritters over to allow even cooking.

Nutrition information per serving: Calories: 81 kcal, Protein: 4 g, Total Carbs: 14 g, Dietary Fibers: 5 g, Total Fat: 2 g

6. Roasted Fennel with Apple Cider Glaze

Serves: 2

Total time: 55 minutes

Ingredients:

- 1 cup reduced sugar apple cider.
- 1 teaspoon fennel seeds
- Olive oil cooking spray
- 2 cups sliced fennel bulbs.

Preparation:

Preheat the oven to 325°F. Combine the apple cider and fennel seeds in a saucepan, and simmer over low heat until the liquid has thickened to a glaze and reduced by half. Strain the glaze from the seeds. Lightly spray an ovenproof dish with cooking spray and arrange the sliced fennel in the dish. Brush the fennel with the glaze. Roast for 30 to 45 minutes, re-coating with the glaze every 10 to 15 minutes. The fennels can be slow-roasted until they are tender and caramelized.

Nutrition information per serving: Calories: 79 kcal, Protein: 1 g, Total Carbs: 11 g, Dietary Fibers: 3 g, Total Fat: 0 g

7. Truffle Cauliflower Bake

Serves: 2

Total time: 45 minutes

Ingredients:

- Olive oil cooking spray (white truffle flavored if possible)
- 2 cups cauliflower florets
- 1 clove garlic, minced.
- 1 cup cherry tomatoes, halved.
- ½ teaspoons truffle salt
- Freshly ground black pepper

Preparation:

Preheat oven to 350°F. Lightly spray an ovenproof serving dish with the white truffle flavored olive oil cooking spray. Toss the cauliflower florets with the minced garlic and cherry tomatoes and arrange them evenly in the dish's base. Season with the truffle salt and freshly ground black pepper, bake for 30 to 40 minutes, or until the cauliflower florets are fork-tender.

Nutrition information per serving: Calories: 45 kcal, Protein: 3 g, Total Carbs: 7 g, Dietary Fibers: 4 g, Total Fat: 0 g

8. Lime-Roasted Eggplants

Serves: 2

Total time: 45 minutes

Ingredients:

- 2 teaspoons salt
- 3 cups cubed eggplants.
- ¼ cup lime juice
- Olive oil cooking spray

Preparation:

Preheat the oven to 350°F. Sprinkle the salt on the cubed eggplants and allow them to rest for 10 minutes to draw out excess water. Rinse the eggplants thoroughly to remove the salt, and pat dry with a clean kitchen towel. Toss the eggplant cubes in the lime juice. Lightly spray an ovenproof dish with the cooking spray and arrange the eggplant cubes in the dish's base. Bake for 25 to 30 minutes, or until the eggplants are cooked through and soft.

Nutrition information per serving: Calories: 39 kcal, Protein: 1 g, Total Carbs: 10 g, Dietary Fibers: 4 g, Total Fat: 0 g

9. Grilled Tomatoes with Black Garlic Spread

Serves: 2

Total time: 45 minutes

Ingredients:

- 3 bulbs black garlic (or try white garlic/wild garlic if you can't find black garlic)
- 3 beef tomatoes

Preparation:

Preheat the oven to 350°F. Cut the tops off the black garlic bulbs so that the tops of the cloves are exposed. Place the bulbs on a small ovenproof dish. Slice the beef tomatoes each into four slices and arrange them on an ovenproof dish. Bake the tomatoes and the garlic bulbs in the oven for 35 to 40 minutes. When done, spread the soft flesh of the garlic on top of the tomato slices to serve.

Nutrition information per serving: Calories: 90 kcal, Protein: 6 g, Total Carbs: 18 g, Dietary Fibers: 0 g, Total Fat: 0 g

10. Tomato and Arugula Egg White Scramble

Serves: 2

Total time: 15 minutes

Ingredients:

- Olive oil cooking spray
- 1 large onion, chopped.
- 2 beef tomatoes, diced.
- 3 large egg whites, whisked.
- 1 cup arugula leaves, shredded.

Preparation:

Lightly spray a non-stick pan with the cooking spray, and heat over medium heat. Add the chopped onions, and sauté until they become translucent. Add the diced tomatoes, and cook until the tomatoes have released their liquids, for about three minutes. Add the whisked egg whites and allow them to sit for a couple of minutes. Add the arugula leaves and scramble the egg whites so that the ingredients are well combined. Serve hot.

Nutrition information per serving: Calories: 92 kcal, Protein: 10 g, Total Carbs: 14 g, Dietary Fibers: 1 g, Total Fat: 1 g

11. Sunshine Pie

Serves: 2

Total time: 65 minutes

Ingredients:

- 1.5 lb. spaghetti squash
- 1 teaspoon olive oil
- 1 garlic clove, minced.
- 1 tablespoon chopped onions.
- ½ cup sliced mushrooms.
- ¼ cup chopped red peppers.
- 1 cup canned chopped tomatoes.
- 1 teaspoon dried oregano
- 1 cup shredded low-fat mozzarella cheese.

Preparation:

Preheat the oven to 375°F. To prepare the spaghetti squash, half the squash and discard its seeds. Place each half face down in a 9x13-inch baking dish. Cover and bake for 30-40 minutes until soft. Remove and allow to cool. When cool enough to handle, scrape out the squash's flesh and mash to a smooth consistency.

Meanwhile, prepare the filling. Heat the olive oil in a large saucepan over medium heat. Add the garlic and onions, and cook for 2 minutes, stirring frequently. Add the mushrooms, bell peppers, chopped tomatoes, and dried oregano to the pan, and bring to a boil. Reduce the heat, and simmer for 15 to 20 minutes until the sauce has thickened, stirring occasionally. To assemble: Transfer the tomato filling into an ovenproof serving dish. Top with the squash, and then the mozzarella cheese. Bake for 25 minutes or until lightly browned. Let cool for 5 minutes before serving.

Nutrition information per serving: Calories: 81 kcal, Protein: 6 g, Total Carbs: 4 g, Dietary Fibers: 1 g, Total Fat: 5 g

12. Kale Fruit Salad

Serves: 2

Total time: 15 minutes

Ingredients:

- 1 small tangerine, segmented.
- 3 cups baby kale leaves, shredded.
- ½ cup pears thinly sliced.

Preparation:

Toss together the tangerine segments, baby kale leaves, and pears in a salad bowl. Allow chilling for 15 minutes for the flavors to blend. Optional: Dress with a bit of apple cider vinegar to balance out the sweet fruit.

Nutrition information per serving: Calories: 82 kcal, Protein: 4 g, Total Carbs: 19 g, Dietary Fibers: 5 g, Total Fat: 1 g

13. Savory Tofu

Serves: 2

Total time: 30 minutes

Ingredients:

- 1 teaspoon minced ginger
- 1 tablespoon oyster sauce
- 1 tablespoon reduced-sodium soy sauce.
- 1 teaspoon white pepper
- ¼ tablespoons pure sesame oil
- 3 ½ oz. extra firm, high-protein, low-fat tofu
- 3 tablespoons chopped scallions.

Preparation:

To make the seasoning Combine the minced ginger, oyster sauce, soy sauce, white pepper, and sesame oil in a bowl. Rinse the tofu, and pat dry with a kitchen towel. Arrange on a heat-proof steaming bowl and drizzle the seasoning over the tofu. Steam the tofu for 15 to 20 minutes until done, and spoon over the seasoning several times throughout the cooking time. Alternatively, heat a little sesame oil in a screaming hot pan and add the tofu for 3-4 minutes until crispy and brown. Top with the chopped scallions to serve.

Nutrition information per serving: Calories: 117 kcal, Protein: 10 g, Total Carbs: 12 g, Dietary Fibers: 0 g, Total Fat: 5 g

14. Baked Sweet Cabbage

Serves: 2

Total time: 65 minutes

Ingredients:

- 2 large cabbage leaves
- 1 teaspoon olive oil
- ½ medium onion, diced.
- 1 small carrot, grated.
- 1 teaspoon dried oregano
- 1 cup canned tomatoes

Preparation:

Preheat oven to 350°F. Bring a pot of water to a boil. Wash the cabbage leaves and blanch them in hot water for 30 seconds. Pat dry and set aside. Heat the olive oil in a non-stick pan over medium heat. Add the onions, carrots, and dried oregano, stirring for a few minutes until the vegetables are slightly soft and caramelized. Divide the vegetable mixture into the center of each cabbage leaf and roll up to seal the vegetables. Arrange the cabbage rolls, seam sides down in a small baking dish. Top with the canned tomatoes and bake for 35 to 40 minutes. Allow cooling for 5 to 10 minutes before serving.

Nutrition information per serving: Calories: 111 kcal, Protein: 2 g, Total Carbs: 11 g, Dietary Fibers: 6 g, Total Fat: 2 g

15. Tomato and Herb Pizzettes

Serves: 5

Total time: 30 minutes

Ingredients:

- 12 cherry tomatoes, halved.
- ¼ teaspoon garlic powder
- 1 teaspoon dried oregano
- 6 light multigrain English muffins, sliced in half.
- 1 cup finely sliced green pepper.
- 4 oz. fat-free mozzarella cheese, sliced into thin disks.
- ¼ cup fresh basil, chopped.
- 2 teaspoons balsamic vinegar

Preparation:

Preheat the oven to 400°F. Line a baking sheet with parchment paper. Layer the baking sheet with the tomato halves. Evenly sprinkle on the garlic powder and oregano. Give the tomatoes a spray with cooking oil. Roast in the oven until the tomato skins begin to split (about 10 minutes). Take the tray out and set it aside. Line another baking sheet with parchment paper. Place the English muffin halves on the baking sheets, cut-side up. Divide the pepper, cheese, and roasted tomatoes onto the muffins. Finally, sprinkle the basil evenly over all 12 pizzas. Bake the pizzas in the oven for 10-12 minutes or until the cheese is all melted and gooey. Drizzle with balsamic vinegar before serving.

Nutrition information per serving: Calories: 191 kcal, Protein: 14 g, Total Carbs: 33 g, Dietary Fibers: 6 g, Total Fat: 2 g

16. Spinach and Mozzarella Bake

Serves: 3

Total time: 40 minutes

Ingredients:

- ½ cup non-fat mozzarella cheese
- 2 cups fresh spinach cooked and drained.
- 1 eggplant, diced.
- 1 zucchini, diced.
- ½ cup tomato paste
- ½ cup frozen peas
- 1 tablespoon dried basil
- 1 tablespoon low-fat parmesan/cheddar cheese

Preparation:

Preheat your oven to 375°F. In a bowl, mix the mozzarella and spinach. In another bowl, mix the eggplant, zucchini, and ½ the tomato paste. Save the rest of the paste for later. You'll need a lasagna dish for the next part. Spoon the mozzarella and spinach mixture into the base. Spoon the vegetable mixture to form the next layer. Cover with the reserved pasta. Sprinkle with basil and hard cheese. Cook for 30 minutes or until golden brown and bubbly. Remove from the oven and slice into portions. Spoon onto your plates and enjoy.

Nutrition information per serving: Calories: 135 kcal, Protein: 24 g, Total Carbs: 24 g, Dietary Fibers: 10 g, Total Fat: 1 g

17. Fresh Chickpea Salad

Serves: 2

Total time: 10 minutes

Ingredients:

- 3/4 cup canned chickpeas, drained
- 1 tablespoon olive oil
- 1 tablespoon balsamic vinegar
- 1 lemon, juiced
- 2 oz. Low-fat feta cheese crumbled.
- 12 cherry tomatoes, halved.

- 1 small cucumber, deseeded and diced.
- ½ green onion finely sliced.
- 18 pitted black olives, halved.
- A pinch of salt and freshly ground black pepper.
- 1 tablespoon chopped fresh mint
- 1 teaspoon chopped fresh oregano
- 2 cups washed raw spinach leaves

Preparation:

Place the chickpeas in a fine sieve. Rinse with plenty of cold water, then leave to drain thoroughly. Mix the oil and vinegar with lemon juice. Place the feta, tomatoes, cucumber, onion, and olives in a large mixing bowl with the chickpeas. Mix, cover, and leave to rest in the fridge for 20-30 minutes if possible. Season the chickpea mixture and add the mint and oregano. Top the spinach leaves with the chickpea salad and serve.

Nutrition information per serving: Calories: 82 kcal, Protein: 3 g, Total Carbs: 8 g, Dietary Fibers: 2 g, Total Fat: 5 g

18. Broccoli Cheddar Bake

Serves: 6

Total time: 65 minutes

Ingredients:

- 4 cups chopped fresh broccoli.
- ½ cup finely chopped onion
- 2 tablespoons water
- 1 ½ cups egg substitute
- 1 cup fat-free milk
- 1 cup shredded cheddar cheese
- ½ teaspoon ground black pepper

Preparation:

Preheat the oven to 350°F. Lightly coat a baking dish with cooking spray. In a non-stick skillet, combine the broccoli, onion, and water. Sauté over medium-high heat until the vegetables are tender, about 5 to 8 minutes. Keep adding water to prevent the vegetables from drying out but use as little water as possible. Drain and set aside when the broccoli is done. In a small bowl, combine milk, egg substitute, and 3/4 cup of cheese. Then add the broccoli mixture and pepper into the same bowl. Stir to mix thoroughly. Shift the mixture into the prepared baking dish. Set the baking dish into a large pan filled with about 1 inch of water. Bake uncovered until a knife inserted in the center comes out clean, about 45 minutes. Remove from the oven and top with the remaining ¼ cup shredded cheese. Let stand about 10 minutes before serving.

Nutrition information per serving: Calories: 173 kcal, Protein: 15 g, Total Carbs: 8 g, Dietary Fibers: 2 g, Total Fat: 9 g

19. Cold Tomato Couscous

Serves: 4

Total time: 15 minutes

Ingredients:

- 5 oz. couscous
- 3 tablespoons tomato sauce
- 3 tablespoons lemon juice
- 1 small-sized onion, chopped
- 1 cup vegetable stock
- ½ small-sized cucumber, sliced
- ½ small-sized carrot, sliced
- ¼ teaspoon salt
- 3 tablespoons olive oil
- ½ cup fresh parsley, chopped

Preparation:

First, pour the couscous into a large bowl. Boil the vegetable broth and slightly add in the couscous while stirring constantly. Leave it for about 10 minutes until the couscous absorbs the liquid. Cover with a lid and set aside. Stir from time to time to speed up the soaking process and break the lumps with a spoon.

Meanwhile, preheat the olive oil in a frying pan, and add the tomato sauce. Add chopped onion and stir until translucent. Set aside and let it cool for a few minutes. Add the oily tomato sauce to the couscous and stir well. Now add lemon juice, chopped parsley, and salt to the mixture and give it a final stir. Serve with sliced cucumber, carrot, and parsley.

Nutrition information per serving: Calories: 249 kcal, Protein: 5.6 g, Total Carbs: 32.8 g, Dietary Fibers: 3.2 g, Total Fat: 11 g

20. Red Orange Salad

Serves: 3

Total time: 15 minutes

Ingredients:

- Fresh lettuce leaves, rinsed
- 1 small cucumber sliced
- ½ red bell pepper, sliced
- 1 cup frozen seafood mix
- 1 onion peeled and finely chopped
- 3 garlic cloves, crushed
- ¼ cup fresh orange juice
- 5 tablespoons extra virgin olive oil
- Salt, to taste

Preparation:

Heat 3 tablespoons of extra virgin olive oil over medium-high temperature. Add chopped onion and crushed garlic. Stir fry for about 5 minutes.

Reduce the heat to a minute and add 1 cup of frozen seafood mix. Cover and cook for about 15 minutes, until soft. Remove from the heat and allow it to cool for a while. Meanwhile, combine the vegetables in a bowl. Add the remaining 2 tablespoons of olive oil, fresh orange juice, and a little salt. Toss well to combine. Top with seafood mix and serve immediately.

Nutrition information per serving: Calories: 206 kcal, Protein: 7 g, Total Carbs: 13.1 g, Dietary Fibers: 1.8 g, Total Fat: 14.6 g

21. Grilled Veal Steak with Vegetables

Serves: 4

Total time: 20 minutes

Ingredients:

- 1 lb. veal steak, about 1 inch thick
- 1 medium red pepper
- 1 medium green pepper
- 1 small onion is finely chopped.
- 3 tablespoons olive oil
- Salt and pepper, to taste

Preparation:

Wash and pat dry the steak with kitchen paper. Heat the olive oil over medium temperature in a non-stick grill pan and fry for about 20 minutes (about ten on each side). Remove from the heat and set aside. Wash and cut vegetables into thin strips. Add some salt and pepper. Add to a grill pan and cook for about 15 minutes, stirring constantly. Serve immediately.

Nutrition information per serving: Calories: 311, Protein: 30.6 g, Total Carbs: 5.3 g, Dietary Fibers: 1.3 g, Total Fat: 18.5 g

22. Sweet Potato and Spinach Turkey Meatballs

Serves: 8

Total time: 30 minutes

Ingredients:

- 2 cups or one peeled medium sweet potato (3/4-inch chunks)
- 1 large egg
- 2 large cloves of garlic (minced)
- 1 small onion is finely chopped.
- 2 cups fresh chopped spinach.
- ½ teaspoons salt
- 1 tablespoon poultry seasoning or Italian seasoning
- 1 tablespoon extra-virgin olive oil
- 1 lb. lean ground turkey
- ½ teaspoons black pepper

Preparation:

Microwave sweet potato for 4-6 minutes until very soft and fork-tender. Allow cooling.

In a large bowl, mash sweet potato. Add turkey, egg, spinach, onion, garlic, herbs, salt, pepper, and oil. Roll into ¼ cup size balls. Brush 2 Tablespoons olive oil onto a baking sheet. Preheat oven to 400°F. Place meatballs 1 inch spaced apart. Brush the remaining one tablespoons of oil onto meatballs. Bake until cooked through and slightly golden, about 20 minutes.

Nutrition information per serving: Calories: 127 kcal, Protein: 14.8 g, Total Carbs: 7 g, Dietary Fibers: 0.3 g, Total Fat: 6.9 g

23. Italian Eggplant Pizzas

Serves: 6

Total time: 45 minutes

Ingredients:

- 1 large eggplant, cut into ¼ to ½ inch rounds.
- 1 tablespoon salt
- 1 tablespoon extra-virgin olive oil
- 2 teaspoons minced garlic
- ½ teaspoon dried oregano
- 1 cup marinara sauce with Italian herbs
- 1 cup fresh basil leaves
- 1 cup shredded part-skim Mozzarella cheese
- ¼ cup shredded Parmigiano-Reggiano Cheese

Preparation:

Preheat the oven to 425°F. Use aluminum foil to line a large, rimmed baking sheet. Put the eggplant rounds on paper towels and sprinkle them with salt. Let them stir for 10 to 15 minutes to help release some water in the eggplant. Pat dry afterward. It's okay to wipe off some of the salt before baking. In a small bowl, mix the olive oil, garlic, and oregano. Place the eggplant rounds 1-inch apart on the baking sheet. Using a pastry brush, coat each side of the eggplant with the olive oil mixture. Bake the eggplant for 15 minutes. Create Pizzas by layering 1 to 2 tablespoons of marinara sauce, 2 basil leaves, about 1 tablespoon of mozzarella cheese, and about ½ tablespoon Parmigiano-Reggiano Cheese on each baked eggplant round. Bake the pizzas for an additional 10 minutes or until the cheese is melted and starting brown. Serve immediately and enjoy.

Nutrition information per serving: Calories: 99 kcal, Protein: 5 g, Total Carbs: 7 g, Dietary Fibers: 2 g, Total Fat: 6 g

24. Roasted Vegetable Quinoa Salad with Chickpeas

Serves: 6

Total time: 45 minutes

Ingredients:

- 1 small eggplant, diced.
- 1 small zucchini, diced.
- 1 small yellow squash, diced.
- ½ cup grape tomatoes halved.
- 1 (15-oz.) can chickpeas, drained and rinsed
- 3 tablespoons extra virgin olive oil, divided.
- 1/3 cup packed quinoa
- 1 cup low-sodium vegetable or chicken broth
- 2 tablespoons freshly squeezed lemon juice
- 1 tablespoon dried basil
- 1 teaspoon dried oregano

Preparation:

Preheat the oven to 425°F. Line a 9x13-inch baking sheet with parchment paper. Spread the eggplant, zucchini, yellow squash, tomatoes, and chickpeas across the baking sheet and toss them with 1 tablespoon of olive oil. Bake for 30 minutes, stirring once halfway. The finished vegetables should be tender, and the tomatoes should be juicy. The chickpeas will be firm and crispy.

While the vegetables and chickpeas are roasting, place the quinoa and broth in a small saucepan over medium-high heat. Cover and bring to boil. Reduce the heat to low and cook for 15 minutes or until the liquid has absorbed. Remove the pan from the heat and fluff the quinoa with a fork or make quinoa according to package instructions. In a small dish, whisk together the lemon juice, garlic, and the remaining 2 tablespoons of olive oil. Mix in the basil and oregano. In a large serving bowl, combine the quinoa, roasted vegetables with chickpeas, and dressing. Gently stir to combine. Serve and enjoy.

Nutrition information per serving: Calories: 200 kcal, Protein: 7 g, Total Carbs: 27 g, Dietary Fibers: 8 g, Total Fat: 9 g

25. Mexican Stuffed Summer squash

Serves: 2

Total time: 40 minutes

Ingredients:

- Non-stick cooking spray
- 1 yellow summer squash
- ½ cup canned fat-free refried pinto beans with 1 teaspoon taco seasoning mixed in (for flavor)
- ½ cup cooked quinoa
- ½ cup shredded Colby Jack Cheese
- 1 small tomato, diced.
- 2 tablespoons sliced black olives.
- 2 scallions, chopped for garnish.

Preparation:

Preheat the oven to 400°F. Coat an 8x8-inch baking dish with the cooking spray. Cut the ends off the summer squash and discard. Cut lengthwise, then use a spoon to remove and discard the seeds. Place the squash halves cut-side down in the baking dish. Gentle poke a couple of holes in the squash to vent. Add 1 tablespoon of water to the dish. Microwave for about 3 minutes or until slightly tender. Discard any leftover water. When cool enough to handle, turn the squash to skin-side down and spread evenly apart in a dish.

Layer ¼ cup of beans in each squash, then ¼ cup of the quinoa. Top the whole thing with Colby Jack cheese. Cover with aluminum foil and bake for 25 minutes. Remove the foil and bake for 5 minutes more or until the cheese is bubbly and the squash is

tender. Garnish each squash with the tomatoes, olives, and scallions just before serving.

Nutrition information per serving: Calories: 190 kcal, Protein: 9 g, Total Carbs: 21 g, Dietary Fibers: 4 g, Total Fat: 8 g

26. Roasted root vegetables

Serves: 6 cups

Total time: 60 minutes

Ingredients:

- Non-stick cooking spray
- 2 medium red beets peeled.
- 2 large parsnips peeled.
- 2 large carrots peeled.
- 1 medium butternut squash (about 2 pounds) peeled and seeded.
- 1 medium red onion
- 2 tablespoons extra-virgin olive oil
- 4 teaspoons minced garlic
- 2 teaspoons dried thyme

Preparation:

Preheat the oven to 425°F. Spray a large, rimmed baking sheet with cooking spray. Roughly chop the beets, Parsnips, carrots, and butternut squash into the 1-inch piece. Cut the onions into half and then each half into 4 chunks. Arrange the vegetables in a single even layer on the baking sheet and sprinkle them with olive oil, garlic, and thyme. Use a spoon to mix the vegetables to coat them with the oil and seasoning. Roast for 45 minutes, stirring the vegetables after every 15 minutes until all the vegetables are tender. Serve immediately.

Nutrition information per serving: Calories: 68 kcal, Protein: 1 g, Total Carbs: 11 g, Dietary Fibers: 1 g, Total Fat: 3 g

27. Eggplant Rollatini

Serves: 8

Total time: 1 hour 5 minutes

Ingredients:

- Non-stick cooking spray
- 1 large eggplant
- 1 tablespoon salt
- 1 teaspoon extra-virgin olive oil
- 1-pound fresh spinach (about 10 cups)
- ½ cup part-skim ricotta cheese
- ¾ cup shredded part-skim mozzarella cheese, divided.
- ¼ cup shredded Parmigiano-Reggiano Cheese
- 1 egg
- ½ cup marinara sauce along with Italian herbs
- 1 teaspoon garlic, minced

Preparation:

Set an oven at 400°F. Coat one or two baking sheets with the cooking spray. Cut the eggplant into ¼-inch pieces lengthwise. Sprinkle the slices with salt and place them on a paper towel. Allow them to sit for 10 minutes to allow some of the water in the eggplant to escape. After that, pat dry. It's fine if any of the salt is removed before baking. Bake for 10 minutes with the eggplants on the baking sheet. Remove the baking sheet from the oven and put it aside to cool. Switch on the oven. Heat a large pot to medium-high. For 1 minute, heat the olive oil.

Add spinach and cook, stirring regularly, for around 3 minutes, or until the spinach leaves have wilted. Allow cooling before serving. In a medium mixing dish, combine the ricotta, ¼ cup mozzarella cheese, Parmigiano-Reggiano, egg, and garlic. Mix well. Gently fold the spinach into the cheese mixture until it has cooled. ¼ cup marinara sauce should be spread around the bottom of an 8x8-inch baking dish. Spread about 2 tablespoons of the cheese mixture onto each eggplant slice, roll it up, and put seam side down in the baking dish. Continue rolling eggplant slices into roll-ups and placing them in the pan until all of them are finished. The remaining ¼ cup marinara and ½ cup mozzarella go on top of the rolled eggplants. Preheat the oven to 350°F. Bake for 30 minutes with the baking sheets covered with aluminum foil. Remove the foil and continue baking for another 10 minutes, or until the cheese is golden brown and bubbly.

Nutrition information per serving: Calories: 160 kcal, Protein: 11 g, Total Carbs: 16 g, Dietary Fibers: 6 g, Total Fat: 7 g

28. Cabbage Rolls

Serves: 6

Total time: 20 minutes

Ingredients:

- 1 head of cabbage, individual leaves removed.
- 1/3 cup brown Minute Rice, or other whole grain of choice
- 1 teaspoon olive oil
- ½ medium onion, diced (if tolerated)
- 2 medium carrots, diced.
- 1 pound 93% lean ground turkey
- 2 teaspoons garlic powder
- 2 teaspoons oregano or Italian seasoning
- 2 cups tomato sauce

Preparation:

Preheat the oven to 350°F. To make cabbage leaves simpler to deal with, wash them and blanch them for 30 seconds. Blanching is a cooking method that involves temporarily immersing food in boiling water (usually for 10 to 60 seconds). Prepare the rice according to the package directions. Meanwhile, heat olive oil in a wide skillet over medium heat. Stir in the onions and carrots until they are slightly softened and caramelized. Add turkey and cook until the turkey is browned in the pan with the vegetables. Add seasonings, powders, rice, and meat; ½ cup of the mixture should be placed in the middle of each cabbage leaf. Roll them up, securing all ends. To keep the cabbage rolls from unrolling, place them in a baking dish seam side down, side by side. Serve the tomato sauce on top of the cabbage rolls, allowing it to spill over to the bottom of the dish, and bake for 35–45 minutes. Allow for a 5- to 10-minute rest before serving.

Nutrition information per serving: Calories: 174 kcal, Protein: 15 g, Total Carbs: 16 g, Dietary Fibers: 4 g, Total Fat: 5.5 g

29. Butternut Squash and Black Bean Enchiladas

Serves: 5

Total time: 55 minutes

Ingredients:

- 2 teaspoons minced garlic
- 1 teaspoon extra virgin olive oil
- 1 diced onion.
- 1 jalapeno pepper seeded and finely diced.
- 1 red bell pepper
- 2 ½ pound or 1 small butternut squash peeled, seeds removed and diced.
- 1 /2 teaspoon low sodium taco seasoning
- 1 teaspoon ground cumin
- 1 (10 oz.) can of diced tomatoes
- ¼ cup water
- 1 (15.5 oz.) can of black beans rinsed and drained
- 1 (10 oz.) can red enchilada sauce
- 8 small whole-wheat tortillas
- 1 shredded Monetary jack cheese
- ½ cup sliced black olives.
- 2 scallions, chopped.

Preparation:

Preheat the oven to 425°F. Place a large skillet over medium-high heat. Heat the olive oil and garlic for 1 minute or until the garlic is fragrant. Add the onions, jalapeno, and bell pepper. Sauté for 2 to 3 minutes. Add the squash, taco seasonings, and cumin. Cook

and stir for 2 minutes until well mixed. Add the tomatoes, beans, and water. Cover the skillet and cook for 30 minutes or until the squash is tender. Spread ¼ cup of sauce on the bottom of a 9 by 13-inch baking dish. Place the tortillas on a clean working surface. Fill each tortilla with about ½ cup of squash mixture. Pour the sauce over the top of the enchiladas. Top with the cheese. Cover with aluminum foil. Bake for 10 minutes or until cheese is melted. Garnish with olives and scallion and serve it.

Nutrition information per serving: Calories: 233 kcal, Protein: 13 g, Total Carbs: 27 g, Dietary Fibers: 6 g, Total Fat: 8 g

30. Cheesy Cauliflower Casserole

Serves: 8

Total time: 55 minutes

Ingredients:

- 1 head cauliflower cut into florets.
- 1 cup low fat cottage cheese
- 1 cup low-fat plain Greek Yogurt
- ½ teaspoon Dijon Mustard
- ¼ teaspoon garlic powder
- 2 oz. shredded aged white cheddar cheese.
- 2 oz. shredded mild cheddar cheese (½ cup)

Preparation:

Preheat the oven to 350°F. Fill a medium pot one-third full of water and place a steamer basket inside. Boil the water over high heat. Add the cauliflower to the steamer basket, cover the pot and reduce the heat to a gentle boil. Steam the cauliflower for 10 to 15 minutes or until the florets are soft and tender. While the cauliflower steams, mix the cheese, yogurt, mustard, and garlic powder in a medium bowl. Drain the cauliflower in a large colander and gently mash it to drain excess water. Stir the cauliflower pieces into cottage cheese mixture and with cheddar cheese. Transfer the cauliflower mixture to an 8x8-inch baking dish, bake for 30 minutes, and serve immediately.

Nutrition information per serving: Calories: 147 kcal, Protein: 13 g, Total Carbs: 8 g, Dietary Fibers: 2 g, Total Fat: 7 g

31. Barley Mushroom Risotto

Serves: 6

Total time: 55 minutes

Ingredients:

- 1 tablespoon extra-virgin olive oil
- 1 teaspoon minced garlic
- 2 leeks cleaned ends removed and chopped.
- 4 cups sliced mushrooms.
- 2 teaspoons dried thyme
- ½ cup pearl barley
- ½ cup dry white vinegar
- 1 ½ cup low sodium vegetable or chicken broth
- 1 cup water
- 3 cups fresh spinach leaves

Preparation:

Place a large skillet over medium heat. Sauté the olive oil and garlic for 1 minute. Add the leeks and cook for 2 to 3 minutes or until tender. Add the mushrooms and cook until tender and browned for about 4 minutes. Stir in thyme and barley. Cook for another 2 minutes. Add the wine and stir. Simmer for about 5 minutes or until the liquid is absorbed. Add water and broth and reduce the heat to low; cover the skillet and simmer for 40 minutes. Stir occasionally to make sure the barley does not stick to the bottom of the pan. Gently stir in the spinach and mix until it is wilted. Serve immediately.

Nutrition information per serving: Calories: 104 kcal, Protein: 3 g, Total Carbs: 16 g, Dietary Fibers: 3 g, Total Fat: 3 g

32. Red Lentil Soup with kale

Serves: 6

Total time: 55 minutes

Ingredients:

- 1 tablespoon extra-virgin olive oil
- 1 cup onion, chopped
- ½ cup carrots, cut into ½ inch chunks.
- ½ cup celery cut it into ¼ inch chunks.
- 1 teaspoon garlic, minced
- 1 cup red lentils
- 1 teaspoon dried thyme
- 1 teaspoon ground cumin
- 2 cups low sodium vegetable broth
- 2 cups water
- 2 large stalks kale, stemmed and leaves chopped.
- 1 bay leaf
- 2 tablespoons freshly squeezed lemon juice
- Low fat plain Greek yogurt

Preparation:

In a large stockpot over medium heat, heat the olive oil. Add the onion, carrots, celery, and garlic, and cook until tender for 5 to 7 minutes. Add the lentils, thyme, and cumin. Mix well and stir for 1 to 2 minutes until all the ingredients are coated well with the seasonings. Add the broth and water to the pot. Bring to simmer, add the kale, and stir well. Add the bay leaf, then cover the pot and simmer for 30 to 35 minutes. Remove the pot from the heat. Remove and discard the bay leaf. Stir in the lemon juice. Use an immersion blender to puree the soup to desired consistency. Garnish soup with a dollop of Greek yogurt and serve.

Nutrition information per serving: Calories: 170 kcal, Protein: 13 g, Total Carbs: 24 g, Dietary Fibers: 3 g, Total Fat: 3 g

33. Cheesy Broccoli Soup

Serves: 8

Total time: 30 minutes

Ingredients:

- 1 tablespoon extra-virgin olive oil
- 1 medium onion chopped.
- 1 tablespoon minced garlic
- 2 cups grated carrots.
- ¼ teaspoon ground nutmeg
- ¼ cup whole wheat pastry flour
- 2 cups low sodium vegetable broth
- 2 cups non-fat or 1 % milk
- ½ cup fat-free half and half
- 3 cups broccoli florets
- 2 cups shredded extra-sharp cheddar cheese.

Preparation:

In the stockpot, heat the olive oil over medium heat. Add the onion and garlic. Stir until fragrant for about 1 minute. Add the carrots and continue to stir until tender for about 2 to 3 minutes. Add the nutmeg and flour. Continue to cook, constantly stirring until browned for about 2 to 3 minutes. Add the broth and milk, whisk continuously until it starts to thicken. Add half and half and mix to combine well. Stir in the broccoli florets. Boil it and reduce the heat to a simmer. Cook for 10 minutes until broccoli is tender. Use an immersion blender to puree it to smooth consistency. Stir in cheddar cheese until melted. Reserve some cheese for topping. Refrigerate any leftovers and eat within 1 week.

Nutrition information per serving: Calories: 193 kcal, Protein: 12 g, Total Carbs: 17 g, Dietary Fibers: 4 g, Total Fat: 9 g

34. Broccoli Egg and Cheese Bake

Serves: 8

Total time: 1 hrs. 30 minutes

Ingredients:

- 6 large eggs
- 4 oz. light margarine
- ½-pound low-fat cheddar cheese
- 6 tablespoons flour
- 2 lb. non-fat cottage cheese
- 10 oz. frozen, chopped broccoli (thawed)
- 1 teaspoon salt
- 1 dash black pepper
- 1 dash paprika (optional)
- ½ cup mushrooms, sliced, canned, or fresh (optional)
- 1 (4-ounce) jar of chopped pimento (optional)

Preparation:

Preheat the oven to 350°F. Combine all ingredients. Spray 2-quart casserole dish with cooking spray. Place combined ingredients in a prepared pan and bake for 90 minutes. Serve hot.

Nutrition information per serving: Calories: 115 kcal, Protein: 12 g, Total Carbs: 5 g, Dietary Fibers: 2 g, Total Fat: 5 g

35. Cottage Cheese Bake

Serves: 8

Total time: 30 minutes

Ingredients:

- 2 cups low-fat or fat-free cottage cheese
- 2 whole eggs
- 1 10-ounce pack of frozen spinach (thawed and drained)
- ½ cup Parmigiano-Reggiano cheese

Preparation:

Preheat oven to 350°F. In a large bowl, mix all ingredients well. Place evenly into an 8x8 pan. Bake for 20 to 30 minutes or until cheese bubbles on the outside. Let sit 5 minutes before serving. Season to taste with salt, pepper, and garlic as desired.

Nutrition information per serving: Calories: 78 kcal, Protein: 11 g, Total Carbs: 3 g, Dietary Fibers: 1 g, Total Fat: 3 g

36. Creamy Pumpkin Mousse

Serves: 4

Total time: 5 minutes

Ingredients:

- 1 teaspoon cinnamon
- 1 4-ounce package of vanilla pudding: fat-free
- ½ cup skim milk
- 2 cups whipped topping: sugar-free
- Allspice, ginger, nutmeg, Splenda, and clove, to taste
- 1 15-ounce can of pumpkin

Preparation:

Mix all ingredients. Whip until creamy smooth.

Nutrition information per serving: Calories: 149 kcal, Protein: 2 g, Total Carbs: 28 g, Dietary Fibers: 3.4 g, Total Fat: 4.4 g

37. Protein-packed Pesto

Serves: 4

Total time: 10 minutes

Ingredients:

- ½ cup water
- 2 tablespoons grated parmesan cheese
- 1 10-ounce package frozen, chopped spinach (thawed and well-drained)
- 1/3 cup 1% cottage cheese
- 1/3 cup fresh basil
- 2 garlic cloves, minced
- 1 tablespoon olive oil

Preparation:

Combine all ingredients in a blender or food processor. Blend or process until smooth. Spoon ½ cup of mixture on poultry or fish.

Nutrition information per serving: Calories: 77 kcal, Protein: 6 g, Total Carbs: 4 g, Dietary Fibers: 1 g, Total Fat: 5 g

38. Cheesy Vegetarian Chili

Serves: 8

Total time: 30 minutes

Ingredients:

- 2 garlic cloves
- 2 teaspoons olive oil
- 1 large green bell pepper (diced)
- 1 cup onion chopped.
- ½ pound of sliced mushrooms
- 1 14.5-ounce can have diced tomatoes or 2 cups fresh tomatoes.
- 8 oz. tomato sauce
- 2 tablespoon chili powder
- 1 medium zucchini (thinly sliced)
- 2 15-ounce cans of red kidney beans (rinsed)
- 1 10-ounce package frozen corn
- 1 cup low-fat shredded Cheddar cheese

Preparation:

Heat olive oil and garlic in a large pan. Add onions, green pepper, and mushrooms. Cook until tender. Add in diced tomatoes, tomato sauce, chili powder, and boil it. Reduce the heat, add in zucchini and kidney beans. Cook for 10 to 15 minutes. Add corn and ½ cup of cheddar cheese. Stir. Simmer on low for additional 10-15 minutes. Serve topped with cheddar cheese.

Nutrition information per serving: Calories: 195 kcal, Protein: 13 g, Total Carbs: 34 g, Dietary Fibers: 9 g, Total Fat: 3 g

39. Cottage Cheese Fluff

Serves: 8

Total time: 5 minutes

Ingredients:

- 1 (8-ounce) whipped topping: sugar-free
- 2 (24-ounce) containers of cottage cheese: fat-free
- 2 (3-ounce) packages gelatin: sugar-free (flavor of your choice)

Preparation:

Mix all ingredients in a large bowl. Optional: add your favorite fruit.

Nutrition information per serving: Calories: 220 kcal, Protein: 22 g, Total Carbs: 24 g, Dietary Fibers: 0 g, Total Fat: 3 g

40. Pumpkin and Black Bean Soup

Serves: 6

Total time: 30 minutes

Ingredients:

- 2 tablespoons olive oil
- 1 medium onion, chopped.
- 4 garlic cloves, minced.
- 1 tablespoon ground cumin
- 1 teaspoon chili powder
- ½ teaspoon black pepper
- 2 15-ounce cans of black beans rinsed and drained.
- 1 cup canned diced tomatoes.
- 2 cups beef broth
- 1 16-ounce can pumpkin puree

Preparation:

Over medium heat, warm the oil in a soup pan, sauté garlic, onions, cumin, pepper, and chili powder until soft. Add black beans, broth, tomatoes, and pumpkin. Simmer uncovered, occasionally stirring for about 25 minutes until soup is a thick consistency. Serve as is, or puree using an immersion blender for a smooth consistency.

Nutrition information per serving: Calories: 290 kcal, Protein: 15 g, Total Carbs: 46 g, Dietary Fibers: 11 g, Total Fat: 6 g

41. Mashed Cauliflower

Serves: 3

Total time: 15 minutes

Ingredients:

- 1 large head Cauliflower
- ¼ cup water
- ½ cup low-fat buttermilk
- 1 tablespoon minced garlic
- 1 tablespoon extra-virgin olive oil

Preparation:

Break the cauliflower into small florets. Place in a large microwave-safe bowl with the water. Cover and microwave for about 5 minutes or until cauliflower are soft. Drain the water from the bowl. In a blender or food processor, puree the buttermilk, cauliflower, garlic, and olive oil on medium speed until the cauliflower is smooth and creamy. Serve immediately.

Nutrition information per serving: Calories: 62 kcal, Protein: 3 g, Total Carbs: 8 g, Dietary Fibers: 3 g, Total Fat: 2 g

42. Coconut Curry Tofu Ball

Serves: 6

Total time: 1 hour 15 minutes

Ingredients:

- 1 (14-ounce) package extra-firm- tofu
- 3 teaspoons coconut oil, divided.
- 4 teaspoons minced garlic
- 1 tablespoon grated ginger
- 1 jalapeno pepper, seeds removed, and finely diced.
- 1 yellow or orange bell pepper, chopped.
- 2 carrots, cut into ½ inch chunks.
- 1 medium bok choy, stems cut into ½ inch pieces, leaves diced.

- 2 tablespoons curry powder
- ½ teaspoon turmeric
- ½ teaspoon ground cumin
- ½ teaspoon ground cinnamon
- 2 cups unflavored, unsweetened coconut milk
- 4 oz. canned tomato sauce
- ½ cup low-sodium vegetables or chicken broth
- Cauliflower rice (optional)

Preparation:

Drain tofu and place it on a paper towel-lined plate or bowl. Cover with several layers of paper towel or a clean dish towel and set a sauté pan on top for added weight. Let the tofu sit for 30 minutes to drain some of its excess water. Place the tofu on a clean cutting board. Halve it lengthwise and then cut into 1x2-inch cubes in a large non-stick pan over medium heat, heat 1 ½ teaspoons of coconut oil. When the oil is very hot, add the tofu cubes and cook until lightly browned on all sides for 10 to 15 minutes. Transfer the tofu to a bowl and set aside. In the same pan over medium heat, add the remaining 1 ½ teaspoons of coconut oil. Once the oil is very hot, add garlic, ginger, jalapeno, bell pepper carrots, and bok choy stems. Sate for 10 minutes or until the vegetables are crisp-tender. Add the curry powder, turmeric, cumin, and cinnamon and stir to coat. Next, mix in the coconut milk, tomato sauce, and broth. Stir until smooth. Gently mix in the tofu and bok choy leaves. Stir to coat and simmer for 5 minutes to 10 minutes or until the leaves are wilted. Prepare the bowls by layering the Cauliflower Rice and curry tofu vegetable mixture. Garnish each bowl with cilantro.

Nutrition information per serving: Calories: 219 kcal, Protein: 15 g, Total Carbs: 24 g, Dietary Fibers: 11 g, Total Fat: 8 g

Chapter 11: Seafood Recipes

1. Grilled Dorados with Arugula Salad

Serves: 2

Total time: 30 minutes

Ingredients:

- 2 x 4 oz. dorado fillets
- ½ lemon, juiced
- 9 cherry tomatoes
- 2 oz. canned anchovies
- 1 teaspoon dried oregano
- 2 cups arugula leaves
- ½ tablespoons capers

Preparation:

Preheat the oven to 400°F. Place the dorado fillets on aluminum foil sheets and bake for 20 minutes or until the fish is cooked through. To make the arugula salad, combine the lemon juice, cherry tomatoes, anchovies, dried oregano, arugula leaves, capers in a bowl, and chill until ready to serve. When the fish is cooked, top with the salad and its juices.

Nutrition information per serving: Calories: 159 kcal, Protein: 27 g, Total Carbs: 5 g, Dietary Fibers: 1 g, Total Fat: 3 g

2. Asian-Style Steamed Monkfish

Serves: 2

Total time: 30 minutes

Ingredients:

- 2 x 4 oz. boneless monkfish medallions
- 1 stalk lemongrass bashed and finely chopped.
- 4 kaffir lime leaves
- 2 tablespoons chopped cilantro.
- 2 teaspoons Shaoxing rice wine
- 1 tablespoon reduced-sodium soy sauce.
- 1 small ginger root, sliced.
- 1 garlic clove, sliced.
- 1 cup chopped scallions.

Preparation:

Arrange the monkfish medallions in a bowl that will fit the steamer snugly. Combine the lemongrass, lime leaves, chopped cilantro, rice wine, soy sauce, ginger slices, garlic slices, and chopped scallions in a bowl. Pour over the monkfish to cover. Steam for 20 to 25 minutes until the fish is cooked through.

Nutrition information per serving: Calories: 148 kcal, Protein: 23 g, Total Carbs: 6 g, Dietary Fibers: 1 g, Total Fat: 2 g

3. One-Pan Cod and Cauliflower in a Spiced Tomato Sauce

Serves: 2

Total time: 30 minutes

Ingredients:

- 1 cup canned chopped tomatoes.
- ¼ teaspoons ground cumin
- 1 teaspoon ground ginger
- ½ teaspoons ground turmeric
- Freshly ground black pepper, to taste
- 6 oz. cod fillets
- 2 cups cauliflower flowerets
- 1 tablespoon chopped chives.

Preparation:

To make the tomato sauce, combine the chopped tomatoes, ground cumin, ground ginger, and ground turmeric in a nonstick pan. Season with black pepper. Bring to a simmer over medium heat until the sauce has thickened slightly, about 10 to 15 minutes. Arrange the cod fillets and cauliflower florets in the tomato sauce, cover the pan with a tight-fitting lid, and continue to simmer over low heat until the fish is cooked through and the cauliflower has softened. Spoon the sauce over the fish and vegetables. (During cooking, the fish should release its juices into the sauce, but if the sauce becomes too dry, add a little stock or water to the pan.) Serve with a sprinkling of fresh chives.

Nutrition information per serving: Calories: 123 kcal, Protein: 18 g, Total Carbs: 11 g, Dietary Fibers: 6 g, Total Fat: 2 g

4. Air fried Mackerel with Gingered Brown Rice

Serves: 2

Total time: 35 minutes

Ingredients:

- 1 tablespoon reduced-sodium soy sauce.
- ½ teaspoons lime juice
- 5 oz. mackerel fillets
- ½ cup uncooked long-grain, brown rice
- 1 teaspoon grated ginger
- 2 tablespoons chopped chives.

Preparation:

Preheat the Air fryer to 350°F. Combine the soy sauce and lime juice to make a marinade. Rub the mackerel fillets with the mixture. Allow the fish to rest for 5 minutes. Arrange the mackerels in the Air Fryer Basket, set the timer for 20 minutes, or wait until the fish is cooked through, flipping over halfway through the cooking time to allow for even cooking.

Meanwhile, cook the ginger-flavored brown rice: Wash the rice until the water runs clear. Submerge the grains in 3/4 cup water and stir in the grated ginger. Bring to a boil, cover, and reduce the heat for 20 minutes or until most of the water has been soaked up. Remove the mackerel from the air fryer and flake with a knife and fork. Serve the flaked air-fried mackerel with a portion of brown rice, and top with the chopped chives.

Nutrition information per serving: Calories: 117 kcal, Protein: 8 g, Total Carbs: 9 g, Dietary Fibers: 1 g, Total Fat: 5 g

5. Herring Salad

Serves: 2

Total time: 20 minutes

Ingredients:

- 3 ½ oz. water
- 1 lime juice
- 3 ½ oz. dry white wine
- 1 teaspoon white peppercorns
- 2 bay leaves
- 1 tablespoon white wine vinegar
- 1 teaspoon salt
- 3 oz. herring fillets
- 1 cup cubed cucumber

Preparation:

Combine the water, lime juice, white wine, peppercorns, bay leaves, white wine vinegar, and salt in a pot, and bring to a rolling boil. Reduce the heat to a simmer and poach the herrings for 12 minutes or until cooked through. Drain from the water and set aside to cool slightly. Flake with a knife and fork. Serve with freshly diced cucumbers.

Nutrition information per serving: Calories: 143 kcal, Protein: 8 g, Total Carbs: 5 g, Dietary Fibers: 1 g, Total Fat: 6 g

6. Sardine Salsa

Serves: 2

Total time: 35 minutes

Ingredients:

- 3 oz. canned sardines in tomato sauce
- 1 cucumber peeled and diced.
- 3 tablespoons chopped shallots.

Preparation:

Use a fork to flake the sardines into a salad bowl. Combine with the cucumber and shallots. Cover, and chill for at least 5 minutes for the flavors to blend before serving.

Nutrition information per serving: Calories: 109 kcal, Protein: 9 g, Total Carbs: 5 g, Dietary Fibers: 3 g, Total Fat: 6 g

7. Salmon Portobello Burgers

Serves: 2

Total time: 35 minutes

Ingredients:

- 4 oz. salmon fillets, skinless and boneless
- 1 small ginger root, sliced.
- ¼ cup cilantro leaves
- 1 cup chopped celery.
- 1 medium red capsicum, chopped.
- 4 large Portobello mushrooms
- Freshly ground black pepper
- Olive oil cooking spray
- 1 lemon, juiced
- 1 cup arugula leaves

Preparation:

To make the salmon patties, Pulse the salmon fillets, ginger, cilantro leaves, celery, and capsicums in a food processor. Scrape out the mixture from the food processor using a spatula, and then using wet hands, form 2 patties. Heat a nonstick pan over high heat. Grill the Portobello mushrooms on the pan until they shrink slightly. Remove from the pan, and season with black pepper. Heat another nonstick pan to medium heat, and lightly spray it with the cooking spray. Pan-fry the salmon patties until they are cooked through on both sides. On each Portobello mushroom, to assemble, layer a salmon patty, drizzle over some lemon juice, sprinkle with arugula leaves, and top with another Portobello mushroom.

Nutrition information per serving: Calories: 128 kcal, Protein: 16 g, Total Carbs: 10 g, Dietary Fibers: 3 g, Total Fat: 3 g

8. Tuna Sashimi with Lime-Chili Quinoa

Serves: 2

Total time: 25 minutes

Ingredients:

- ½ cup quinoa
- 1 cup low sodium chicken stock
- 2 teaspoons grated lime zest
- 1 teaspoon cayenne pepper
- 2 limes juice
- 6 oz. raw sashimi-quality tuna thinly sliced.

Preparation:

To cook the lime-chili quinoa, bring the quinoa and chicken stock to a boil over high heat. Reduce the heat to medium and stir in the lime zest. Cover with a tight-fitting lid and simmer until the quinoa is cooked. Allow to cool slightly, add the cayenne pepper and lime juice, and fluff with a fork to mix the seasoning. To assemble, Top the quinoa with the tuna slices and serve.

Nutrition information per serving: Calories: 279 kcal, Protein: 23 g, Total Carbs: 33 g, Dietary Fibers: 4 g, Total Fat: 4 g

9. Seared Salmon Fillets and Sautéed Leeks

Serves: 2

Total time: 35 minutes

Ingredients:

- 2 x 4 oz. salmon fillets, skinless and boneless
- Olive oil cooking spray
- 1.5 cups chopped leeks.
- 1 lemon juice

Preparation:

Preheat the oven to 400°F. Arrange the salmon fillets on aluminum foil sheets and bake for 20 to 30 minutes until the salmon is cooked through. Meanwhile, lightly spray a nonstick pan with olive oil cooking spray and heat over high heat. Add the chopped leeks, and sauté for 1 minute. Lower the heat to low, and allow the leeks to cook, occasionally stirring, until they are softened. The leeks can cook for the duration that the salmons are in the oven but be sure to cook on low and occasionally stir to prevent the leeks from sticking to the pan or charring. To serve, Top the salmon fillets with the leeks and drizzle generously with the lemon juice.

Nutrition information per serving: Calories: 212 kcal, Protein: 29 g, Total Carbs: 11 g, Dietary Fibers: 1 g, Total Fat: 5 g

10. Salmon and Sweet Corn Soup

Serves: 2

Total time: 25 minutes

Ingredients:

- 2 cups vegetable stock
- 1 tablespoon fresh thyme
- 6 oz. salmon fillets, skinless and boneless
- 1 cup yellow corn kernels
- Freshly ground black pepper

Preparation:

In a soup pot, bring the fish stock and fresh thyme to a boil over high heat. Reduce the heat and add the salmon fillets. Cover the pot with a lid and continue simmering until the fish is cooked (12 minutes or according to package directions). Add the corn kernels and bring them to a boil again. Serve hot, and season with freshly ground black pepper.

Nutrition information per serving: Calories: 220 kcal, Protein: 26 g, Total Carbs: 20 g, Dietary Fibers: 2 g, Total Fat: 5 g

11. Seared Teriyaki Salmon with a Black Bean and Green Mango Salad

Serves: 2

Total time: 25 minutes

Ingredients:

- ¼ cup canned black beans.
- ¼ chopped shallots.
- 1 tablespoon fresh cilantro, chopped.
- Juice from ½ lemon
- ½ green mango, sliced.
- 1 tablespoon apple cider vinegar
- 1 tablespoon reduced-sodium teriyaki sauce.
- 1 teaspoon grated ginger
- 5 oz. salmon fillet, skinless and boneless
- Olive oil cooking spray

Preparation:

To make the black bean and mango salad, combine the black beans, shallots, fresh cilantro, lemon juice, sliced green mango, apple cider vinegar in a salad bowl and chill until ready to serve. Combine the teriyaki sauce with the grated ginger and rub it into the salmon fillets. Lightly spray a nonstick pan with the cooking spray, and heat over medium heat. Sear the salmon fillets for 5 to 6 minutes on each side until they are cooked through. Serve hot with chilled black beans and green mango salad.

Nutrition information per serving: Calories: 208 kcal, Protein: 19 g, Total Carbs: 24 g, Dietary Fibers: 5 g, Total Fat: 5 g

12. Tuna and Veggie Fritters

Serves: 2

Total time: 18 minutes

Ingredients:

- 1 tablespoon flaxseed meal
- 2 ½ tablespoons water
- ¼ cup grated zucchini.
- ¼ cup grated potatoes.
- ¼ cup grated carrots.
- 1 tablespoon chopped chives.
- 4 oz. canned tuna in water
- ¼ teaspoons lemon juice
- 1 tablespoon brown rice flour

Preparation:

Combine the flaxseed meal with the water, and let it rest until it thickens. Combine the vegetables, tuna, and lemon juice, and form fritters of the desired size with your hands. Preheat the Air fryer to 350°F. Lightly dredge the fritters with the flax egg mixed earlier and dust with the brown rice flour. Arrange the fritters in the Air fryer Basket, set the timer for 8 minutes, or wait until the fritters are cooked through, flipping them over halfway during the cooking time to allow for even cooking.

Nutrition information per serving: Calories: 109 kcal, Protein: 13 g, Total Carbs: 9 g, Dietary Fibers: 3 g, Total Fat: 3 g

13. Potato and Cod Stew

Serves: 2

Total time: 30 minutes

Ingredients:

- 1 cup fish stock
- ½ cup water
- 1 bay leaf
- ½ teaspoons ground turmeric
- ½ teaspoons paprika
- 1 teaspoon dried oregano
- 1 medium potato, diced.
- 2 beef tomatoes, diced.
- 6 oz. cod fillets, boneless and skinless
- 1 tablespoon fresh parsley

Preparation:

Bring the fish stock and water to a boil in a medium pot over high heat. Add the bay leaf, ground turmeric, paprika, dried oregano, potato, and beef tomatoes to the soup, and simmer on medium-low. Add the cod fillets to the soup and continue to simmer until the fish is cooked through (about 15 minutes). If a thicker stew is preferred, continue to simmer uncovered until the stew is reduced. Top with fresh parsley to serve.

Nutrition information per serving: Calories: 186 kcal, Protein: 19 g, Total Carbs: 26 g, Dietary Fibers: 4 g, Total Fat: 1 g

14. Baked Lemon and Parsley-Crusted Sea Bass

Serves: 2

Total time: 30 minutes

Ingredients:

- ½ slice whole-wheat bread, toasted and crumbled into breadcrumbs
- 1 tablespoon fresh parsley, chopped
- ½ lemon juice
- 2 6-oz. sea bass fillets

Preparation:

Preheat the oven to 425°F. Combine the breadcrumbs, parsley, and lemon juice, and coat the top of the sea bass fillets with the breadcrumbs. Lay the sea bass fillets on aluminum foil pieces and bake for 20 minutes or until the fish is cooked through. Serve hot and slice in half if using one fillet. Accompany with your favorite vegetables or side salad.

Nutrition information per serving: Calories: 71 kcal, Protein: 15 g, Total Carbs: 1 g, Dietary Fibers: 0 g, Total Fat: 1 g

15. Thai-Style Cod

Serves: 4

Total time: 15 minutes

Ingredients:

- 2 stalks lemongrass bruised and chopped
- ¼ cup ginger root, sliced
- ½ cup snow peas
- 1 tablespoon fresh cilantro
- 2 x 6 oz. cod fillets
- 2 tablespoons fish sauce

- 1 lime, juiced

Preparation:

Preheat the oven to 425°F. Cut two pieces of parchment paper large enough to form parcels for the cod. In each parchment parcel center, arrange the lemongrass, ginger, snow peas, and fresh cilantro. Place the cod fillets on top of the vegetables. Season the cod with fish sauce and lime juice. Fold the parchment paper to enclose the cod fillets loosely. Bake for 10 minutes and allow the packets to cool for about 5 minutes before opening and serving with all the delicious juices.

Nutrition information per serving: Calories: 96 kcal, Protein: 16 g, Total Carbs: 6 g, Dietary Fibers: 1 g, Total Fat: 1 g

16. Chinese-Style Halibut with Wild Rice and Bok Choy

Serves: 3

Total time: 25 minutes

Ingredients:

- ½ cup bok choy
- 6 oz. halibut fillet
- 1 tablespoon reduced-sodium soy sauce.
- 1 teaspoon sesame oil
- 4 scallion stems, chopped.
- 1 tablespoon fresh cilantro leaves
- 1 cup cooked wild rice.

Preparation:

On a flat plate that can fit the steamer snugly, arrange the bok choy on the plate's sides, and the halibut fillets in the plate's center. Combine the soy sauce, sesame oil, scallions, and cilantro leaves and drizzle over the halibut fillets. Steam for 15 to 20 minutes or until the fish is cooked through. Flake the halibut with a knife and fork. Spoon the sauce and the flaked halibut over the wild rice to serve.

Nutrition information per serving: Calories: 212 kcal, Protein: 28 g, Total Carbs: 13 g, Dietary Fibers: 1 g, Total Fat: 5 g

17. Tilapia, Garlic, and Tomato Bake

Serves: 2

Total time: 30 minutes

Ingredients:

- Olive oil cooking spray
- 1 cup cherry tomatoes, halved
- 2 garlic cloves
- 1 tablespoon balsamic vinegar
- 2 4-oz. tilapia fillets
- 2 tablespoons fresh basil, shredded

Preparation:

Preheat the oven to 425°F. Lightly spray an ovenproof dish with olive oil cooking spray and arrange the cherry tomatoes and garlic cloves on the dish. Drizzle the balsamic vinegar over the tomatoes. Roast the tomatoes and garlic for 15 minutes. Add the fish fillets on top of the tomato juices, bake for another 10 minutes, or wait until the fish is cooked through. Top with fresh basil to serve.

Nutrition information per serving: Calories: 131 kcal, Protein: 22 g, Total Carbs: 5 g, Dietary Fibers: 1 g, Total Fat: 2 g

18. BBQ Sole Fillets with Parsley, Mint, and Tomato Salsa

Serves: 4

Total time: 30 minutes

Ingredients:

- Juice of 2 lemons
- 1 beef tomato finely diced
- 2 tablespoons chopped shallots
- 2 cups chopped parsley.
- 1 cup chopped mint.
- 4 x sole fillets barbecued or broiled.

Preparation:

To make the parsley, mint, and tomato salsa: Combine the lemon juice, diced tomatoes, chopped shallots, chopped parsley, and chopped mint in a bowl, and chill for at least 30 minutes, or until ready to serve. Flake the barbecued sole fillets and add to the salsa just before serving.

Nutrition information per serving: Calories: 133 kcal, Protein: 20 g, Total Carbs: 7 g, Dietary Fibers: 2 g, Total Fat: 3 g

19. Grilled Cod with Sweet Potato Mash and Cumin Yogurt

Serves: 2

Total time: 40 minutes

Ingredients:

- Olive oil cooking spray
- 2 6-oz. cod fillets
- 2 cups cubed sweet potatoes.
- ½ cup low-fat plain yogurt
- 1 teaspoon ground cumin

Preparation:

Preheat the oven to 350°F. Lightly spray an ovenproof dish with cooking spray and arrange the cod fillets on the dish. Bake for 20 to 30 minutes, or until the fish is cooked through. While the fish is cooking, cook the sweet potatoes in a pot of boiling water until they are softened. Drain from the water and mash the sweet potatoes. Season the yogurt with ground cumin. To serve, arrange the cod on the sweet potato mash, and top with the cumin yogurt.

Nutrition information per serving: Calories: 268 kcal, Protein: 35 g, Total Carbs: 25 g, Dietary Fibers: 3 g, Total Fat: 3 g

20. Low-Fat Fish Tacos with Kale Leaves

Serves: 2

Total time: 25 minutes

Ingredients:

- ¼ cup chopped scallions
- ¼ cup chopped cilantro

- 2 tablespoons fat-free sour cream
- 1 lime juice
- ½ clove garlic, minced
- 6 oz. Cod (or other white fish fillets), skinless and boneless, cubed
- 1 teaspoon ground cumin
- 1 teaspoon coriander seeds
- ½ teaspoons paprika
- ½ teaspoons red pepper flakes
- 2 small whole wheat tortillas
- 1 cup kale leaves, shredded

Preparation:

To make the sauce, combine the chopped scallions, cilantro, sour cream, lime juice, minced garlic in a bowl, and set aside. Season the fish fillet cubes with ground cumin, coriander seeds, paprika, and red pepper flakes. Cook the fish under a hot broiler for 4 to 5 minutes on each side or until the fish is thoroughly cooked through. Remove and place to one side. When the fish has slightly cooled, mix with the sauce until well combined. Gently toast the tortillas under the broiler for 1-2 minutes. To assemble, spoon the fish onto the tortillas and top with the shredded kale leaves.

Nutrition information per serving: Calories: 227 kcal, Protein: 21 g, Total Carbs: 27 g, Dietary Fibers: 6 g, Total Fat: 5 g

21. Wild Salmon Salad

Serves: 2

Total time: 10 minutes

Ingredients:

- 2 medium-sized cucumbers, sliced
- A handful of iceberg lettuce, torn
- ¼ cup sweet corn
- 1 large tomato roughly chopped
- 8 oz. smoked wild salmon, sliced
- 4 tablespoons freshly squeezed orange juice

Dressing:

- 1 ¼ cup liquid yogurt, 2% fat
- 1 tablespoon fresh mint finely chopped
- 2 garlic cloves, crushed
- 1 tablespoon sesame seeds

Preparation:

Combine vegetables in a large bowl. Drizzle with orange juice and top with salmon slices. Set aside. In another bowl, whisk together yogurt, mint, crushed garlic, and sesame seeds. Drizzle over salad and toss to combine. Serve cold.

Nutrition information per serving: Calories: 249 kcal, Protein: 5.6 g, Total Carbs: 32.8 g, Dietary Fibers: 3.2 g, Total Fat: 11 g

22. Baked fish with pea puree

Serves: 2 large servings

Total time: 20 minutes

Ingredients:

- 1 teaspoon olive oil
- 1 teaspoon butter
- 1 teaspoon finely grated lemon rind
- ½ fresh lemon juice
- 300 g white fish fillets
- 1 spring onion (coarsely chopped)
- 2 teaspoons chopped dill.

Pea puree:

- ½ cup hot chicken stock
- 250 g frozen baby peas
- 1 spring onion (coarsely chopped)
- 1 teaspoon butter

Preparation:

Preheat oven to 356°F. Cut 2 pieces of baking paper large enough to wrap each fish fillet. Place fish, olive oil, butter, lemon juice, lemon rind, one spring onion, and dill onto one baking paper piece. Season with salt and pepper. Repeat for the second fish fillet. Bring the sides of the baking paper up and fold twice to seal. Fold in the ends and tuck under the parcels to seal in the juices. Bake fish parcels for 10-15 minutes. To make the pea puree, bring the stock, peas, and one spring onion to a boil in a medium saucepan. Cook for 5 minutes. Drain, reserving the stock. Return the peas to the pan. Add the butter, use a stick blender to process, adding a little of the reserved stock if required. Divide the pea puree among serving plates. Top with the fish and drizzle over the juices.

Nutrition information per serving: Calories: 1228 kcal, Protein: 38 g, Total Carbs: 11 g, Dietary Fibers: 4 g, Total Fat: 12.5 g

23. Baked Halibut with tomatoes

Serves: 6

Total time: 40 minutes

Ingredients:

- 3 tablespoons extra virgin olive oil
- 1 Vidalia onion, chopped.
- 1 tablespoon minced garlic
- 1 (10 oz.) container grape tomatoes
- 3 tablespoons capers
- ¾ cup dry white vinegar, divided.
- 1 ½ pounds thick-cut halibut fillet, deboned.
- Salt
- Freshly ground black pepper

Preparation:

Preheat oven to 350°F. In a Dutch oven or large oven-safe skillet over medium-high heat, the olive oil. Add the onion and sauté until browned and softened for 3 to 5 minutes. Add the garlic and cook until fragrant for 1 to 2 minutes. Add the tomatoes and cook for 5 minutes or until they start to soften. Once the tomatoes start to soften, carefully use a potato masher to gently crush the tomatoes just enough to release their juices. Add ½ cup of the wine to the pan and stir. Cook 2 to 3 minutes until slightly thickened. Stir in the capers. Push the vegetables to the pan's sides, leaving the pan's center open for the fish. Place the fish in the pan and sprinkle it with the

oregano, salt, pepper, then scoop the tomato mixture over the fish. Pour in the remaining ¼ cup of wine. Place in the oven and bake for about 20 minutes, uncovered or until the fish flakes easily with a fork or reaches an internal temperature of 145°F. Serve.

Nutrition information per serving: Calories: 237 kcal, Protein: 24 g, Total Carbs: 6 g, Dietary Fibers: 1 g, Total Fat: 10 g

24. BBQ Roasted Salmon

Serves: 4

Total time: 20 minutes

Ingredients:

- ¼ cup pineapple juice
- 2 tablespoons fresh lemon juice
- 4 salmon fillets (6 oz. each)
- 2 tablespoons brown sugar
- 4 teaspoons chili powder
- 2 teaspoons grated lemon rind
- 3/4 teaspoon ground cumin
- ½ teaspoon salt
- ¼ teaspoon cinnamon

Preparation:

Preheat oven to 400°F. Combine the first three ingredients in a Ziploc bag. Marinate in the refrigerator for one hour, turning occasionally. Remove salmon from bag and discard marinade. Combine the remainder of the ingredients and rub over the fish. Place fillets in a baking dish coated with cooking spray. Bake for 12 to 15 minutes or until desired doneness. Serve with lemon slice garnish.

Nutrition information per serving: Calories: 225 kcal, Protein: 34 g, Total Carbs: 7 g, Dietary Fibers: 3 g, Total Fat: 6 g

25. Red Snapper Veracruz

Serves: 6

Total time: 30 minutes

Ingredients:

- 10 to 12 multicolored bell peppers, stemmed, seeded, and thinly sliced.
- 1(10-ounce) container cherry tomatoes, halved
- 1 cup fresh cilantro roughly chopped.
- 2 tablespoons capers
- 2 limes, juiced
- 2 tablespoons extra-virgin olive oil
- 1 Jalapeño pepper, stem, and seeds removed, finely diced
- 4 (4-ounce) snapper fillets

Preparation:

Preheat a grill to medium-low. Alternatively, preheat the oven to 425°F. In a small mixing bowl, combine the mini bell peppers, tomatoes, cilantro, capers, lime juices, olive oil, and jalapeno pepper to make the salsa. Set aside. Put four large aluminum foil sheets (about 8 ½ by 11 inches in size) on a work surface. Place a fish fillet on a foil sheet and top it with one-fourth of the salsa. Fold over the foil, so it covers the fish entirely and rolls the edges to tightly seal and prevent any air (and liquid) from escaping. Repeat for the remaining three fillets and salsa. Put the foil packets on the grill and close the lid. (The grill temperature should reach no hotter than 450°F). Cook for 8 to 10 minutes or until the fish is opaque. The fish is done when it flakes easily with a fork or reaches an internal temperature of 145°F. If using the oven, place the foil packets on a nonstick baking sheet and bake for 12 to 15 minutes or until the fish flakes easily with a fork.

Nutrition information per serving: Calories: 161 kcal, Protein: 15 g, Total Carbs: 7 g, Dietary Fibers: 1 g, Total Fat: 8 g

26. Fried-less Friday Fish Fry with Cod

Serves: 4

Total time: 30 minutes

Ingredients:

- ¾ cup cornmeal
- ¾ cup whole-wheat breadcrumbs
- 1 ½ teaspoon lemon pepper seasoning
- ½ teaspoon onion powder
- ½ teaspoon garlic powder
- ¾ teaspoon ground cayenne pepper
- 2 eggs
- 4 (4-ounce) cod fillets
- 1 ½ tablespoon extra-virgin olive oil

Preparation:

Preheat oven to 450°F. Combine cornmeal, breadcrumbs, lemon pepper seasoning, onion powder, garlic powder, and cayenne pepper in a large sealing bag. Shake to mix and set aside. In a small bowl, lightly beat the eggs. Carefully add fish fillets to the bag to coat it with the dry mixture. Next, dip it into the eggs, then coat it a second time in the dry mixture. Set aside on a plate and repeat with the remaining fillets. Place a large oven-safe skillet over medium heat. Add the oil and allow it to heat for 1 minute. Carefully add the fish to the skillet. Brown it on one side for 2 minutes and then gently turn to brown the other side for another 2 minutes. Transfer the skillet to the oven. Bake for 6 to 7 minutes, or until golden brown and flaky.

Nutrition information per serving: Calories: 297 kcal, Protein: 27 g, Total Carbs: 28 g, Dietary Fibers: 3 g, Total Fat: 9 g

27. Tuna Noodle Less Casserole.

Serves: 10

Total time: 55 minutes

Ingredients:

- Nonstick cooking spray
- 1 medium red onion chopped
- 1 red bell pepper, chopped
- 1 ½ cups diced tomato
- 3 cups fresh green beans

- 1/3 cup olive oil-based mayonnaise
- 1 (14.5 oz.) can condense cream mushroom soup
- ½ cup low-fat milk
- 1 cup shredded cheddar cheese
- ½ teaspoon freshly ground black pepper 8 (5-ounce) cans water-packed albacore tuna, drained

Preparation:

Preheat the oven to 425°F. Coat a large skillet with the cooking spray and place it over medium heat. Add the onion, red bell pepper, tomatoes, and sauté for about 5 minutes or until the vegetables are tender and tomatoes start to soften. Remove the skillet from the heat and set it aside. Cut off the stem ends of the green beans and snap them into 3 to 4-inch pieces. Fill a large saucepot 1/3 full of water and place a steamer basket inside. Place the pot over high heat and bring the water to a boil. Add the green beans to the steamer basket, cover the pot and reduce the heat to medium. Steam the green beans for 5 minutes. Immediately remove them from the heat, drain them, and set them aside. Coat a 9x13-inch baking dish with the cooking spray. In a large bowl, mix the mayonnaise, condensed soup, milk, and cheese. Season the mixture with black pepper. Add tuna, green beans, and sauteed vegetables to the bowl and mix to combine. Pour the mixture into the baking dish. Bake for 30 minutes or until the edges start to brown. Serve.

Nutrition information per serving: Calories: 147 kcal, Protein: 15 g, Total Carbs: 6 g, Dietary Fibers: 2 g, Total Fat: 7 g

28. Lemon Parsley Crab Cakes

Serves: 4

Total time: 55 minutes

Ingredients:

- 3 tablespoons whole-wheat breadcrumbs
- 1 egg lightly beaten
- ½ teaspoon Dijon mustard
- 1 ½ tablespoon olive oil-based mayonnaise
- ¼ teaspoon ground cayenne pepper
- 2 teaspoons chopped fresh parsley
- ½ lemon juice
- 2 (6-ounce) cans lump crabmeat, drained, and cartilage removed
- Nonstick cooking spray

Preparation:

In a medium bowl, mix the breadcrumbs, eggs, mustard, mayonnaise, cayenne pepper, parsley, and lemon juice. Very gently fold in the lump crabmeat. Using a ¼ cup measuring cup, shape the mixture into 4 individual patties. Put the patties in the refrigerator and let them sit for 30 minutes. Preheat the oven to 500°F while the crab cakes rest in the refrigerator. Coat a baking sheet with the cooking spray. Place the crab Cakes on the baking sheet and bake on the oven's center rack for 10 minutes or until brown. Serve immediately.

Nutrition information per serving: Calories: 148 kcal, Protein: 21 g, Total Carbs: 5 g, Dietary Fibers: 0 g, Total Fat: 4 g

29. Shrimp Cocktail Salad

Serves: 4

Total time: 15 minutes

Ingredients:

- 1 lemon halved and seeded.
- 1 tablespoon black peppercorns
- 1 teaspoon dried thyme
- 1 bay leaf
- 1-pound unpeeled shrimp
- ½ cup seafood sauce
- 3 tablespoons low-fat plain Greek yogurt
- ½ cup olive oil-based Mayonnaise
- 1 large head romaine lettuce, chopped.
- ½ seedless cucumber, chopped.

Preparation:

Fill a large pot with water. Squeeze the juice from the lemon halves into the water, and add the black peppercorns, thyme, and bay leaf. Place the pot over high heat and bring to boil. While the water is heating, create an ice bath by filling a large bowl with ice and water. Set aside. Add the shrimp to the boiling water and cook them for 2 to 3 minutes or until they just turn pink. Drain the shrimp in a colander and immediately put them in the ice bath to cool. Once cool, peel the shrimp and remove the tails. In a large bowl, combine the seafood sauce, yogurt, and mayonnaise. Mix well. Add the cooked shrimp to the dressing and stir to coat. Divide the lettuce among four plates. Add the cucumber and top it with the dressed shrimp. Serve immediately.

Nutrition information per serving: Calories: 163 kcal, Protein: 17 g, Total Carbs: 4 g, Dietary Fibers: 1 g, Total Fat: 6 g

30. Seafood Cioppino

Serves: 8

Total time: 60 minutes

Ingredients:

- 2 teaspoon minced garlic
- 1 tablespoon extra-virgin olive oil
- 2 leeks, washed and cut into ¼ inch slices, both white and green parts
- 2 celery stalks cut into ¼ inch pieces.
- 1 green bell pepper diced.
- 4 cups water
- 1 ½ cups dry white wine
- 1 (10-ounce) container grape tomatoes
- 1 large tomato, chopped into ¼ inch pieces.
- ½ teaspoon dried thyme
- ½ teaspoon dried basil
- 1 bay leaf
- 1 tablespoon chopped fresh parsley.
- ½ lemon juice
- 2 lb. shrimp, deveined.
- 1 (6-ounce) can lump crabmeat, drained, and cartilage removed
- ½ pound scallops
- 1 teaspoon freshly ground black pepper.

Preparation:

Place a large pot or Dutch oven over medium heat. Sauté the garlic in olive oil for 1 to 2 minutes. Add the leeks and stir for about 2 minutes or until tender. Add the celery and green pepper and cook for about 5 minutes or until tender. Pour in water, wine tomatoes, thyme, basil, bay leaf, parsley, and lemon juice. Bring to a boil, then cover, reduce the heat to low, and let simmer for 25 minutes. Remove and discard the bay leaf. Add the shrimp, crabmeat, and scallops. Bring back to a simmer and cook for 5 to 10 minutes, or until the shrimp are no longer pink and the scallops are opaque. Stir in the black pepper. Ladle into soup bowls and serve.

Nutrition information per serving: Calories: 171 kcal, Protein: 21 g, Total Carbs: 5 g, Dietary Fibers: 0 g, Total Fat: 4 g

31. Slow Roasted Pesto Salmon

Serves: 4

Total time: 25 minutes

Ingredients:

- 4 (6-oz.) salmon fillets
- 1 teaspoon extra virgin oil
- 4 tablespoon basil pesto

Preparation:

Preheat the oven to 275°F. Line a rimmed baking sheet with aluminum foil and brush the foil with olive oil. Place the salmon fillets skin-side down on the baking sheet. Spread 1 tablespoon of pesto on each fillet. Roast the salmon for about 20 minutes or just until opaque in the center. Serve immediately.

Nutrition information per serving: Calories: 182 kcal, Protein: 20 g, Total Carbs: 1 g, Dietary Fibers: 0 g, Total Fat: 10 g

32. Herb Crusted Salmon

Serves: 4

Total time: 25 minutes

Ingredients:

- 2 (4-ounce) salmon fillets
- 2 teaspoons minced garlic
- 1 tablespoon dried parsley
- ½ teaspoon dried thyme
- 2 teaspoons freshly squeezed lemon
- 4 tablespoons grated Parmigiano-Reggiano cheese

Preparation:

Preheat the oven to 425°F. Line a rimmed baking sheet with parchment paper. Place the salmon skin-side down on the baking sheet and cover with a second piece of parchment paper. Bake for 10 minutes. Meanwhile, mix the garlic, parsley, thyme, lemon juice, and Parmigiano-Reggiano cheese in a small dish. Discard the parchment paper covering the salmon. Use a pastry brush to carefully cover the fillets with the herb-cheese mixture. Bake the salmon uncovered for about 5 minutes more. The salmon is done when the fish flakes easily with a fork. Serve immediately.

Nutrition information per serving: Calories: 197 kcal, Protein: 27 g, Total Carbs: 9 g, Dietary Fibers: 1 g, Total Fat: 10 g

33. Baked Cod with fennel and Kalamata Olives

Serves: 4

Total time: 45 minutes

Ingredients:

- 2 teaspoons extra-virgin olive oil
- 1 fennel bulb sliced paper-thin
- ¼ cup dry white wine
- 1/8 cup freshly squeezed orange juice
- 1 teaspoon freshly ground black pepper
- 4 (4-ounce) cod fillets
- 4 slices fresh orange
- ¼ cup Kalamata olives pitted.
- 2 bay leaves

Preparation:

Preheat the oven to 400°F. Place a large Dutch oven or oven-safe skillet over medium heat and add the olive oil. Add the fennel and cook, stirring occasionally until softened 8 to 10 minutes. Add the wine. Bring it to simmer and cook for 1 to 2 minutes. Stir in the orange juice and pepper and simmer for 2 minutes more. Remove the skillet from the heat and arrange the cod on the top of the fennel mixture. Place the orange slices over the fillets. Position the olives and bay leave around the fish. Roast for 20 minutes or until the fish is opaque. The fish is done when it flakes easily. Serve warm.

Nutrition information per serving: Calories: 186 kcal, Protein: 21 g, Total Carbs: 8 g, Dietary Fibers: 3 g, Total Fat: 5 g

Chapter 12: Dessert Recipes

1. Almond Butter Banana Cream

Serves: 6

Total time: 15 minutes

Ingredients:

- 2 teaspoons vanilla extract
- 4 frozen bananas (chunks)
- ½ cup non-dairy milk: unsweetened
- ½ cup almond butter

Preparation:

Add the frozen bananas and non-dairy milk to a food processor. Process them at low. Turn off the food processor and scrape sides as needed, and mix up the bananas several times with a spoon throughout this step. Process until bananas are creamy. This works best if you take the bananas out of the freezer 10-15 minutes before making the ice cream. If you don't have time, that's OK too, you'll just need to scrape the sides more often. Add the almond butter and vanilla extract to the food processor and process on low until mixed in. Add the mix-ins and pulse until evenly distributed. Enjoy as a soft-serve or transfer to a dish and place in the freezer for 5-6 hours or overnight for a scoop-friendly nice cream. The cream will become very hard, so you'll want to let it sit at least 30 minutes out of the freezer before scooping it into a dish or a cone. Top the cream as you desire.

Nutrition information per serving: Calories: 205 kcal, Protein: 6 g, Total Carbs: 22 g, Dietary Fibers: 4 g, Total Fat: 12 g

2. Apple Cake

Serves: 2

Total time: 25 minutes

Ingredients:

- 2 tablespoons wholemeal plain flour
- ¼ tablespoons granulated sweetener
- ½ teaspoons ground cinnamon
- 1 ½ teaspoons baking powder
- 1 egg
- 1 tablespoon Vanilla skim milk/skim milk + 1 teaspoon vanilla extract
- ½ tablespoons low-fat butter, melted.
- ½ tablespoons applesauce

- 1 cup cooking apples, peeled, cored, and cut into thin slices.

Preparation:

Preheat the oven to 400°F, and lightly spray a mini-loaf tin with low-fat cooking spray.

To make the batter:

Mix the wholemeal flour with sugar, ground cinnamon, and baking powder. Make a well in the center and add the egg, vanilla skim milk and vanilla extract. Stir in.

Stir in the melted low-fat butter and applesauce. Fold in the apple slices. Pour the batter into the tin and bake for 20 to 25 minutes, or until the cake has risen and is firm and golden. When the cake is done, allow it to cool slightly in the pan.

Nutrition information per serving: Calories: 139 kcal, Protein: 5 g, Total Carbs: 16 g, Dietary Fibers: 3 g, Total Fat: 5 g

3. Pecan Cookies

Serves: 10

Total time: 25 minutes

Ingredients:

- ½ cup pecan butter
- 1 ½ cup Kamut flour
- 6 tablespoons no-calorie sweetener (e.g., Splenda Brown Sugar Blend)
- ¼ cup low-fat almond milk
- 1 teaspoon vanilla extract
- ½ teaspoons salt

Preparation:

Preheat the oven to 350°F, and line a cookie sheet with parchment paper. Combine the pecan butter, kamut flour, sweetener, almond milk, vanilla extract, and salt in a mixing bowl. Divide the dough into 10 cookies. Bake the cookies for 20 minutes. Transfer to a cookie rack to cool completely before serving.

Nutrition information per serving: Calories: 90 kcal, Protein: 3 g, Total Carbs: 15 g, Dietary Fibers: 2 g, Total Fat: 2 g

4. Vegan Strawberry Crumbles

Serves: 2

Total time: 25 minutes

Ingredients:

For the filling:

- 16 oz. fresh strawberries
- ¼ teaspoons lemon juice
- 1/3 cup no-calorie sweetener
- 1 tablespoon cornstarch

For the crumble topping:

- ½ cup quick oats
- ¼ teaspoons pumpkin pie spice
- 1 tablespoon low-fat margarine
- 1/8 teaspoons salt

Preparation:

Preheat the oven to 350°F.

To make the filling:

Mix the strawberries with the lemon juice in a bowl, and add the sweetener and cornstarch. Mix well to combine.

To make the crumble topping:

Pulse together the quick oats, pumpkin pie spice, margarine, and salt until it resembles a coarse meal texture.

To assemble:

Divide the filling between the ramekins and the top with the crumble topping. Bake for 35 minutes. Turn off the oven and allow the ramekins to cool in the oven.

Nutrition information per serving: Calories: 167 kcal, Protein: 4 g, Total Carbs: 35 g, Dietary Fibers: 5 g, Total Fat: 3 g

5. Pumpkin Cheesecake

Serves: 6

Total time: 1 hr.

Ingredients:

- 8 oz. low-fat soft cheese
- 1 scoop vanilla protein powder
- 1 teaspoon vanilla extract
- ½ teaspoons baking soda
- 1 ½ teaspoons pumpkin pie spice
- ¼ cup no-calorie sweetener, as desired
- ½ cup non -fat vanilla Greek yogurt
- 15 oz. canned unsalted pumpkin purée

Preparation:

Preheat your oven to 350°F. Beat the cream cheese until it becomes smooth and stir in the protein powder, vanilla extract, baking soda, pumpkin pie spice, and sweetener. Add the yogurt and pumpkin purée, and mix well to combine. Pour the batter into a glass pie plate, and bake for an hour.

Nutrition information per serving: Calories: 134 kcal, Protein: 9 g, Total Carbs: 13 g, Dietary Fibers: 2 g, Total Fat: 5 g

6. Easy Crêpes

Serves: 2

Total time: 15 minutes

Ingredients:

- ¼ cup skim milk
- 1/3 cup water
- 2 tablespoons Margarine melted.
- 1 tablespoon vanilla extract
- ½ cup all-purpose flour
- A drop of liquid sweetener/Stevia
- Coconut oil spray

Preparation:

Whisk all the ingredients together, and chill for 2 hours (if you can) before cooking. Lightly spray a nonstick frying pan with cooking spray and place over medium heat. Add 1-2 tablespoons of batter at a time, and swirl to make a crépe. Flip when the edges begin to get crispy. Enjoy it.

Nutrition information per serving: Calories: 167 kcal, Protein: 5 g, Total Carbs: 24 g, Dietary Fibers: 1 g, Total Fat: 5 g

7. Healthy Chocolate Mousse

Serves: 4

Total time: 10 minutes

Ingredients:

- 2 cups unsweetened coconut cream
- 4 tablespoons unsweetened cocoa powder
- 2 teaspoons vanilla essence
- Stevia, as desired

Preparation:

Combine all the ingredients in a food processor fitted with a metal blade. Cover and process until smooth and creamy. Divide the mousse into dessert cups and chill until ready to serve.

Nutrition information per serving: Calories: 35 kcal, Protein: 1 g, Total Carbs: 3.5 g, Dietary Fibers: 2.5 g, Total Fat: 3 g

8. Blueberry Yogurt Cups

Serves: 2

Total time: 5 minutes

Ingredients:

- 1 cup low-fat yogurt
- 1 teaspoon vanilla extract
- ¼ cup fresh blueberries
- 1 teaspoon chia seeds

Preparation:

Stir the vanilla extract into the yogurt. Divide the yogurt into 2 chilled cups. Top with the fresh blueberries and chia seeds to serve

Nutrition information per serving: Calories: 92 kcal, Protein: 12 g, Total Carbs: 8 g, Dietary Fibers: 1 g, Total Fat: 1 gSuperfood dark chocolate

Serves: 18 bars

Total time: 30 minutes

Ingredients:

- 6 oz. dark chocolate chips (60% cacao or higher)
- ¼ cup pumpkin seeds (pepitas) chopped
- ¼ cup unsweetened shredded coconut
- ¼ cup chopped pecans.
- ¼ cup unsweetened dried wild blueberries
- 1 teaspoon sea salt

Preparation:

Line 1 or 2 baking sheets with parchment paper. Fill a large pot with water and bring it to a boil. Reduce the heat to a simmer and place a stainless steel heat-proof bowl over the top of boiling water. Add the chocolate chips and stir until melted and smooth. Use a spoon to drizzle the melted chocolate on the sheet pan in small circles. Add the pumpkin seeds, coconut, pecans, and dried blueberries to each chocolate circle. Each should hold about ¾ tablespoons of toppings total. Sprinkle with the sea salt. Let the chocolate harden at room temperature or in a refrigerator. Keep them in an airtight container and eat within 2 weeks to maintain maximum freshness.

Nutrition information per serving: Calories: 102 kcal, Protein: 3 g, Total Carbs: 8 g, Dietary Fibers: 2 g, Total Fat: 7 g

9. Chocolate Chia Pudding

Serves: 4

Total time: 1 hr. 15 minutes

Ingredients:

- 2 cups unsweetened soy milk
- 10 drops liquid stevia
- ¼ cup unsweetened cocoa powder
- ¼ teaspoon ground cinnamon
- ¼ teaspoon vanilla extract
- ½ cup chia seeds
- ½ cup fresh raspberries, for garnish

Preparation:

In a small bowl, whisk together the soy milk, stevia, cocoa powder, cinnamon, and vanilla until well combined. Stir in the chia seeds. Divide between 4 small serving dishes. Cover and refrigerate for at least 1 hour or overnight. When ready to serve, garnish with raspberries.

Nutrition information per serving: Calories: 182 kcal, Protein: 11 g, Total Carbs: 14 g, Dietary Fibers: 14 g, Total Fat: 9 g

10. Peanut Butter cookies

Serves: 15 cookies

Total time: 30 minutes

Ingredients:

- Nonstick cooking spray
- 1 cup natural smooth peanut butter
- 1 large egg
- ½ cup stevia baking blend
- ½ teaspoon vanilla extract

Preparation:

Preheat the oven to 350°F. Coat a nonstick baking sheet with the cooking spray or parchment paper. In a medium bowl, use a hand mixer to combine the peanut butter, egg, stevia, and vanilla. Roll the batter into 1-inch spheres and assemble them on a baking sheet. Flatten them to about ¼ inch thickness. Use a fork to create imprints of a crisscross pattern on the cookie. Bake for about 12 minutes. The cookies are done until golden brown. Cool for 5 minutes, then move to a baking rack to finish cooling.

Nutrition information per serving: Calories: 107 kcal, Protein: 4 g, Total Carbs: 4 g, Dietary Fibers: 1 g, Total Fat: 9 g

11. Chocolate Brownies with Almond Butter

Serves: 16 brownies

Total time: 30 minutes

Ingredients:

- Nonstick cooking spray
- ½ cup cocoa powder
- 1 tablespoon ground flaxseed
- ½ teaspoon ground instant coffee
- ¼ teaspoon baking soda
- ½ cup agave nectar
- ½ cup almond butter
- 2 large eggs
- ¼ cup melted coconut oil
- 1 teaspoon vanilla extract

Preparation:

Preheat the oven to 325ºF. Coat an 8x8-inch glass baking dish with the cooking spray. Place the cocoa powder, flaxseed, instant coffee, baking soda, almond butter, coconut oil, eggs, vanilla extract, and agave nectar in a high-speed blender or food processor. Blend on medium-high until smooth. Pour the batter into the baking dish. Bake for 25 minutes or until a toothpick inserted in the middle comes out clean. Let cool for 10 minutes before cutting into 16 squares.

Nutrition information per serving: Calories: 124 kcal, Protein: 3 g, Total Carbs: 11 g, Dietary Fibers: 2 g, Total Fat: 9 g

12. Lemon Blackberry Frozen Yogurt

Serves: 4 cups

Total time: 10 minutes

Ingredients:

- 4 cups frozen blackberries
- ½ cup low-fat Greek yogurt
- 1 lemon juice
- 2 teaspoons liquid stevia
- Fresh mint leaves, for garnish

Preparation:

In a blender or a food processor, add the blackberries, yogurt, lemon juice, and stevia. Blend until smooth for about 5 minutes. Serve immediately or freeze in an airtight container and use within 3 weeks. Garnish with fresh mint leaves.

Nutrition information per serving: Calories: 68 kcal, Protein: 3 g, Total Carbs: 15 g, Dietary Fibers: 5 g, Total Fat: 0 g

13. Low-Calorie Cherry Chocolate Ice Cream

Serves: 3

Total time: 10 minutes

Ingredients:

- 2 cups cherries, fresh
- ½ banana
- ½ cup unsweetened almond milk
- 3 tablespoons dairy-free chocolate chips

Preparation:

Wash and dry the cherries, and remove all the pits. Place in a freezer bag or glass container, and freeze for at least three hours. If you don't have the time, you can use frozen cherries. Peel a banana, and place half in the freezer. Pour ¼ cup of the almond milk into ice cube trays (save the other ¼ cup), and freeze those as well, for at least three hours. Place the frozen cherries, half a frozen banana, ice cubes, and ¼ cup almond milk in a food processor, and process until completely smooth, several minutes. Stir in chocolate chips, and enjoy immediately!

Nutrition information per serving: Calories: 126 kcal, Protein: 2.1 g, Total Carbs: 22.3 g, Dietary Fibers: 2.8 g, Total Fat: 4 g

14. Skinny Mug Brownie

Serves: 3

Total time: 5 minutes

Ingredients:

- 1 tablespoon cocoa powder, unsweetened
- 2 packets Truvia (may substitute for other sweeteners)
- 2 tablespoons all-purpose flour (may substitute for Almond Flour)
- 3 tablespoons almond milk (may substitute for regular milk or yogurt)

Preparation:

Place all ingredients in a microwave-safe mug. Mix with a fork or small whisk. Microwave on high for 60 seconds. Enjoy.

Nutrition information per serving: Calories: 97 kcal, Protein: 1.2 g, Total Carbs: 9.2 g, Dietary Fibers: 2.2 g, Total Fat: 2.2 g

15. Carrot Cake

Serves: 2

Total time: 20 minutes

Ingredients:

- ¼ cup flour
- Just over ½ teaspoons cinnamon
- ¼ teaspoons baking powder
- 1/8 teaspoons baking soda
- 1/3 cup canned carrots, drained
- 1/8 teaspoons salt
- 1 ½ tablespoons brown sugar
- Pinch of uncut stevia /1 tablespoon sugar
- 1 tablespoon milk of choice
- optional ½ teaspoons ginger or 2 teaspoons flax meal
- 1 tablespoon oil or more milk of choice
- ¼ teaspoons pure vanilla extract

Preparation:

In a small bowl, mix dry ingredients (not carrots). If you have a blender or Magic Bullet, mix all wet ingredients and blend. Mix dry mixture into the wet mixture, and stir. Pour this mixture into a greased little dish. In the case of the microwave, cook for 1 minute and 20 seconds, or cook in the oven at 350°F for around 15 minutes. Let cool before trying to pop out.

Nutrition information per serving: Calories: 70 kcal, Protein: 2.5 g, Total Carbs: 17 g, Dietary Fibers: 3 g, Total Fat: 0.5 g

16. Mini Plum Cakes

Serves: 12

Total time: 20 minutes

Ingredients:

- 3/4 cup all-purpose flour
- ¼ flaxseed meal
- 1 ½ teaspoons baking powder
- ¼ teaspoon kosher salt
- 3 tablespoons unsalted butter, at room temperature
- 2 tablespoons avocado
- 1/3 cup sugar
- 1 large egg
- 2/3 cup low-fat milk
- 1 teaspoon finely grated lemon zest
- 1 teaspoon vanilla extract
- 1 plum (or any stone fruit), pitted and cut into thin slices
- 2 tablespoons raw sugar (optional)

Preparation:

Preheat the oven to 350° F. Use nonstick spray to coat the muffin pan. Whisk baking powder, flaxseed meal, flour, and salt in a bowl. Put aside. Use an electric processor to beat avocado, butter, and sugar in another bowl until light and fluffy, about 2 minutes. Add egg, lemon zest, and vanilla and beat until combined. With the mixer on low speed, add dry ingredients in 3 additions alternating with milk in 2 additions, beginning and ending with dry ingredients. Pour batter evenly among muffin cups. Sprinkle plum slices and raw sugar on top. Bake for 20-25 minutes until golden. Transfer pan to a wire rack; let pan cool for 5 minutes. Transfer cakes to rack and let cool completely.

Nutrition information per serving: Calories: 113 kcal, Protein: 3 g, Total Carbs: 14 g, Dietary Fibers: 1 g, Total Fat: 5 g

17. Lemonade Cupcakes

Serves: 24

Total time: 30 minutes

Ingredients:

- 1 15.25 oz. box white cake mix.
- 1 cup water
- 1/3 cup unsweetened applesauce
- 1 tablespoon lemon zest
- 1 ½ tablespoon sugar-free lemonade mix
- 1 8 oz. tub light whipped topping

Preparation:

Preheat oven to 350ºF. Line muffin cups with liners (paper). In a medium mixing bowl, combine water, cake mix, lemon zest, applesauce, and 1 tablespoon of the sugar-free lemonade mix. Spoon batter evenly into cupcake cups. Bake until a toothpick inserted into the center comes out clean, about 17 minutes. Transfer cupcakes immediately to a rack to cool. While cupcakes are cooling, make the frosting by combining the whipped topping and remaining ½ tablespoons sugar-free lemonade mix. Once cupcakes are completely cool, top with frosting and serve.

Nutrition information per serving: Calories: 100 kcal, Protein: 0.8 g, Total Carbs: 16.7 g, Dietary Fibers: 0.2 g, Total Fat: 3 g

18. Strawberry Watermelon Protein Pops

Serves: 12

Total time: 15 minutes

Ingredients:

- 2 cups seeds removed and cubed watermelon.
- 2 cups quartered fresh or frozen strawberries,
- ¼ cup strawberry-flavored protein powder: whey isolate
  - Optional: ¼ cup Splenda or 2 tablespoons Truvia

Preparation:

Place all ingredients in a container of an electric blender. Cover and mix it until smooth. Put it into popsicle molds and freeze it until popsicles are solid frozen for about six hours. To extract popsicles, take out each popsicle from the mold with the handle attached. If stubborn, run under a little warm water.

Nutrition information per serving: Calories: 28 kcal, Protein: 2.5 g, Total Carbs: 4 g, Dietary Fibers: 1 g, Total Fat: 0 g

19. Cheesecake-Stuffed Strawberries

Serves: 6

Total time: 20 minutes

Ingredients:

- 12 fresh strawberries
- ⅛ teaspoon vanilla extract
- 4 tablespoons fat-free cream cheese, softened
- 3 teaspoons Stevia (or any zero-calorie sweetener)
- 1 low-fat graham cracker crushed into crumbs

Preparation:

Cut the strawberries' tops, and with a sharp knife, cut an X, do not cut through the strawberry. Gently remove a little strawberry from the center. In a small bowl, mix cream cheese, Stevia, and vanilla. Place mixture into a pastry bag or a plastic bag with the tip cut off and pipe in the filling. Roll the top of strawberries in graham cracker crumbs.

Nutrition information per serving: Calories: 34 kcal, Protein: 1 g, Total Carbs: 8 g, Dietary Fibers: 0 g, Total Fat: 0 g

20. Vegan Honeydew Melon Fries with Lemon Poppyseed Cherry Dip

Serves: 4

Total time: 10 minutes

Ingredients:

- ½ large honeydew melon, cut into French-fry shapes

Dip:

- ¾ cup plain non-dairy yogurt
- 1 tablespoon lemon zest
- ¼ cup lemon juice
- 1 teaspoon poppy seeds
- 1-2 teaspoons maple syrup
- ½ cup frozen cherries thawed

Garnish:

- ½ teaspoon poppy seeds
- 2 tablespoons cherries frozen and dried pulverized in a blender.
- 1 teaspoon lemon zest

Preparation:

Mix the yogurt, poppy seeds, lemon zest, lemon juice, and maple syrup for the dip. Blend the cherries and pour them on the dip. To serve, garnish the fries with cherry dust, lemon zest, and poppy seeds and serve it with dip.

Nutrition information per serving: Calories: 138 kcal, Protein: 2 g, Total Carbs: 31 g, Dietary Fibers: 3 g, Total Fat: 1 g

21. Blueberry and Ricotta Baked Custard

Serves: 5

Total time: 30 minutes

Ingredients:

- 1.5 teaspoons Splenda (4 packets)
- 15 oz container of skim ricotta cheese
- 2.5 teaspoons vanilla extract
- 3/4 cup wild (mini) blueberries
- 4 large eggs

Preparation:

Preheat oven to 400°F. Line 10 muffin wells with foil muffin cup liners. In a medium bowl, whisk all ingredients, skip berries until smooth. Then add the berries into "batter" and pour batter into muffin pan covering 3/4 full. For 25 minutes, bake it or until an inserted toothpick comes out clean. Let cool in pan or cooling rack.

Nutrition information per serving: Calories: 157 kcal, Protein: 4.4 g, Total Carbs: 22.5 g, Dietary Fibers: 0.6 g, Total Fat: 5.6 g

22. Frozen Strawberry Yogurt Pops

Serves: 5

Total time: 10 minutes (3 hours freezing)

Ingredients:

- ½ cup almonds, chopped into small pieces
- ½ cup roughly crushed plain bran flakes or Fiber One Original cereal
- 2 tablespoons coconut oil, melted
- 1 ½ cups fat-free vanilla or lemon-flavored Greek yogurt
- 1 ½ cups chopped strawberries

Preparation:

In a small bowl, combine almonds, cereal, and coconut oil until well incorporated. Evenly distribute almond mixture into the bottom of each popsicle well and spoon yogurt over almond mixture. Top each cup with chopped strawberries, then place in the freezer for at least 3 hours or until completely frozen (option to freeze overnight).

Nutrition information per serving: Calories: 72 kcal, Protein: 5.8 g, Total Carbs: 12.5 g, Dietary Fibers: 0.7 g, Total Fat: 0.1 g

23. Pumpkin Ricotta Custard

Serves: 1

Total time: 5 minutes

Ingredients:

- ¼ cup part-skim ricotta cheese
- 2 tablespoons canned pumpkin puree (not pumpkin pie filling)
- ¼ teaspoons pumpkin pie spice
- 1/8 teaspoons vanilla extract

Preparation:

Mix all ingredients in a bowl. Perfect for the fall.

Nutrition information per serving: Calories: 74.1 kcal, Protein: 6.6 g, Total Carbs: 8.0 g, Dietary Fibers: 1.7 g, Total Fat: 2.2 g

24. Watermelon Pizza

Serves: 4

Total time: 10 minutes

Ingredients:

- 2 large round slices of watermelon about 1 inch thick
- 3/4 cup low-fat or fat-free plain Greek yogurt
- 1 teaspoon honey
- 1 teaspoon vanilla extra
- 1 cup fresh strawberries, sliced
- 1 cup fresh blackberries, sliced in half (You may use fresh blueberries if blackberries are unavailable. You can also use bananas or raspberries with, or instead, of strawberries)
- A handful of fresh mint leaves, rough chopped, optional

Preparation:

Combine yogurt, honey, and vanilla in a bowl, mix well. Divide yogurt in half, and spread equal amounts on each watermelon round. Decorate each watermelon round with berries and sprinkle with mint leaves, if using. Cut each watermelon round into 8 slices and serve.

Nutrition information per serving: Calories: 150 kcal, Protein: 10 g, Total Carbs: 21 g, Dietary Fibers: 2 g, Total Fat: 4 g

25. Easy Sugar-free Cheesecake

Serves: 8

Total time: 20 minutes (1 hr. refrigeration)

Ingredients:

- 1 prepared graham cracker crumb crust,
- 1 – 4 serving pkg. sugar-free lemon gelatin
- 1 cup boiling water,
- 2 – 8 oz. pkg. fat-free cream cheese
- 2 teaspoons vanilla extract,
- 1 cup Fat-Free Cool Whip
- Lemon slices, optional

Preparation:

Dissolve lemon gelatin in boiling water. Let cool until thickened but not set. In a large bowl, beat cream cheese and vanilla until smooth. Blend in lemon gelatin. Fold in Cool Whip Free. Pour filling into crust. Refrigerate overnight. Garnish with lemon slices if desired.

Nutrition information per serving: Calories: 312 kcal, Protein: 6.4 g, Total Carbs: 25.2 g, Dietary Fibers: 2.8 g, Total Fat: 21.4 g

26. Pumpkin Fluff

Serves: 4

Total time: 10 minutes

Ingredients:

- 1 can of pumpkin (15 oz.),
- 1 teaspoon pumpkin pie spice,
- 1 cup skim milk
- 1 cup fat-free Cool Whip,

- 1 small package sugar-free vanilla pudding mix

Preparation:

In a small bowl, mix milk, pumpkin, and spice until well blended. Add pudding mix and beat for 2 minutes. Add cold whip and refrigerate. Serve cold.

Nutrition information per serving: Calories: 79 kcal, Protein: 1 g, Total Carbs: 15 g, Dietary Fibers: 1 g, Total Fat: 2 g

27. Strawberry Lemon High Protein Jell-O

Serves: 4

Total time: 10 minutes

Ingredients:

- 2 Scoops or 2 Packets Strawberry Sorbet
- 1 Package Jell-O Sugar-Free Lemon Gelatin
- 2 Cups Water

Preparation:

Follow package directions for dissolving Jell-O in 1 cup of boiling water. After dissolving, set aside to cool for 3 to 5 minutes. In a different bowl, measure 1 cup of cold water. Add two scoops or packets of Strawberry Sorbet to cold water, one scoop or packet at a time, stirring slowly to dissolve. Stir sorbet mix in cold water with dissolved Jell-O. Cool quickly. The protein will settle to make a smooth consistency at the bottom. Serve it.

Nutrition information per serving: Calories: 60 kcal, Protein: 12 g, Total Carbs: 2 g, Dietary Fibers: 0 g, Total Fat: 0 g

28. Low Fat Panna Cotta

Serves: 4

Total time: 10 minutes (3 hrs. chill)

Ingredients:

- ½ tablespoons gelatin
- 1 tablespoon water
- 1 cup skim milk
- 2 tablespoons pure maple syrup
- 1 cup low-fat buttermilk

- 1 cup low-fat Greek yogurt

Preparation:

In a small bowl, mix the gelatin with the water and let stand until softened, about 5 minutes. In a small saucepan, bring the milk to a simmer with the maple syrup. Remove from the heat and stir in the softened gelatin until it is dissolved. Whisk the buttermilk with the yogurt in a medium bowl. Drizzle in the warm milk and whisk continuously until the panna cotta mixture is smooth. Pour the panna cotta mixture into six 4-ounce ramekins, and refrigerate until set, about 3 hours.

Nutrition information per serving: Calories: 111 kcal, Protein: 8 g, Total Carbs: 19 g, Dietary Fibers: 0 g, Total Fat: 1 g

29. Pumpkin Pancakes with Apple Compote

Serves: 2

Total time: 20 minutes

Ingredients:

- 1 apple cored and chopped.
- ½ tablespoons lemon juice
- 2 eggs, whites only
- 1 ½ teaspoon ground cinnamon
- ¼ cup pumpkin purée
- Vegetable oil spray

Preparation:

To make the apple compote: Stew the apples with the lemon juice over low heat until the apples are softened. Mash them with a fork and chill until ready to serve.

To make the pumpkin pancakes: Whisk together the egg whites, ground cinnamon, and pumpkin purée in a mixing bowl. Spray a nonstick frying pan with vegetable oil spray and pour ½ the batter into the pan. Cook for 4 to 5 minutes. When bubbles start to form, flip the pancake, and cook for another 1 to 2 minutes. Repeat for the remaining batter.

Nutrition information per serving: Calories: 111 kcal, Protein: 12 g, Total Carbs: 18 g, Dietary Fibers: 6 g, Total Fat: 0 g

Conclusion

Imagine becoming satisfied after a meal without consuming almost as much without gaining significant weight in the process. That is the purpose of gastric sleeve surgery, which is now one of the more common bariatric or weight-loss surgery forms. The gastric sleeve is a minimally invasive treatment that reduces hunger and limits the amount of food one may consume. Since the gastric sleeve is not for anyone that is overweight, if you are seriously obese and have some medical disorder that will benefit from losing weight, you might be a candidate for this life-changing operation. Before you start, you must first understand the risks and benefits. If you qualify, there are many health advantages to consider, which could overshadow any possible side effects. Following the operation, the patient must adhere to a strict diet to enable the body to heal and adjust to a smaller stomach. Following that, the patient would commit to a lifetime of balanced eating. Gastric sleeve surgery generally requires a dedication to a healthy way of life. Bariatric surgery is a relatively secure and efficient form of weight control for managing morbid obesity. It is much more effective when paired with dietary care, which can be complex, continuous, and varies between surgical procedures. Through continuous assessment of nutritional status, avoidance of food shortages, and maximization of long-term weight reduction, the physician's coordinated treatment, which includes collaboration with the bariatric dietitian and other health management team members, optimizes the advantages and health effects for the patient.

Although fad diets frequently promote cutting out any ingredients or substituting unhealthy items, gastric sleeve patients can still enjoy their favorite. While bariatric-friendly meals are smaller and involve fewer carbohydrates, they can still be flavorful and have the nutrition our bodies need to remain healthy and strong.

This book will help you make better post-operative diet decisions and stay on track with your weight-loss goals. Patients can eat regularly and remain balanced with the help of dietary supplements, cereals, bariatric-friendly meals, and snacks.

You'll feel good while on the way to achieving your targets if you remain stick to your gastric sleeve diet. It will require dedication and discipline, so you won't have to go it alone. This book guides you through the whole process, from the initial treatment to healing and beyond, and makes a post-surgery diet simple by including healthy choices for all stages of recovery.

Made in the USA
Columbia, SC
26 February 2022

56859771R00087